60 Hikes within 60 MILES

SEATTLE

INCLUDING BELLEVUE, EVERETT, AND TACOMA

Andrew Weber and Bryce Stevens

 **MENASHA RIDGE PRESS**
Birmingham, Alabama

Copyright © 2006 Andrew Weber and Bryce Stevens
All rights reserved
Printed in the United States of America
Published by Menasha Ridge Press
Distributed by The Globe Pequot Press
First edition, first printing

Library of Congress Cataloging-in-Publication Data

Weber, Andrew, 1971–
    60 Hikes within 60 Miles, Seattle : including Bellevue, Everett, and Tacoma /
Andrew Weber and Bryce Stevens.—1st ed.
        p. cm.
    ISBN 10: 0-89732-610-5
    ISBN 13: 978-0-89732-610-0
    1. Hiking—Washington (State)—Seattle Region—Guidebooks. 2. Seattle
Region (Wash.)—Guidebooks. I. Stevens, Bryce, 1969–. II. Title. III. Title:
Sixty Hikes within sixty miles, Seattle.

GV199.42.W22S43 2006
796.5109797'72—dc22

                                                                2006044402

Cover design by Grant M. Tatum
Text design by Karen Ocker
Cover photo © Andrew Weber
All other photos by Andrew Weber and Bryce Stevens
Maps by Andrew Weber, Bryce Stevens, and Steve Jones

Menasha Ridge Press
P.O. Box 43673
Birmingham, AL 35243
www.menasharidge.com

for Gerhard Weber, who loved the special places of the world
—Andrew Weber

For my parents, who introduced me to the natural world
through camping trips as a child
—Bryce Stevens

TABLE OF CONTENTS

TABLE OF CONTENTS

ACKNOWLEDGMENTS

This book would not be possible without the tireless efforts of countless volunteers, employees, and representatives from a host of organizations, including The Mountaineers, Washington State Trails Association, Washington Department of Natural Resources, National Forest Service, National Park Service, and various county and city departments of Parks and Recreation, who make the Seattle-area trail system one of the finest in the world. Nor would it be possible without the museum staff and the amateur and professional historians and archivists who allowed me to share and learn from their passions in order to bring the rich history of the Pacific Northwest to life. Their contributions to this book were immeasurable, even though they are almost certainly unaware of what they've done.

Also, I would like to express my boundless gratitude to my friends, family, and coworkers, who provided unlimited patience, tolerance, and support while this project was underway. And I would like to thank Russell Helms and the entire staff at Menasha Ridge Press, who presented Bryce and me with this unique opportunity and guided the work to completion. Without their leadership, this book would never have made it out of the wilderness.

—*Andrew Weber*

I would like to thank everyone who has joined me on excursions in the past, making these outdoor adventures fun and memorable. There are too many to name here, but the list includes Gary Dow, Dan Brady, Murray Kahn, Doug Colbeck, Jamie Nations, Jens Hansen, Rob Holmes, Neal Bozeman, and, of course, Andrew Weber. This group and many others have explored Washington with me on foot, mountain bikes, sea kayaks, snowshoes, skis, snowboards, parachutes, and even bungee cords. Thanks to these people, I have the knowledge base required to assemble a variety of hikes in the parks and mountains around the wonderful city of Seattle.

Finally, my greatest thanks go to those who wanted to hike with me while researching this book, but stayed at home most of the time—my patient wife Julie, and my sons Kyle and Andrew.

—*Bryce Stevens*

FOREWORD

Welcome to Menasha Ridge Press's *60 Hikes within 60 Miles*, a series designed to provide hikers with information needed to find and hike the very best trails surrounding cities usually underserved by good guidebooks.

Our strategy was simple: First, find a hiker who knows the area and loves to hike. Second, ask that person to spend a year researching the most popular and very best trails around. And third, have that person describe each trail in terms of difficulty, scenery, condition, elevation change, and all other categories of information that are important to hikers. "Pretend you've just completed a hike and met up with other hikers at the trailhead," we told each author. "Imagine their questions, be clear in your answers."

Authors Andrew Weber and Bryce Stevens have selected 60 of the best hikes in and around the Seattle metropolitan area. From the driftwood-strewn shores of Puget Sound to the snowy heights of the Cascade Mountains, Weber and Stevens provide hikers (and walkers) with a great variety of hikes—and all within roughly 60 miles of Seattle.

You'll get more out of this book if you take a moment to read the Introduction explaining how to read the trail listings. The "Topographic Maps" section will help you understand how useful topos will be on a hike, and will also tell you where to get them. And though this is a "where-to," not a "how-to" guide, those of you who have hiked extensively will find the Introduction of particular value.

As much for the opportunity to free the spirit as well as to free the body, let these hikes elevate you above the urban hurry.

All the best,
The Editors at Menasha Ridge Press

ABOUT THE AUTHORS

ANDREW WEBER

Thanks to a family scattered around the globe, Andrew Weber has become a world traveler for life, counting the Canadian Rockies, the beaches of New Zealand, and the deserts of southern Africa among his favorite places. He has been exploring the outdoors of the Pacific Northwest for more than a decade, including a successful climb of Mount Rainier in 2005 and a solo circumnavigation of the Wonderland Trail around the mountain in 2002. He currently resides in Seattle, where he works as a Web publisher and a freelance journalist and photographer. Andrew has written about a wide range of topics, including cultural events, the arts, the National Basketball Association and the National Football League. This is his first book.

BRYCE STEVENS

A lifelong Washingtonian, Bryce Stevens grew up in the Yakima area, graduated from the University of Washington, and has lived in Seattle for two decades. He has thoroughly explored the Cascade Range, the Olympic Mountains, and the lowlands of Puget Sound, all while hiking, backpacking, climbing, mountain biking, backcountry snowboarding, and sea kayaking. He discovered his love of outdoor photography while canyoneering in southeastern Utah in 2001 and has returned to the spectacular region every year since. In 1999 he cofounded **www.trails.com,** an online trail-information resource and topographic-mapping service that he continues to help run today. Bryce lives in the Maple Leaf neighborhood of Seattle with his wife, Julie, and their two sons, Kyle and Andrew.

PREFACE

Seattle is connected to the outdoors like few other places in the world. On a clear day, either or both of the Cascade and Olympic mountains can be seen from just about any high point in the city. Advertising for the Space Needle, arguably Seattle's most prominent man-made attraction, emphasizes its view of distant Mount Baker rather than of the downtown area nearby. Whenever the seemingly endless gray days of winter lead to speculation on the suitability of Seattle as a place to live, it can take only a glimpse of Mount Rainier to remind people why they choose to make their homes here. "The Mountain is out," locals say, when Rainier emerges from the clouds to make such an appearance, as if greeting an old friend who has been away.

Not surprisingly for a place so in love with the natural environment, reams of paper and gallons of ink have been consumed in an effort to catalog Washington's trails. This could well lead someone to ask whether anyone really needs another Washington hiking guidebook. Aren't there enough already?

Many celebrated trails in Washington are nowhere near Seattle at all, far outside any reasonable range for a day trip from the city. What has been lacking—and is now available here—is a true Seattle hiking guidebook.

From easy walks in local city parks to demanding hikes and scrambles in the mountains, there is something here for everyone. Within this book's modest 60-mile radius, beaches, tide pools, old-growth forests, high peaks, swimming holes, alpine meadows, lakes, glaciers, and more all invite exploration. Many of the things to be found on the featured trails are obvious: forests, rivers, and mountains. But there are more-subtle treasures, too, in historical and cultural gems. Walk a few steps down a path traveled by the pioneer settlers and feel a link with history unavailable in any museum. Or take a cursory glance at many Washington maps for an introduction to the Chinook language, which predates the settlers by centuries and provides names for countless geographic features. Even veteran hikers are sure to make some new discoveries and find something in this book they didn't already know about. (Who would have guessed that Stevens Pass has a link to the Panama Canal?) Or maybe you need a good reason to revisit some old favorites and see how familiar places have changed over time.

The most important message this book can send is that wilderness is not only found way out there; it's also right here, for those who know where to look. Islands in Puget Sound, the lowlands of South King County, and the Kitsap Peninsula—all worthy of visits in their own right and good places to escape the crowds—are just a few of the quietly overlooked hiking destinations highlighted within these pages.

White morning glory at Redmond
Watershed Park and Preserve

There is also no reason summer needs to be viewed as the one-and-only hiking season. Plenty of trails are open year-round and offer special seasonal attractions. Who can forget a waterfall at its maximum flow when it crests after a week of winter rain? Or an ancient forest at its most evocative when thick fog lends an otherworldly atmosphere to the giant trees? This guidebook shows the way.

▶ ABOUT THE HIKES

If Seattle stood at the center of a plain, a 60-mile circle could be drawn to encompass all the hikes in this book. The resulting overview map might well resemble a pepperoni pizza, with the featured trails distributed evenly around the city. However, the Seattle region has a rugged and interesting topography, bounded by Puget Sound to the west and the Cascade Mountains to the east, preventing any such easy apportionment of the "60 Hikes Within 60 Miles" promised by the title.

Accordingly, although the hikes described are generally scattered over a wide area, there are a few places where they are concentrated, as dictated by the necessities of the landscape. It is also an unfortunate geographic reality that the peaks of the Olympics, despite beckoning to Seattle from only 40 miles away, are nonetheless too remote for inclusion. Although it is blessed with some magnificent trails, the Olympic Peninsula requires several hours to reach by road, ferry, or both, and therefore had to be left out.

Of the featured 60 hikes, approximately one-third are located in urban or suburban areas, another third are in rural areas, and the remaining third are in the wilderness. About 40 can be hiked year-round, including many in the mountains.

If you hike one trail from this book each week without fail, regardless of weather or other commitments, it would take you more than a year to complete them all. And that doesn't even take into consideration the destinations that frequently include

Cascades of Dingford Creek along the Middle Fork Snoqualmie River

multiple hiking options. In the era of ever-escalating gas prices, this book provides great opportunities for outdoor recreation within about an hour's drive or less.

Thankfully, the same terrain that restricts where trails can be found also makes hiking here so unique and rewarding. If the waters of Puget Sound largely limit the number of hikes to the west of the city, the ones that are available are nonetheless exceptional. The remaining hikes in this book—the vast majority—run in a broad arc on the eastern side of the urban area, stretching from Mount Rainier in the south to the Boulder River Wilderness in the north.

▶ SEATTLE PARKS

The hikes in this group definitively prove that it is not necessary to venture far from home to find a good trail. You can't help but be amazed at the natural attractions to be discovered here, practically in your own backyard. Many parks preserve pieces of the landscape like it used to be, before urban development began. Some, like Schmitz Preserve Park and Seward Park, still harbor stands of old-growth forest. Carkeek Park and Discovery Park both offer great beach access. And unique Blake Island State Park presents a special challenge and reward for those intrepid enough to journey across the water.

▶ BELLEVUE AND THE EASTSIDE

Despite the rapid growth of Bellevue and the suburban area, many great natural pockets remain on the Eastside, from Saint Edward State Park and O. O. Denny County Park on the shores of Lake Washington to the panoramic heights of the Issaquah Alps. Mercer Slough Nature Park and Redmond Watershed Park and Preserve both feature interesting wetlands and the wildlife that goes with it, while the many trails on Cougar, Squak, and Tiger mountains provide the closest hikes to Seattle with a "big-mountain" feel. The interesting industrial history of the region can also be found, awaiting discovery along Coal Creek.

▶ INTERSTATE 90 AND THE SNOQUALMIE PASS AREA

Snoqualmie Pass is the first area most people think of for hiking near Seattle. That's no surprise, given that the trail up Mount Si is a virtual rite of passage for anyone who's ever laced up a pair of hiking boots in the Puget Sound region. The I-90 corridor serves as a grand gateway to the Cascade Mountains, where towering peaks with names like Granite and Defiance challenge all comers and provide commensurate rewards in the form of great views from their summits for hikers tough enough to reach them. The steep trail up Mailbox Peak might be the king of them all; this truly demanding hike favored by mountain climbers in off-season training is covered with a carpet of wildflowers in the warmer months and offers a panoramic view at the top. If that's not enough, many of the waterfalls that inspired the name "Cascades" are in abundance along the trails around Snoqualmie Pass, and they are the main attractions at places like Twin Falls, Snoqualmie Falls, and Franklin Falls.

▶ KITSAP PENINSULA AND WHIDBEY ISLAND

Most hikers who look out over Puget Sound are inevitably drawn to the Olympic Mountains, distracted from the treasures at their feet by the prominent peaks on the horizon. Whidbey Island's untamed shoreline offers up two wild beaches at Useless Bay and Ebey's Landing, the latter also providing great views over the Strait of Juan de Fuca from its stunning high-bluff trail. On the Kitsap Peninsula, the horseshoe-shaped Hood Canal reaches its end at the ecologically rich Theler Wetlands. Kitsap is also home to Green Mountain, an exceptional high point on the generally low-lying terrain between the Olympic Peninsula and the mainland. The peak provides a great view over much of the sound from an unusual perspective that few people see.

▶ EVERETT, EDMONDS, AND US 2 STEVENS PASS AREA

For residents of the cities north of Seattle, Stevens Pass is a local version of Snoqualmie Pass, complete with easy access along US 2. Both passes have their own distinct flavor and attractions, though. Unlike Snoqualmie, where hikers can ascend the significant mountains with relative ease, few trails reach the top of the sharp and forbidding peaks around Stevens, whose summits are best left to serious climbers. Hikers should be content to view jagged Baring Mountain and Mount Index from the Heybrook Ridge Lookout or the shores of Lake Serene, one of the finest swimming holes in the Cascades. The region's rich pioneer history also awaits exploration along trails that feel like tours through a living museum. Look for abandoned mine shafts and equipment along Silver Creek and near the Mineral City Town Site, and for the remnants of a once-mighty railroad line on the fascinating Iron Goat Trail.

▶ GRANITE FALLS AND THE MOUNTAIN LOOP HIGHWAY

The town of Granite Falls serves as entry portal to the rugged mountains of northern

PREFACE

Snohomish County. With no suitable crossing to the east, the only road that manages significant penetration into the area is forced to bend back on itself, creating the Mountain Loop Highway. Yet the mountains here are accessible on foot, allowing hikers to reach great locations that cars cannot. Magnificent groves of old-growth forest populate the areas near Heather Lake and Bear Lake. The Boulder River Trail runs deep into the wilderness of the same name. And the hike up Mount Pilchuck is a true Puget Sound classic, culminating in a spectacular view of the entire region from the summit lookout.

▶ TACOMA, OLYMPIA, ENUMCLAW, AND WA 410

Lacking any easily recognizable landmarks, the region encompassed by southern King County, Pierce County, and the lower end of Puget Sound is often overlooked by hikers. Yet this "forgotten frontier" does offer some worthy trails and an eclectic mix of outdoor attractions. Point Defiance features interesting history alongside great views of the South Sound, not to mention some old-growth trees—the main attraction at Federation Forest State Park. Bird-watchers will love the Nisqually National Wildlife Refuge. And the Mud Mountain Dam and Recreation Area provides an interesting look at the White River (and man's attempts to control it), while Pinnacle Peak stands like a lone sentinel above the surrounding flatlands, a geologic oddity demanding further investigation.

▶ MOUNT RAINIER NATIONAL PARK

Words cannot do justice to the natural wonders that pervade the area around Washington's most famous landmark. Ancient forests, thundering waterfalls, and giant glaciers are just a few of the spectacular features to be found throughout the 236,000 acres that make up Mount Rainier National Park. Head to the aptly named Spray Falls to see one of the most beautiful waterfalls in the state, and continue up to the high alpine meadows at Spray Park for an unforgettable wildflower display. Just to the north, the view from the top of Tolmie Peak makes the mountain and its massive ice flows seem close enough to touch. And if you are truly tempted to do so, follow the Carbon River Trail through lowland forest to the toe of the mighty Carbon Glacier, a one-of-a-kind experience.

PREFACE

▶ GET OUT AND EXPLORE ON YOUR OWN

Tell someone you are writing a guidebook—a hiking guidebook of all things—and you are sure to be flooded with advice, questions, and ideas. Everyone has something to say, and Seattle residents invariably show their passion for the outdoors in the strength of their opinions. You must include this hike, someone's favorite; you cannot include that other one, the secret hike no one knows about. You have to write in this particular style, or use a photo from this vantage point, or include these features on the map.

Beneath all of the advice lies a not-too-well-hidden subtext: Who are you to write a guidebook for me? And indeed, the question is a good one. Every individual has a unique experience on the trails, the product of countless factors like physical fitness, personal preference, and even particular mood on a given day. Nobody owns the trails, and we are all free to enjoy them in our own way—and this is the reason most of us go hiking in the first place. No guidebook could hope to capture all of the ways people experience the outdoors, and none should even try.

I was reminded of this on a hike one cloudy Mother's Day, when I stumbled across a half dozen moms with several bottles of champagne and a basket of strawberries escaping six husbands and who knows how many kids at a secluded viewpoint in the Issaquah Alps. A guidebook might have led them to the spot, but it certainly didn't tell them this was the thing to do when they got there.

Let these audacious women be your inspiration, and use this book as a sampler for your own adventures; it is nothing more than a brief introduction to hiking in the Pacific Northwest. No one could ever hope to produce an exhaustive accounting of the vast outdoor resources to be found in this remarkable corner of the planet—or tell you how they should be enjoyed, which is the best reason to go exploring on your own. Make the most of this unique, wonderful region. There is no other place like it anywhere in the world.

HIKING RECOMMENDATIONS

▶ HIKES LESS THAN 3 MILES

Annette Lake and Asahel Curtis Nature Trail
Boulder River Wilderness: Boulder River Trail
Camp Long
Carkeek Park
Cedar River Trail: Landsburg Park to Big
  Bend Natural Area
Flaming Geyser State Park
Franklin Falls and Old Snoqualmie Pass
  Wagon Road Trail
Heybrook Ridge and Lookout Tower
Hood Canal and Theler Wetlands
John MacDonald Tolt River County Park
Meadowdale County Park and Beach

Mercer Slough and Bellefields Nature Parks
O. O. Denny County Park Loop
Pinnacle Lake and Bear Lake
Pinnacle Peak County Park: Cal Magnusson
  Trail
Saint Edward State Park
Schmitz Preserve Park
Seward Park
Twin Falls Natural Area and Olallie State
  Park
Washington Park Arboretum and Foster
  Island Trail
Woodland Park and Green Lake Park

▶ HIKES 3 TO 6 MILES

Barclay Lake, Stone Lake, and Eagle Lake
Blake Island State Park
Coal Creek Park
Cougar Mountain Regional Wildland Park:
  Licorice Fern Trail
Cougar Mountain Regional Wildland Park:
  Wilderness Creek and Wilderness Peak Loop
Discovery Park: Beaches, Bluffs, and
  Lighthouse
Ebey's Landing State Park and National
  Historic Reserve
Federation Forest State Park
Green Mountain State Forest: Gold Creek,
  Beaver Pond, and Wildcat Trail Loop
Heather Lake
Iron Goat Trail
Lake Serene and Bridal Veil Falls
Lime Kiln Trail at Robe Canyon
  Historic Park
Little Si Trail

Mount Pilchuck State Park: Mount Pilchuck
  Lookout
Mount Rainier National Park: Mowich Lake,
  Eunice Lake, and Tolmie Peak
Mount Rainier National Park: Spray Falls and
  Spray Park
Nisqually National Wildlife Refuge
Pinnacle Lake and Bear Lake
Point Defiance Park
Rattlesnake Ledge and Rattlesnake Mountain
Redmond Watershed Park and Preserve
Seward Park
Snoqualmie Falls Viewpoint via Preston-
  Snoqualmie Rail-Trail
Spencer Island Natural Wildlife Reserve
Tiger Mountain State Forest: Chirico Trail
Tiger Mountain State Forest: West Tiger
  Mountain Three Loop
Useless Bay Tidelands
Wallace Falls State Park

▶ HIKES LONGER THAN 6 MILES

Annette Lake and Asahel Curtis Nature Trail
Barclay Lake, Stone Lake, and Eagle Lake
Bare Mountain
Boulder River Wilderness: Boulder River Trail

Granite Mountain Lookout Tower
Green Mountain State Forest: Gold Creek,
  Beaver Pond, and Wildcat Trail Loop

HIKING RECOMMENDATIONS

▶ HIKES LONGER THAN 6 MILES (CONTINUED)

Ira Spring Trail to Mason Lake, Mount
  Defiance, and Bandera Mountain
Iron Goat Trail
Lake Serene and Bridal Veil Falls
Lime Kiln Trail at Robe Canyon Historic Park
Mailbox Peak
McClellan Butte
Middle Fork Snoqualmie River Trail
Mount Rainier National Park: Carbon River
  and Carbon Glacier
Mount Rainier National Park: Spray Falls and
  Spray Park
Mount Si Trail
Mud Mountain Dam and Recreation Area:
  Mud Mountain Lake and White River Trail
Rattlesnake Ledge and Rattlesnake Mountain
Silver Creek and Mineral City Town Site
Squak Mountain State Park: Double Peak
  Loop
Tiger Mountain State Forest: Poo Poo Point
  Trail

▶ HIKES WITH MOUNTAIN-BIKING OPPORTUNITIES

Blake Island State Park
Cedar River Trail: Landsburg Park to Big
  Bend Natural Area
Green Mountain State Forest: Gold Creek,
  Beaver Pond, and Wildcat Trail Loop
John MacDonald Tolt River County Park
Lime Kiln Trail at Robe Canyon Historic Park
Meadowdale County Park and Beach
Middle Fork Snoqualmie River Trail
Mud Mountain Dam and Recreation Area:
  Mud Mountain Lake and White River Trail
Redmond Watershed Park and Preserve
Saint Edward State Park
Snoqualmie Falls Viewpoint via Preston-
  Snoqualmie Rail-Trail
Wallace Falls State Park

▶ HIKES WITH WATERFALLS

Boulder River Wilderness: Boulder River Trail
Coal Creek Park
Cougar Mountain Regional Wildland Park:
  Licorice Fern Trail
Franklin Falls and Old Snoqualmie Pass
  Wagon Road Trail
Ira Spring Trail to Mason Lake, Mount
  Defiance, and Bandera Mountain
Lake Serene and Bridal Veil Falls
Mount Rainier National Park: Carbon River
  and Carbon Glacier
Mount Rainier National Park: Spray Falls and
  Spray Park
Silver Creek and Mineral City Town Site
Snoqualmie Falls Viewpoint via Preston-
  Snoqualmie Rail-Trail
Twin Falls Natural Area and Olallie State Park
Wallace Falls State Park

▶ HIKES WITH LAKES

Annette Lake and Asahel Curtis Nature Trail
Barclay Lake, Stone Lake, and Eagle Lake
Heather Lake
Ira Spring Trail to Mason Lake, Mount
  Defiance, and Bandera Mountain
Lake Serene and Bridal Veil Falls
Mount Rainier National Park: Mowich Lake,
  Eunice Lake, and Tolmie Peak
Pinnacle Lake and Bear Lake
Saint Edward State Park
Seward Park
Tiger Mountain State Forest: West Tiger
  Mountain Three Loop
Woodland Park and Green Lake Park

HIKING RECOMMENDATIONS

▶ HIKES ALONG RIVERS

Boulder River Wilderness: Boulder River Trail
Cedar River Trail: Landsburg Park to Big
 Bend Natural Area
Federation Forest State Park
Flaming Geyser State Park
Franklin Falls and Old Snoqualmie Pass
 Wagon Road Trail
John MacDonald Tolt River County Park
Lime Kiln Trail at Robe Canyon Historic Park

Middle Fork Snoqualmie River Trail
Mount Rainier National Park: Carbon River
 and Carbon Glacier
Mud Mountain Dam and Recreation Area:
 Mud Mountain Lake and White River Trail
Nisqually National Wildlife Refuge
Silver Creek and Mineral City Town Site
Twin Falls Natural Area and Olallie State Park
Wallace Falls State Park

▶ HIKES WITH HISTORIC SITES

Blake Island State Park
Camp Long
Coal Creek Park
Discovery Park: Beaches, Bluffs, and
 Lighthouse
Ebey's Landing State Park and National
 Historic Reserve
Flaming Geyser State Park
Franklin Falls and Old Snoqualmie Pass
 Wagon Road Trail

Iron Goat Trail
Lime Kiln Trail at Robe Canyon Historic Park
Mount Pilchuck State Park: Mount Pilchuck
 Lookout
Nisqually National Wildlife Refuge
Point Defiance Park
Silver Creek and Mineral City Town Site
Spencer Island Natural Wildlife Reserve
Squak Mountain State Park: Double Peak
 Loop

▶ BUSY HIKES

Annette Lake and Asahel Curtis Nature Trail
Barclay Lake, Stone Lake, and Eagle Lake
Camp Long
Carkeek Park
Cedar River Trail: Landsburg Park to Big
 Bend Natural Area
Coal Creek Park
Discovery Park: Beaches, Bluffs, and
 Lighthouse
Franklin Falls and Old Snoqualmie Pass
 Wagon Road Trail
Granite Mountain Lookout Tower
Heather Lake
Hood Canal and Theler Wetlands
Ira Spring Trail to Mason Lake, Mount
 Defiance, and Bandera Mountain
Lake Serene and Bridal Veil Falls

Meadowdale County Park and Beach
Mercer Slough and Bellefields Nature
 Parks
Mount Pilchuck State Park: Mount Pilchuck
 Lookout
Mount Rainier National Park: Carbon River
 and Carbon Glacier
Mount Rainier National Park: Mowich Lake,
 Eunice Lake, and Tolmie Peak
Mount Rainier National Park: Spray Falls and
 Spray Park
Mount Si Trail
Nisqually National Wildlife Refuge
Pinnacle Peak County Park: Cal Magnusson
 Trail
Point Defiance Park
Rattlesnake Ledge and Rattlesnake Mountain
Redmond Watershed Park and Preserve

HIKING RECOMMENDATIONS

HIKING RECOMMENDATIONS

▶ SCENIC HIKES (CONTINUED)

Point Defiance Park
Silver Creek and Mineral City Townsite

Spencer Island Natural Wildlife Reserve
Twin Falls Natural Area and Olallie State Park

▶ HIKES WITH WILDFLOWERS

Barclay Lake, Stone Lake, and Eagle Lake
Ebey's Landing State Park and National
   Historic Reserve
Green Mountain State Forest: Gold Creek,
   Beaver Pond, and Wildcat Trail Loop
Ira Spring Trail to Mason Lake, Mount
   Defiance, and Bandera Mountain
Iron Goat Trail

Mailbox Peak
Mount Rainier National Park: Mowich Lake,
   Eunice Lake, and Tolmie Peak
Mount Rainier National Park: Spray Falls and
   Spray Park
Mud Mountain Dam and Recreation Area:
   Mud Mountain Lake and White River Trail

▶ GOOD HIKES FOR YOUNG CHILDREN

Annette Lake and Asahel Curtis Nature Trail
Barclay Lake, Stone Lake, and Eagle Lake
Blake Island State Park
Camp Long
Carkeek Park
Coal Creek Park
Discovery Park: Beaches, Bluffs, and
   Lighthouse
Ebey's Landing State Park and National
   Historic Reserve
Federation Forest State Park
Franklin Falls and Old Snoqualmie Pass
   Wagon Road Trail
Heather Lake
Heybrook Ridge and Lookout Tower
Hood Canal and Theler Wetlands
Iron Goat Trail
Lime Kiln Trail at Robe Canyon Historic Park
Meadowdale County Park and Beach
Mercer Slough and Bellefields Nature Parks

Mount Rainier National Park: Spray Falls and
   Spray Park
Mud Mountain Dam and Recreation Area:
   Mud Mountain Lake and White River Trail
Nisqually National Wildlife Refuge
O. O. Denny County Park Loop
Point Defiance Park
Redmond Watershed Park and Preserve
Saint Edward State Park
Schmitz Preserve Park
Seward Park
Spencer Island Natural Wildlife Reserve
Tiger Mountain State Forest: Chirico Trail
Twin Falls Natural Area and Olallie
   State Park
Useless Bay Tidelands
Wallace Falls State Park
Washington Park Arboretum and Foster
   Island Trail
Woodland Park and Green Lake Park

▶ HIKES WITH BIRD-WATCHING

Ebey's Landing State Park and National His-
   toric Reserve
Hood Canal and Theler Wetlands
Mercer Slough and Bellefields Nature Parks
Nisqually National Wildlife Refuge

Spencer Island Natural Wildlife Reserve
Washington Park Arboretum and Foster
   Island Trail
Woodland Park and Green Lake Park

HIKING RECOMMENDATIONS

▶ GOOD HIKES FOR RUNNERS

Annette Lake and Asahel Curtis Nature Trail
Barclay Lake, Stone Lake, and Eagle Lake
Boulder River Wilderness: Boulder River Trail
Cedar River Trail: Landsburg Park to Big
  Bend Natural Area
Coal Creek Park
Cougar Mountain Regional Wildland Park:
  Licorice Fern Trail
Cougar Mountain Regional Wildland Park:
  Wilderness Creek and Wilderness Peak Loop
Discovery Park: Beaches, Bluffs, and
  Lighthouse
Green Mountain State Forest: Gold Creek,
  Beaver Pond, and Wildcat Trail Loop
Heather Lake
Ira Spring Trail to Mason Lake, Mount
  Defiance, and Bandera Mountain
Iron Goat Trail
Lime Kiln Trail at Robe Canyon Historic Park
McClellan Butte
Middle Fork Snoqualmie River Trail
Mount Pilchuck State Park: Mount Pilchuck
  Lookout

Mount Rainier National Park: Carbon River
  and Carbon Glacier
Mount Rainier National Park: Mowich Lake,
  Eunice Lake, and Tolmie Peak
Mount Rainier National Park: Spray Falls and
  Spray Park
Mount Si Trail
Mud Mountain Dam and Recreation Area:
  Mud Mountain Lake and White River Trail
Point Defiance Park
Redmond Watershed Park and Preserve
Saint Edward State Park
Seward Park
Snoqualmie Falls Viewpoint via Preston-
  Snoqualmie Rail-Trail
Tiger Mountain State Forest: Poo Poo Point
  Trail
Tiger Mountain State Forest: West Tiger
  Mountain Three Loop
Twin Falls Natural Area and Olallie State
  Park
Wallace Falls State Park
Woodland Park and Green Lake Park

▶ HIKES WITH OLD-GROWTH FOREST

Annette Lake and Asahel Curtis Nature Trail
Bare Mountain
Boulder River Wilderness: Boulder River Trail
Federation Forest State Park
Franklin Falls and Old Snoqualmie Pass
  Wagon Road Trail
Lake Serene and Bridal Veil Falls

McClellan Butte
O. O. Denny County Park Loop
Pinnacle Lake and Bear Lake
Point Defiance Park
Schmitz Preserve Park
Seward Park
Wallace Falls State Park

▶ HIKES WITH GREAT VIEWPOINTS

Bare Mountain
Ebey's Landing State Park and National
  Historic Reserve
Granite Mountain Lookout Tower
Green Mountain State Forest: Gold Creek,
  Beaver Pond, and Wildcat Trail Loop
Heybrook Ridge and Lookout Tower
Ira Spring Trail to Mason Lake, Mount
  Defiance, and Bandera Mountain

Iron Goat Trail
John MacDonald Tolt River County Park
Little Si Trail
Mailbox Peak
McClellan Butte
Mount Pilchuck State Park: Mount Pilchuck
  Lookout
Mount Rainier National Park: Mowich Lake,
  Eunice Lake, and Tolmie Peak

HIKING RECOMMENDATIONS

▶ HIKES WITH GREAT VIEWPOINTS (CONTINUED)

Mount Si Trail
Mud Mountain Dam and Recreation Area:
  Mud Mountain Lake and White River Trail
Point Defiance Park
Rattlesnake Ledge and Rattlesnake Mountain
Snoqualmie Falls Viewpoint via Preston-
  Snoqualmie Rail-Trail

Tiger Mountain State Forest:
  Chirico Trail
Tiger Mountain State Forest: Poo Poo Point
  Trail
☑Tiger Mountain State Forest: West Tiger
  Mountain Three Loop

▶ YEAR-ROUND HIKES

Blake Island State Park
Boulder River Wilderness: Boulder River Trail
Camp Long
Carkeek Park
Cedar River Trail: Landsburg Park to Big
  Bend Natural Area
Coal Creek Park
Cougar Mountain Regional Wildland Park:
  Licorice Fern Trail
Cougar Mountain Regional Wildland Park:
  Wilderness Creek and Wilderness Peak Loop
Discovery Park: Beaches, Bluffs, and
  Lighthouse
Ebey's Landing State Park and National
  Historic Reserve
Federation Forest State Park
Flaming Geyser State Park
Green Mountain State Forest: Gold Creek,
  Beaver Pond, and Wildcat Trail Loop
Heybrook Ridge and Lookout Tower
Hood Canal and Theler Wetlands
John MacDonald Tolt River County Park
Lime Kiln Trail at Robe Canyon Historic Park
Little Si Trail
Meadowdale County Park and Beach
Mercer Slough and Bellefields Nature Parks
Middle Fork Snoqualmie River Trail
Mud Mountain Dam and Recreation Area:
  Mud Mountain Lake and White River Trail

Nisqually National Wildlife Refuge
O. O. Denny County Park Loop
Pinnacle Peak County Park: Cal Magnusson
  Trail
Point Defiance Park
Rattlesnake Ledge and Rattlesnake Mountain
Redmond Watershed Park and Preserve
Saint Edward State Park
Schmitz Preserve Park
Seward Park
Snoqualmie Falls Viewpoint via Preston-
  Snoqualmie Rail-Trail
Spencer Island Natural Wildlife Reserve
Squak Mountain State Park: Double Peak
  Loop
Tiger Mountain State Forest: Chirico Trail
Tiger Mountain State Forest: Poo Poo Point
  Trail
Tiger Mountain State Forest: West Tiger
  Mountain Three Loop
Twin Falls Natural Area and Olallie State
  Park
Useless Bay Tidelands
Wallace Falls State Park
Washington Park Arboretum and Foster
  Island Trail
Woodland Park and Green Lake Park

60 Hikes

within **60 MILES**

SEATTLE

INCLUDING BELLEVUE, EVERETT, AND TACOMA

INTRODUCTION

Welcome to *60 Hikes within 60 Miles: Seattle.* If you're new to hiking or even if you're a seasoned trail-smith, take a few minutes to read the following introduction. We explain how this book is organized and how to use it.

▶ HIKE DESCRIPTIONS

Each hike contains seven key items: an "In Brief" description of the trail, a key at-a-glance box, directions to the trail, trailhead coordinates, a trail map, an elevation profile, and a trail description. Many also include a note on nearby activities. Combined, the maps and information provide a clear method to assess each trail from the comfort of your favorite reading chair.

LOCATING A TRAIL
After narrowing down the general area of the hikes on the overview map (see inside front cover), the directions given in the narratives will enable you to find the trailheads.

IN BRIEF
A "taste of the trail." Think of this section as a snapshot focused on the historical landmarks, beautiful vistas, and other sights you may encounter on the hike.

KEY AT-A-GLANCE INFORMATION
The information in the key at-a-glance boxes gives you a quick idea of the statistics and specifics of each hike.

LENGTH The length of the trail from start to finish (total distance traveled). There may be options to shorten or extend the hikes, but the mileage corresponds to the described hike. Consult the hike description to help decide how to customize the hike for your ability or time constraints.

CONFIGURATION A description of what the trail might look like from overhead. Trails can be loops, out-and-backs (trails on which one enters and leaves along the same path), figure eights, or a combination of shapes.

DIFFICULTY The degree of effort an "average" hiker should expect on a given hike. For simplicity, the trails are rated as "easy," "moderate," or "difficult."

SCENERY A short summary of the attractions offered by the hike and what to expect in terms of plant life, wildlife, natural wonders, and historic features.

EXPOSURE A quick check of how much sun you can expect on your shoulders during the hike.

TRAFFIC Indicates how busy the trail might be on an average day. Trail traffic, of course, varies from day to day and season to season. Weekend days typically see the most visitors. Other trail users that may be encountered on the trail are also noted here.

TRAIL SURFACE Indicates whether the trail surface is paved, rocky, gravel, dirt, boardwalk, or a mixture of elements.

INTRODUCTION

HIKING TIME   The length of time it takes to hike the trail. A slow but steady hiker will average 2 to 3 miles an hour, depending on the terrain.

ACCESS   A notation of any fees or permits that may be needed to access the trail or park at the trailhead.

Trails in the Cascade Range often require a National Forest Pass for parking: a day pass is $5, and the annual pass is $30. If you plan to hike frequently each year, it is worth buying the annual pass. Both passes can be purchased at National Forest offices, outdoor retailers, and other local vendors; they also are available online through the National Forest Web site (**www.fs.fed.us/r6/feedemo** or **www.nature nw.org**).

A daily or annual permit is also required to park at any Washington state park: the daily permit is $5, an annual permit is $50 (price increases to $7 daily and $70 annually in 2008). Daily permits can be obtained at all state park trailhead parking areas, and annual permits can be obtained at park offices when staffed or online at the Washington State Parks Web site (**www.parks.wa.gov**).

Mount Rainier National Park requires an entrance fee of $15, which covers everybody in one vehicle for seven days. An annual pass to the park costs $30. Both options are available at the park entrance stations during normal park business hours. More information on hours and fees for the park are available online at **www.nps.gov/mora.**

City and county parks typically do not require any permits or parking fees.

MAPS   Here you'll find a list of maps that show the topography of the trail, including Green Trails Maps and USGS topo maps.

FACILITIES   What to expect in terms of restrooms and water at the trailhead or nearby.

DIRECTIONS TO THE TRAIL

Used in conjunction with the overview map, the driving directions will help you locate each trailhead. Once at the trailhead, park only in designated areas.

TRAILHEAD COORDINATES

The trailhead coordinates can be used in addition to the driving directions if you enter the coordinates into your GPS unit before you set out. See the section below on GPS trailhead coordinates to understand GPS unit settings.

TRAIL DESCRIPTIONS

The trail description is the heart of each hike. Here, the authors provide a summary of the trail's essence and highlight any special traits the hike has to offer. The route is clearly outlined, including landmarks, side trips, and possible alternate routes along the way. Ultimately, the hike description will help you choose which hikes are best for you.

NEARBY ACTIVITIES

Look here for information on nearby activities or points of interest. This includes nearby parks, museums, restaurants, or even a brew pub where you can get a well-deserved beer after a long hike. Note that not every hike has a listing.

▶ WEATHER

As you can see from the table below of average daily temperatures by month for the Seattle-Tacoma area, the average highs never reach 80°F and the average lows are well above the freezing point. However, this does not mean that it can't get very hot on some summer days or uncomfortably cold on some winter days, especially at higher elevations. What it does mean is that most of the year you can hike without dealing with extreme temperatures—though you might get wet.

For better or worse, Seattle is nearly synonymous with rain. Yet that perception is surely due to the high number of overcast and drizzly days each year, rather than the actual measured rainfall of about 39 inches. On average, Seattle gets less rain than Miami, Atlanta, Houston, Boston, New York, Philadelphia, Indianapolis, and Washington, D.C. However, Seattle beats all those cities when totaling the number of annual rainy days (around 160). You are most likely to get wet in Seattle from October through March. December is the wettest month with about six inches of accumulated precipitation each year, on average, and July is the driest with less than one inch.

Summer days in the Puget Sound region can be hot on occasion, but typically the air doesn't feel as humid as it does in many other parts of the United States. This is a particular benefit to hiking around Seattle, because heat plus humidity can spell danger when exercising outdoors. Use common sense when hiking on hot days, and rest in the shade if necessary. Stay hydrated by drinking water throughout the hike, and you will minimize any chances of heat-related conditions.

In the winter months, the Cascade Range is typically buried under a blanket of snow. This includes the higher-elevation hikes along I-90, US 2, and the Mountain Loop Highway, and in Mount Rainier National Park. The foothills, including the Issaquah Alps, do get snow in the winter, but it rarely lingers for more than a week or two. That is why this book contains 40 hikes that are considered accessible year-round, even though some of the trails may be snow-covered part of the year. Usually these trails are still hikable in snowy conditions, which may, in fact, be the best time of the year to explore them. If you want to find solitude and experience a different outdoor setting, then venture a couple miles from any trailhead when there is snow on the ground. Just keep in mind that trails may be muddy and slippery under these conditions. Dress warmly and be prepared with the ten essentials. (See "Ten Essentials" section below.)

Seattle's spring and fall are both mild and pleasant. When it's not raining, these are great days to be outside. Spring blooms and fall leaves make the scenery spectacular. And the trails in the Cascades are usually clear of snow by late June, so nearly every trail in this book should be hikable by then.

INTRODUCTION

AVERAGE DAILY TEMPERATURES BY MONTH—SEATTLE-TACOMA
30-YEAR AVERAGE IN DEGREES F

	JAN	FEB	MAR	APR	MAY	JUN
HIGH	46°	50°	53°	58°	64°	70°
LOW	36°	37°	39°	42°	47°	52°
	JUL	AUG	SEP	OCT	NOV	DEC
HIGH	75°	76°	70°	60°	51°	46°
LOW	55°	56°	52°	46°	40°	36°

▶ ALLOCATING TIME

On flat or lightly undulating terrain, the authors averaged 3 miles per hour when hiking. That speed drops in direct proportion to the steepness of a path, and it does not reflect the many pauses and forays off-trail in pursuit of yet another viewpoint, wildflower, or photograph. Give yourself plenty of time. Few people enjoy rushing through a hike, and fewer still take pleasure in bumping into trees after dark. Remember, too, that your pace naturally slackens over the back half of a long trek.

▶ MAPS

Green Trails Maps, with their signature green trails overlaid onto easy-to-read topographic backgrounds, are a local favorite for hiking in the Washington Cascades. The maps are usually scaled at 1:69,500, making them less detailed than typical USGS maps, but they do show a large area which can still be helpful in the backcountry and along the trails. They are also good for identifying nearby peaks and other prominent geographic landmarks. Some of the most-recently published Green Trails Maps cover the Issaquah Alps, including Tiger Mountain, Squak Mountain, Cougar Mountain, and Rattlesnake Mountain (map numbers 203S, 204S, and 205S). These maps are especially useful because the scale is 1:24,000 and because they are more up-to-date than the USGS maps are.

The USGS names listed in this section are for the applicable USGS 7.5 minute quadrangle maps (1:24,000 scale). Many of these maps are out of date, so roads or trails may not be shown in the current location, if they are shown at all. However, the topographic detail of the 7.5 minute series is nonetheless extremely valuable for backcountry navigation. See the section below on Topo Maps for more information on reading topo maps.

▶ TOPO MAPS

The maps in this book have been produced with great care and, used with the hiking directions, will direct you to the trail and help you stay on course. However, you will find superior detail and valuable information in the United States Geological Survey's 7.5 minute series topographic maps. Topo maps are available online in many locations. A well-known free service is located at **www.terraserver.microsoft.com** and another free service with fast click-and-drag browsing is located at **www.topofinder.com.** You can view and print topos of the entire United States from these Web sites, and view aerial photographs of the same area at terraserver. Several online services such as **www.trails.com** charge annual fees for additional features such as shaded-relief, which makes the topography stand out more. If you expect to print out many topo maps each year, it might be worth paying for shaded-relief topo maps. The downside to USGS topos is that most of them are outdated, having been created 20 to 30 years ago. But they still provide excellent topographic detail.

If you're new to hiking, you might be wondering, "What's a topographic map?" In short, a topo indicates not only linear distance but elevation as well, using contour lines. Contour lines spread across the map like dozens of intricate spider webs. Each line represents a particular elevation, and at the base of each topo, a contour's interval designation is given. If the contour interval is 200 feet, then the distance between each contour line is 200 feet. Follow five contour lines up on the same map, and the elevation has increased by 1,000 feet.

Let's assume that the 7.5 minute series topo reads "Contour Interval 40 feet," that the short trail we'll be hiking is two inches in length on the map, and that it crosses five contour lines from beginning to end. What do we know? Well, because the linear scale of this series is 2,000 feet to the inch (roughly two and three-quarters inches representing 1 mile), we know our trail is approximately four-fifths of a mile long (two inches are 2,000 feet). But we also know we'll be climbing or descending 200 vertical feet (five contour lines are 40 feet each) over that distance. And the elevation designations written on occasional contour lines will tell us if we're heading up or down.

In addition to the outdoor shops listed in the Appendix, you'll find topos at major universities and some public libraries, where you might try photocopying the ones you need to avoid the cost of buying them. But if you want your own and can't find them locally, visit the United States Geological Survey Web site at **http://topomaps.usgs.gov.**

▶ GPS TRAILHEAD COORDINATES

To collect accurate map data, each trail was hiked with a handheld GPS unit. The data collected was then downloaded and plotted onto a digital USGS topo map. In addition to rendering a highly specific trail outline, this book also includes the GPS coordinates for each trailhead. The survey datum used to arrive at the coordinates is NAD27. For readers who own a GPS unit, whether handheld or onboard a vehicle, the coordinates provided on the first page of each hike may be entered into the GPS unit. Just make sure your GPS unit is set to navigate using the correct format and with NAD27 datum.

INTRODUCTION

The coordinates for trails in this book are provided in degrees, with minutes as decimal (for example, latitude N 47 35.477 and longitude W 122 11.523).

Most trailheads that begin in parking areas can be navigated to by car. However, some hikes still require a short walk to reach the trailhead from a parking area. In those cases, a handheld unit would be necessary to continue the GPS-navigation process. That said, however, readers can easily access all trailheads in this book by using the directions given, the overview maps, and the trail maps, which show at least one major road leading into the area. But for those who enjoy using the latest GPS technology to navigate, the necessary data has been provided.

▶ TRAIL ETIQUETTE

Whether you're on a city, county, state, or national park trail, always remember that great care and resources (from nature as well as from your tax dollars) have gone into creating these trails. Treat the trail, wildlife, and fellow hikers with respect.

- Hike on open trails only. Respect trail and road closures (ask if not sure), avoid possible trespassing on private land, and obtain all permits and authorization as required. Also, leave gates as you found them or as marked.

- Leave only footprints. Be sensitive to the ground beneath you. This also means staying on the existing trail and not blazing any new trails. Be sure to pack out what you pack in. No one likes to see the trash someone else has left behind.

- Never spook animals. An unannounced approach, a sudden movement, or a loud noise startles most animals. A surprised animal can be dangerous to you, to others, and to themselves. Give them plenty of space and time to adjust to your presence.

- Plan ahead. Know your equipment, your ability, and the area in which you are hiking—and prepare accordingly. Be self-sufficient at all times; carry necessary supplies for changes in weather or other conditions (see "The Ten Essentials" below). A well-executed trip is a satisfaction to you and to others.

- Be courteous to other hikers, bikers, or equestrians you encounter on the trails.

▶ HIKING WITH CHILDREN

No one is too young for a hike in the woods or through a city park. Be mindful, though. Flat, short trails are best with an infant. Toddlers who have not quite mastered walking can still tag along, riding on an adult's back in a child carrier. Use common sense to judge a child's capacity to hike a particular trail, and always rely on the possibility that the child will tire quickly and need to be carried. To determine which

INTRODUCTION

trails are suitable for children, a list of good hikes for children is provided in the "Hiking Recommendations" section earlier in this book.

▶ THE TEN ESSENTIALS

One of the first rules of hiking is to be prepared for anything. The simplest way to be prepared is to carry the "Ten Essentials." In addition to carrying the items listed below, you need to know how to use them, especially navigation items. Always consider worst-case scenarios like getting lost, hiking back in the dark, broken gear (for example, a broken hip strap on your pack or a water filter getting plugged), twisting an ankle or sustaining some other serious injury, and thunderstorms or inclement conditions. The items listed below don't cost a lot of money, don't take up much room in a pack, and don't weigh much, but they might just save your life.

WATER: durable bottles, and water treatment like iodine or a filter

MAP: preferably a topo map and a trail map with a route description

COMPASS: a high-quality compass

FIRST-AID KIT: a good-quality kit including first-aid instructions (see details below)

KNIFE: a multitool device with pliers is best

LIGHT: flashlight or headlamp with extra bulbs and batteries

FIRE: windproof matches or lighter and fire starter

EXTRA FOOD: you should always have food in your pack when you've finished hiking

EXTRA CLOTHES: rain protection, warm layers, gloves, warm hat

SUN PROTECTION: sunglasses, lip balm, sunblock, sun hat

▶ FIRST-AID KIT

A kit may contain more items than you might think. These are just the basics:

Ace bandages or Spenco joint wraps

Antacid (for stomach upset)

Antibiotic ointment (Neosporin or the generic equivalent)

Aspirin and/or acetaminophen

Band-Aids

Benadryl or the generic equivalent, diphen-hydramine (an antihistamine, in case of allergic reactions)

Butterfly-closure bandages

Emergency mylar "space" blanket (for shock victims and emergency shelter)

Epinephrine in a prefilled syringe (for those known to have severe allergic reactions to such things as bee stings)

First-aid manual

Gauze (one roll)

Gauze compress pads (a half dozen 4 x 4 inch)

Hydrogen peroxide or iodine swabs

Insect repellent

Moistened towelettes and antiseptic wipes

Moleskin/Spenco "Second Skin"

Needle or safety pin

Triangle bandage (has many first-aid uses such as a sling or tourniquet)

Tweezers

Whistle (more effective in signaling rescuers than your voice)

INTRODUCTION

▶ WATER

"How much is enough? One bottle? Two? Three? But think of all that extra weight!" Well, one simple physiological fact should convince you to err on the side of excess when it comes to deciding how much water to pack: A hiker working hard in 90-degree heat needs approximately ten quarts of fluid every day—that's two and a half gallons (12 large water bottles or 16 small ones). In other words, pack along one or two bottles even for short hikes.

Serious backpackers hit the trail prepared to purify water found along the route. This method, while less dangerous than drinking it untreated, comes with risks. Purifiers with ceramic filters are the safest but are also the most expensive. Many hikers pack along the slightly distasteful tetraglycine-hydroperiodide (a.k.a. iodine tablets, sold under the names Potable Aqua, Coughlan's, and others).

Probably the most common waterborne bug that hikers face is giardia, which may not affect you until one to four weeks after ingestion. It will have you passing noxious rotten-egg-smelling gas, vomiting, shivering with chills, and living in the bathroom. But there are other parasites to worry about that are harder to kill than giardia, including E. coli and Cryptosporidium.

For most people, the pleasures of hiking make carrying water a relatively minor price to pay to remain healthy. If you're tempted to drink "found water," do so only if you understand the risks involved. Better yet, hydrate prior to your hike, carry (and drink) six ounces of water for every mile you plan to hike, and hydrate again after you're finished.

SEATTLE PARKS

CAMP LONG

KEY AT-A-GLANCE INFORMATION

LENGTH: 1.1 miles

CONFIGURATION: Loop with many side trip options available

DIFFICULTY: Easy

SCENERY: Picturesque pond, stream, and fields; seasonal views of Seattle

EXPOSURE: Mostly shaded

TRAFFIC: Moderate

TRAIL SURFACE: Dirt, gravel, and paved

HIKING TIME: 1-2 hours

ACCESS: Hikable year-round, Tuesday–Sunday, 10 a.m.–6 p.m.; closed on Sundays December–February; no fee for parking or park access

MAPS: USGS Seattle South

FACILITIES: Restrooms and water at visitor center

SPECIAL COMMENTS: Historic Boy Scout camp with old lodge and cabins for rent, climbing rock, and glacier-roping practice course. To rent one of the cabins or shelters, the Environmental Learning Center, or the fire circle, contact the Camp Long office via the Internet at **www.seattle. gov/parks/environment/reserve.htm** or call (206) 684-7434; information on open hours, equipment rentals, and climbing classes on Schurman Rock is also available.

Camp Long

Latitude: North 47d33.329m

Longitude: West 122d22.509m

▶ IN BRIEF

Originally established as an outdoor training ground for the Boy Scouts, Camp Long has grown into one of West Seattle's premier parks. The scouting facilities were opened to the general public in 1984. And now everyone is welcome to hike the trails, camp in the shelters, and even climb on famous Schurman Rock, where many serious Cascade mountaineers first tested and developed their skills.

▶ DESCRIPTION

At just less than 70 acres, Camp Long is far from a significant park if measured by size alone. Yet, as the old saying goes, good things come in small packages. For density of attractions, few parks can match this often-overlooked West Seattle reserve.

All outings at Camp Long should start at the visitor center. Built by the Works Progress Administration (WPA) during the Great Depression, the structure was modeled after Oregon's Multnomah Falls Lodge, which was completed more than a decade earlier in 1925; the heavy stones used in construction at Camp Long had once paved Seattle's E Madison Street, which was being resurfaced at the time.

▶ DIRECTIONS

From Interstate 5 just south of downtown Seattle, take Exit 163A, West Seattle Bridge— Columbian Way. Stay to the right on the off-ramp and continue onto the West Seattle Bridge, which becomes Fauntleroy Way SW when it ascends up to West Seattle. At the first traffic light, turn left onto 35th Avenue SW and drive about 0.5 miles up the hill to SW Dawson Street. At this intersection, turn left into Camp Long and continue through the gate to the parking lot on the right.

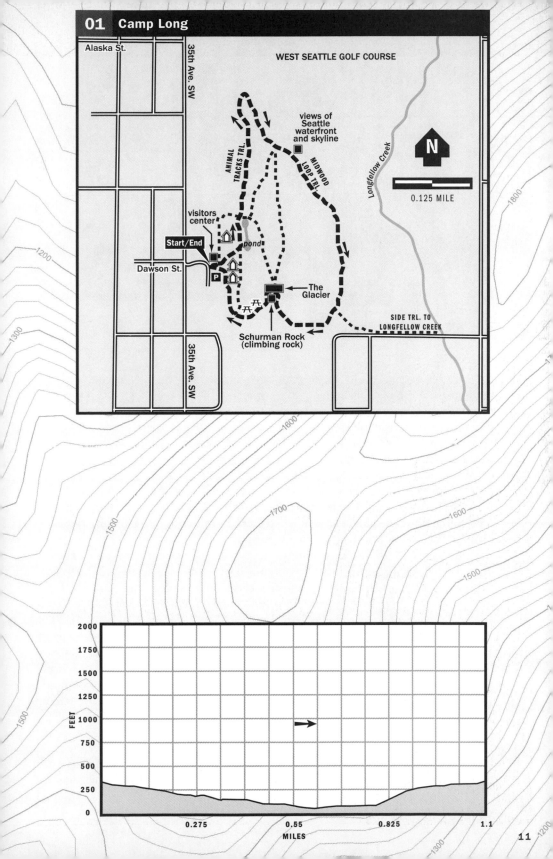

Alaska St.

35th Ave. SW

WEST SEATTLE GOLF COURSE

Longfellow Creek

N

0.125 MILE

ANIMAL TRACKS TRL.

views of
Seattle
waterfront
and skyline

MIDWOOD
LOOP TRL.

visitors
center

Start/End

pond

Dawson St.

P

The Glacier

Schurman Rock
(climbing rock)

SIDE TRL. TO
LONGFELLOW CREEK

35th Ave. SW

1800

1200

1300

1600

1700

1600

1500

1500

1500

1300

1200

2000
1750
1500
1250
1000
750
500
250
0

FEET

0.275   0.55   0.825   1.1

MILES

Climbers on Schurman Rock

Growing right next to the lodge door is an interpretive garden of native plants, modeling a forest-edge plant community typical of the area. Ecologists call this type of environment an ecotone, the meeting of two different landscapes to create a particularly high diversity of species. (The same phenomenon occurs in oceans, where unusual densities of marine life congregate where warm and cold currents mix together.) Many of the plants visible in Camp Long's ecotone can also be seen in the interior of the park.

Inside the visitor center, you'll find information on the history and natural environment of the park on a series of helpful displays. The facility also features a great hall (to the left of the entrance) that is often used for educational gatherings and also hosts the occasional wedding or other ceremony.

An easily completed loop around the perimeter of Camp Long on a series of named trails provides the best hiking option. To get started, circle around the back of the visitor center and pass by several of the camping cabins. Much like the lodge itself, these buildings were built by the Works Progress Administration (WPA), using reclaimed materials from around the city as part of an environmental recycling ethic that the camp continues to promote today.

Head down a gentle slope toward a pond, then turn left along the service road next to the water to find the beginning of the Animal Tracks Nature Trail, in front of the number-seven cabin. Here you should look for a giant stone compass sunk into the ground, another WPA project no doubt built to help young Boy Scouts develop wilderness-navigation skills. This fascinating relic can become obscured by low-lying plants, fallen leaves, and ground cover, but is well worth the effort to find.

The Animal Tracks Trail, which follows a ridge to the northern end of the park, offers occasional views of downtown Seattle, the docks at Harbor Island, and the Space Needle through gaps in the trees. (The forest is a mix of red alder, big leaf maple, and various other species, including western red cedar, although there is no old-growth; the understory is characterized by sword ferns, ivy, Oregon grape, and blackberry bushes.) The trail bends sharply around to the right at its northern point and heads downhill. Stay to the left at a junction (the general rule for hiking the perimeter in the clockwise direction) and cross a creek, the outflow from the wetlands next to the pond you saw at the outset.

Turn left at a second junction to join the Midwood Loop Trail, which runs along the eastern edge of the park closest to the West Seattle Golf Course. Red foxes, frequently spotted on the nearby golf course grounds, can sometimes be observed here.

Shortly before the Midwood Loop Trail ends, a narrow, unmarked trail heads into the trees to the left. This junction connects Camp Long to the Longfellow Creek Trail, a 4-mile-long urban creek corridor through West Seattle; it provides an option for anyone wishing to add to their total hiking distance, although the route frequently travels along roads and sidewalks.

Past the junction, the trail climbs up a short hill to reach the bottom of "The Glacier," a manufactured-rock surface where climbers are likely to be practicing their rope and ice-travel techniques. The Glacier is an add-on to Schurman Rock, just up the stone steps to the left, which tends to be the focus of more-advanced climbing and belaying activity.

Schurman Rock is named for Camp Long cofounder and scout leader Clark Schurman, who envisioned creating a climbing surface that emulated many different types of rocks and challenges typical of the Olympic and Cascade ranges, and for whom Camp Schurman on Mount Rainier's Emmons Glacier is also named. Completed in 1939, Schurman was the first artificial climbing rock in North America. And it has been the staging ground for many great young climbers who later moved on to bigger things. The rock got a major face-lift in 2003, thanks to a consortium of public and private outdoor groups, so it will continue to help train climbers long into the future. In fact, some of them may be practicing on the day of your hike, making the picnic tables and grassy area next to the rock a great place to relax and watch them at work. When you are ready to wrap up your hike, cross the lawn to reach the service road through the trees, and follow it back to the parking lot.

▶ NEARBY ACTIVITIES

The West Seattle Golf Course, adjacent to Camp Long to the east, once hosted the 1953 U.S. Amateur Public Links Championships and has a beautiful layout with great views of downtown Seattle. To schedule a tee time or get more information, visit the West Seattle Golf Club on the Web at **www.westseattlegolf.com/west.asp** or by phone at (206) 935-5187.

CARKEEK PARK

KEY AT-A-GLANCE INFORMATION

LENGTH: 3.5 miles around the perimeter (many more trails in the park interior)

CONFIGURATION: Figure 8 with several options

DIFFICULTY: Easy to moderate

SCENERY: Wildlife (salmon in Pipers Creek when spawning), woodlands, beach, and sea life

EXPOSURE: Wooded park with many shady areas

TRAFFIC: Busy often, but South Ridge trails see little traffic

TRAIL SURFACE: Mixture of gravel, dirt, boardwalk, and paved

HIKING TIME: 1–2 hours or longer with side trips

ACCESS: Hikable year-round, daily, 6 a.m.–10 p.m.; no fees for parking or park access

MAPS: Printed maps on information board near bridge over the railroad tracks, USGS Seattle North

FACILITIES: Restrooms and water near the northern park play area

Carkeek Park

Latitude: North 47d42.742m

Longitude: West 122d22.658m

IN BRIEF

Occupying a stretch of Puget Sound shoreline in northwestern Seattle, Carkeek Park presents a mix of well-developed fields and play areas, an extensive network of trails, and a wide expanse of rocky beach to explore. High bluffs above the water allow all comers to enjoy views usually reserved for the residents of the upscale Blue Ridge neighborhood where the park is nestled.

DESCRIPTION

Carkeek is no secret to many Seattle residents. On any weekend in good weather, expect to compete for space on the playing fields and for parking. People come here for good reason: The park has a variety of attractions, and despite the crowds plenty of peace and solitude can be found out on the trails by anyone willing to put forth a little effort.

From the entrance, the road winds through woods and fields to the upper parking lot next to the playground. If this lot is full, various other less-formal parking opportunities can be found farther along the one-way loop road. There is sure to be space somewhere.

DIRECTIONS

Starting on I-5 north of downtown Seattle, take Exit 173, Northgate Way, and go west. Northgate Way eventually becomes N 105th Street and continues west across WA 99. At the next major intersection after WA 99, cross Greenwood Avenue and veer slightly left onto Holman Road. In a short distance at a sign for Carkeek Park, turn right onto Third Avenue NW. Then turn left onto NW 110th Street, which soon becomes NW Carkeek Park Road. From here, signs guide you into the parking areas of Carkeek Park and the one-way loop road. Try to park in the upper lot nearest the beach or continue down to the lower parking lots if necessary.

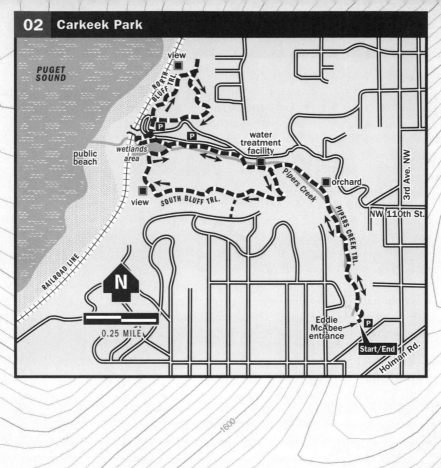

PUGET SOUND

NORTH BLUFF TRL.

view

public beach

wetlands area

water treatment facility

Pipers Creek

orchard

3rd Ave. NW

NW 110th St.

view

SOUTH BLUFF TRL.

PIPERS CREEK TRL.

RAILROAD LINE

N

0.25 MILE

Eddie McAbee entrance

Start/End

Holman Rd.

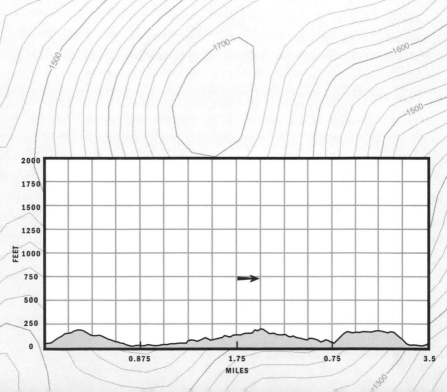

2000
1750
1500
1250
1000
750
500
250
0

FEET

0.875   1.75   0.75   3.5

MILES

Many visitors never venture too far beyond their cars. Adjacent to the parking lot are grass fields that host frequent volleyball, softball, and Frisbee games, and a group of public picnic areas with outdoor grills also stands nearby. A charming playground, which features a slide where kids pass through a giant salmon, will keep children occupied for hours.

Several hiking opportunities are available from the upper parking lot. Despite Carkeek's limited size, the woods north and south of the park road are interlaced with a substantial network of trails. It is possible to get disoriented with so many options, but because of the restricted space no one will stay lost for very long. The easiest way to see the park is to explore on your own; a pamphlet with a trail map should be available at a billboard in the southwest corner of the upper parking lot, next to the beach-access bridge.

Note that Seattle Parks and Recreation is trying to decrease the number of informal trails by specifically graveling maintained trails and letting the rest return to nature, so try to stay on the official trails if you can. Bicycles are allowed only on the Piper's Creek Trail. And dogs are forbidden on the beach and must be leashed at all times everywhere else.

THE BEACH

From the upper playfield, you can access Carkeek Park's beach via a footbridge that crosses some railroad tracks. Kids are sure to be delighted if a train thunders underneath, especially because the vantage offers the chance to see the speeding cars up close, an impressive sight since many freight trains stretch more than a mile in length.

The view west from the beach encompasses Bainbridge Island and the Kitsap Peninsula with the jagged Olympic Mountains beyond. And all kinds of boats—from small day-sailers to giant tankers making for the Strait of Juan de Fuca—provide perspective.

The beach sits on Puget Sound, and the water is too cold for an extended swim (though a quick dip or wade can provide relief on a hot summer day). Exploration, therefore, is the main attraction for many park users. Low tide reveals crabs, anemones, starfish, and many other small marine animals hidden in the tide pools and among the rocks. And the exposed sand allows you to wander up or down the shoreline, possibly as far as Golden Gardens Park over a mile away on Shilshole Bay to the southwest.

THE NORTH BLUFF

To reach the northern side of the park, look for a trailhead along the fence behind the picnic tables. The gravel trail climbs quickly onto the North Bluff, where several viewpoints open above the cliff and expose the steep drop to the beach below. The trail eventually dead-ends at the North Meadow, an open grassy area on a hill with a remarkable view of the sound. Houses are visible nearby, too, as the meadow borders on private property.

Retreat a short distance and you'll find wooden stairs down to the left. Descend into darker woods, composed largely of big leaf maples and red alders; ferns, salal, and other undergrowth cover the forest floor along the route.

Complete the obvious perimeter loop (no more than 0.7 miles) to return to the park road and then your car. Various spur trails lead through the center of the loop and can be used to lengthen your hike.

PIPER'S CREEK AND THE SOUTH RIDGE

The most extensive hiking opportunities at Carkeek are found on the Piper's Creek Trail and the adjoining trails of the South Ridge. Piper's Creek flows through the center of the park, emptying into Puget Sound, and its namesake trail runs alongside for about 1 mile up to an alternate park entrance.

The trail starts just below the upper parking lot; look for a footpath sign and some steps downward. As with the North Bluff, there are many options here. You will know when you have reached Piper's Creek, though, and the right trail is easy to find.

A small wetland lies at the mouth of the creek. The trail surface turns to boardwalk to pass through the lowland bog, with its carpet of algae and high reeds, before returning to gravel. Chum and coho salmon run the creek to spawn in season, an amazing spectacle given the creek's minimal flow and the heavy development nearby.

After following the edge of the grassy lower meadow for about 0.3 miles, the trail passes a small water-treatment plant, then enters a broad ravine. The second-growth forest here is similar in composition to the woods on the North Bluff, although the occasional giant stump testifies to the size of the western red cedars and western hemlocks that grew here before being cut down in the early 20th century.

Upon entering the ravine, the trail starts a gradual uphill climb. Soon some apple trees appear on the left, marking the remnants of the Piper Homestead Orchard. A. W. Piper, the land's owner, was a politician and artist who opened a bakery and candy company in 1876. He and his wife, Minna, sold produce and flowers they grew in the orchard from a wagon in Pike Place Market downtown until the property was sold and developed into a park in 1929.

The trail continues its steady ascent for another half mile until reaching the head of the ravine at the Eddie McAbee Park entrance on NW 100th Place. There is only room for a few cars here, but this side entry can be a great alternate access to the park.

Return down Piper's Creek Trail to just before the water-treatment facility and find the South Ridge Trail to the left. Even on a busy summer day you can expect to have this area of the park to yourself. This trail leads uphill to the southern edge of the ravine, then winds along the top of the ridge back toward the beach. Many side paths lead off into the adjacent residential area as the trail negotiates a series of short rises. Other spurs lead back down to Piper's Creek, but it is easy to stay on the ridge.

After a half mile you will reach the South Bluff and a high overlook. There is no doubt you are at the park boundary, as you emerge from the trees and find yourself practically in someone's backyard. Find the South Bluff Trail, which drops quickly through the woods along the top of the cliff. Be careful here, especially if you have children with you—the sharp drop-off to the beach and sandy tread can be hazardous. From the bottom of the South Bluff it is an easy walk back to your car.

▶ NEARBY ACTIVITIES

Golden Gardens Park offers another great place to explore the Puget Sound shoreline; it includes a sandy bathing beach (although the water isn't any warmer than the water at Carkeek) and a public fishing pier. Reach Golden Gardens by driving to the extreme western end of NW 85th Street and then head down the hill. For more information, visit the Carkeek Web site at **www.cityofseattle.net/parks/parkspaces/carkeek. htm**, or the Golden Gardens Web site at **www.ci.seattle.wa.us/parks/parkspaces/ Golden.htm**.

DISCOVERY PARK: BEACHES, BLUFFS, AND LIGHTHOUSE

KEY AT-A-GLANCE INFORMATION

LENGTH: 3 miles (round-trip)

CONFIGURATION: Loop with many options to extend the hike

DIFFICULTY: Easy to moderate

SCENERY: Historic Fort Lawton grounds, sandy beaches, lighthouse; views of Puget Sound, Seattle, and Mount Rainier.

EXPOSURE: Shaded on upper trails; exposed on beach trails

TRAFFIC: High

TRAIL SURFACE: Mixture of dirt, paved, gravel, and boardwalk

HIKING TIME: 2–4 hours

ACCESS: Hikable year-round; no fees for parking or park access

MAPS: USGS Seattle North

FACILITIES: Restrooms and water at trailhead

Discovery Park: Beaches, Bluffs, and Lighthouse

Latitude: North 47d39.9m

Longitude: West 122d24.691m

▶ IN BRIEF

Occupying a prominent point between Shilshole and Elliott bays, this former military installation is the largest park in the city of Seattle. Blessed with 534 acres of forests, fields, bluffs, and beaches, and even a picturesque lighthouse with excellent views of northern Puget Sound, Discovery Park is a great destination for the entire family.

▶ DESCRIPTION

Discovery Park has more than 10 miles of trails, including a prominently marked Loop Trail that circles most of the open fields and old military housing in the park's southern end. However, because this trail never reaches the beach—arguably the park's leading attraction—a better and more representative loop is described here. This hike descends through the wooded areas in the northern half of the park, travels along the beach to the lighthouse, then returns up the bluff, offering many options for further exploration along the way.

From the North Parking Lot, begin by heading west along the paved road, which is closed to vehicles. Stay on this road through the first junction at the end of the grassy picnic area, where another road branches to the left.

▶ DIRECTIONS

From I-5 north of downtown Seattle, take Exit 169, NE 45th Street, and drive west. Continuing west, 45th Street becomes 46th Street, then drops down into the city of Ballard and becomes Market Street. In Ballard, go left on 15th Avenue NW and immediately cross the Ballard Bridge. Make the first right after the bridge onto W Emerson Street, then make another right onto Gilman Avenue W. Gilman Avenue W eventually becomes W Government Way and goes into the Discovery Park east entrance. Once inside the park, stay to the right and drive to the North Parking Lot.

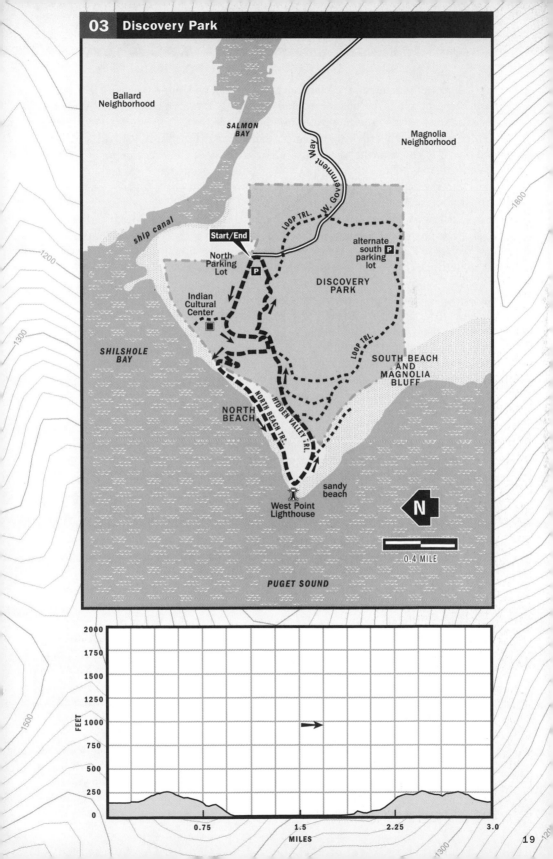

Ballard
Neighborhood

SALMON
BAY

Magnolia
Neighborhood

Government Way

ship canal

LOOP TRL.

Start/End

North
Parking
Lot

alternate
south
parking
lot

DISCOVERY
PARK

Indian
Cultural
Center

LOOP TRL.

SHILSHOLE
BAY

SOUTH BEACH
AND
MAGNOLIA
BLUFF

NORTH
BEACH

NORTH BEACH TRL.

HIDDEN VALLEY TRL.

West Point
Lighthouse

sandy
beach

N

0.4 MILE

PUGET SOUND

A second junction in the road heads up a small rise to the Daybreak Star Indian Cultural Center. Run by the United Indians of All Tribes Foundation (UIATF), this organization provides social services to Native Americans. The site for the Cultural Center was obtained following a heated standoff between Native American activists and the U.S. government in spring of 1970 after the military decommissioned Fort Lawton. Bernie Whitebear, a former Green Beret and longtime advocate for Native American causes, led a so-called invasion and occupation of the fort, arguing that the property was on historic Native American land. The city of Seattle, however, wanted to turn Fort Lawton into a public park. After several months and significant media attention, a compromise agreement was reached, ceding 20 acres of the newly formed Discovery Park to the UIATF with a 99-year renewable lease from the city. Whitebear went on to head the UIATF for three decades, until his death in 2000 at the age of 62.

The Cultural Center's striking architecture blends modern and traditional Native American design, and offers an impressive view from a high bluff out over Shilshole Bay, making it a quick and worthy side trip. Simply follow the road around to the northern side of the building—its best façade—and look for a wooden overlook platform on the far side of the lawn. From this viewpoint, the masts at Shilshole Marina resemble a forest of thin trees near the Lake Washington Ship Canal entrance; on a clear day Mount Baker can be seen far away to the north.

After this short detour, continue back on the main road, which curves around to the left and starts heading south. About a quarter mile past the Cultural Center, the official Loop Trail intersects the road. Turn right on the Loop Trail until you reach a second road, then turn right again and follow the road back to the north, close to where it dead-ends. This somewhat awkward, roundabout route is the result of a landslide that washed away a better access path sometime in the past.

On the opposite side of a small picnic area to the left is a gap in a chain-link fence. And on a green wooden post is a sign directing hikers to the North Beach Trail. Follow this path as it descends through trees on a steep trail with some wooden stairs, bending to the right and dropping 200 feet in about an eighth of a mile.

The trail turns left, above a long breakwater of heavy boulders, along the shore toward the lighthouse. Even with only moderate wind, sizable swells often crash against the rocks here, despite the short run of open water and considerable shelter provided by Bainbridge Island and the Kitsap Peninsula across Puget Sound.

After a half mile, the breakwater gives way to a stretch of sandy beach below the lighthouse. The trail cuts inland, but the beach itself provides a more interesting way to get around the point, except during bad weather or at extreme high tide. Lots of shells, driftwood, and other flotsam lie on the sand, providing fun for beachcombers of all ages who search for treasures along the shore. And marine wildlife—including crabs, barnacles, starfish, and sea anemones—is frequently visible at low tide. This approach also provides excellent views of the lighthouse itself, known as the West Point Lighthouse, and its attached radar installation.

The far side of the point (where the sandy beach continues southeast for another half mile) has treasures all its own, offering interesting views of West Seattle, Mount Rainier, Puget Sound, and the Olympic Mountains. This area is known as the South Beach, and it is certainly worth exploring. Be wary of the tides, though, as people have been known to get trapped here below the steep walls of Magnolia Bluff.

West Point Lighthouse at Discovery Park

When you are ready to continue hiking, look for the trail heading uphill on the northern side of the lighthouse access road. The path follows the road for a few hundred yards before reaching a junction (signed for the Hidden Valley Trail) across from an excellent viewpoint over South Beach from the top of the bluff.

Take the Hidden Valley Trail and climb up through the woods, crossing several intersections until it ends on the park's official Loop Trail, just short of another road. Note that once you cross this road, you are back on the same short section of the Loop Trail you hiked earlier, except now you're traveling in the opposite direction.

Stay on the Loop Trail as it winds up and down through a pleasant forest for a half mile and crosses two more paved roads (long closed to traffic) in one of the nicest sections of the upper park. At a third paved road, head left down the hill to return to the North Parking Lot, where you began.

To extend your hike, the best bet is to follow the official Loop Trail as far as you wish to go, potentially adding several more miles if you complete the entire circuit. Another option is to take the South Beach Trail away from the beach rather than the Hidden Valley Trail, as described earlier, then continue all the way around the Loop Trail in a counterclockwise direction. This will allow you to see the open southern half of the park without ever having to retrace your steps.

▶ NEARBY ACTIVITIES

For more than 75 years, the Fisherman's Terminal has been the best place in Seattle to buy fresh fish straight off the boat. Nowadays, a comfortable façade and a host of eateries greet visitors to the working docks, providing multiple opportunities to sample the North Pacific catch of the day. To reach the Fisherman's Terminal, turn left from Gilman Avenue W onto W Emerson Place and cross a bridge over the train tracks; the entrance is on the left.

SCHMITZ PRESERVE PARK

 KEY AT-A-GLANCE INFORMATION

LENGTH: 1 mile (round-trip; side trip options)

CONFIGURATION: Loop

DIFFICULTY: Easy

SCENERY: Old-growth forest contrasted with enormous logging stumps in an urban park; a cascading stream

EXPOSURE: Shaded

TRAFFIC: Moderate

TRAIL SURFACE: Dirt, gravel, and some boardwalk

HIKING TIME: 1–2 hours

ACCESS: Hikable year-round; no fees for parking or park-access

MAPS: USGS Seattle South

FACILITIES: No restroom or water facilities

Schmitz Preserve Park

Latitude: North 47d34.654m

Longitude: West 122d24.121m

▶ **IN BRIEF**

This unassuming little park hides a singular example of old-growth forest in the middle of the city. With a good network of trails through a quiet, secluded valley, Schmitz Preserve Park makes a great place for a quick escape to the woods, despite its limited size.

▶ **DESCRIPTION**

Almost a century after it was established in 1908, Schmitz Park, originally a 30-acre parcel of land donated by Ferdinand and Emma Schmitz, remains true to its founders' intent—to be kept as an example of the local forest as it was discovered by Seattle's first settlers.

The pioneers of the Denny Party, who landed just down the hill at Alki Point in November 1851, would undoubtedly still feel at home in Schmitz, even if they would find the rest of Seattle completely unrecognizable. Ironically, the park has come to represent Seattle's past, though the name *Alki* comes from a Chinook word indicating the future.

Now expanded to more than 50 acres, Schmitz Park continues to protect the region's natural heritage. In fact, it does such a good job that the University of Washington Forestry Department uses the park as a prime example of Pacific Northwest old-growth forest, proudly displaying it to visiting Asian forest managers. The

▶ **DIRECTIONS**

From I-5 just south of downtown Seattle, take Exit 163A, W Seattle Bridge—Columbian Way. Stay to the right on the off-ramp and continue onto the West Seattle Bridge. Take the Admiral Way exit, then continue for about 2 miles and turn left onto SW Stevens Street just before a bridge. Park along SW Stevens Street, and find the trailhead near the intersection with Admiral Way.

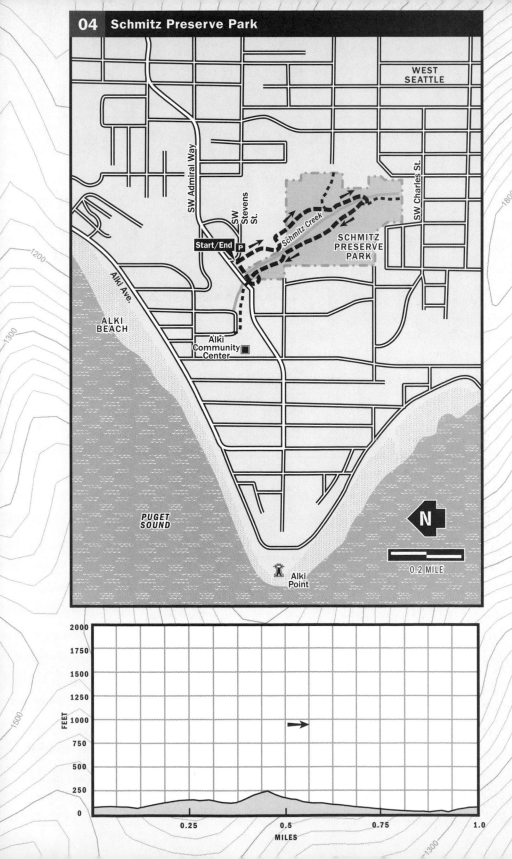

WEST
SEATTLE

SW Admiral Way

SW
Stevens
St.

SW Charles St.

Schmitz Creek

SCHMITZ
PRESERVE
PARK

Start/End

P

Alki Ave.

ALKI
BEACH

Alki
Community
Center

PUGET
SOUND

N

0.2 MILE

Alki
Point

FEET

2000
1750
1500
1250
1000
750
500
250
0

0.25   0.5   0.75   1.0
MILES

Western red cedar bark at
Schmitz Preserve

future of the global environment will undoubtedly be determined in Asia, home to more than half of the world's population and most of its fastest growing economies. Already today, dust clouds from desertification in western China occasionally reach the U.S. Pacific Coast, exacerbating smog and other air-pollution problems and underlining the truly global effects of environmental degradation. One can only hope the university's visitors will be as committed to good land stewardship as the Schmitz family was back in 1908.

At one time it was possible to drive on a road to the center of the park, but that changed following a landslide in 2002 that gave Schmitz a makeover. Now all cars must be parked on adjacent surface streets, although many visitors come from the surrounding communities and walk to the park from home, forgoing their cars altogether.

The trails here are unsigned but easy to follow, and there is no chance of getting lost for any length of time. A narrow loop with multiple side trails leading out to nearby streets and neighborhoods runs through the center of the park. If you mistakenly end up on one of these side trails, simply retrace your steps to rejoin the main route.

Start hiking down the hill on the old gravel road, which soon becomes a dirt single-track trail. Head left along Schmitz Creek to begin the clockwise loop; this small stream defines the park's central ravine and is marked by several small waterfalls along the way.

A few mammoth stumps indicate that minimal logging did occur here in the late 1800s, nonetheless some truly giant trees remain. A particularly impressive western red cedar, its deeply grooved bark showing the passage of time, stands on a rise just off the trail to the left. Watch for other ancient trees with blackened bark, revealing forest fires that swept through West Seattle in years past.

A boardwalk runs through the wetlands along the creek, winding through skunk cabbage, water parsley, and various ferns. Metal laths on the elevated boards help keep the footing secure even when the surface is wet, which is most of the time because of the shelter and cooling shade of the tree canopy.

The trail reaches the southern end of the park then doubles back to the right, climbing the valley wall. Pileated woodpeckers are common here, and can easily be heard or seen taking their toll on the trees nearby. The woodpeckers are only one of a large range of bird species that live in the mixed-conifer forest, which also is home to Steller's jays, song sparrows, and black-capped chickadees.

Eventually, the loop trail reaches an old road (now closed to vehicles) along the creek. Continue down the road to find a stairway on the left that'll take you to the Schmitz Park Bridge, built in 1936, overhead. Head up the stairs and cross the bridge to return to your car. The road continues under the bridge and heads downhill to the Alki Community Center, an alternate place to begin the hike.

▶ NEARBY ACTIVITIES

Try a meal at the Luna Park Cafe, a neighborhood staple at 2918 SW Avalon Way, just past the end of SW Admiral Way under the West Seattle Bridge. With hearty meals and an extensive children's menu, it's easy to see why Luna Park has long been a family favorite; an extensive renovation in 2005 only helped add to the atmosphere. Call the café at (206) 935-7250 for more information.

SEWARD PARK

KEY AT-A-GLANCE INFORMATION

LENGTH: 6.6 miles (2.4 miles of paved shoreline trail and 2.2 miles of interior dirt trails)

CONFIGURATION: Loop with other options

DIFFICULTY: Easy

SCENERY: Views of the surrounding area and Lake Washington; old-growth forest and other picturesque plant life; lakeshore beaches

EXPOSURE: Shaded on interior trails, exposed on shoreline trail

TRAFFIC: Heavy on shoreline trail, moderate on interior trails

TRAIL SURFACE: Dirt in interior, paved around perimeter

HIKING TIME: 1–3 hours

ACCESS: Hikable year-round; no fees for parking or park-access

MAPS: USGS Seattle South and Bellevue South

FACILITIES: Restrooms and water at the parking areas (some may be closed in winter)

Seward Park

Latitude: North 47d33.106m

Longitude: West 122d15.231m

▶ IN BRIEF

Before Lake Washington was lowered by the opening of the ship canal in 1917, the peninsula now occupied by Seward Park was almost an island. Today, the park is an island of a different sort. Resisting the Seattle development that has spread around it for almost a century, Seward is now one of the last significant vestiges of old-growth forest within the city limits. A paved circular loop follows the island's lakefront shoreline and connects to a network of single-track trails beneath the ancient trees.

▶ DESCRIPTION

Seward Park was named for William Seward, who was appointed as secretary of state by Abraham Lincoln in 1861. An outspoken critic of slavery and an ardent supporter of the Union during the Civil War, Seward became a highly visible and symbolic enemy of the Confederacy. His further abuse of power as head of the government program to eliminate so-called disloyals in the North cemented his reputation among Southerners as a man to be feared and hated. In fact, Seward became a supplemental target of the assassination

▶ DIRECTIONS

From I-5 south of downtown Seattle, take Exit 163, S Columbian Way, which soon becomes 15th Avenue S. In a short distance, S Columbian Way veers left (east) off of 15th Avenue S and continues to an intersection with Beacon Avenue S. Turn right (south) on Beacon Avenue S. In just more than a half mile, turn left (east) onto S Orcas Street, which eventually ends at Seward Park. Turn right into the park entrance, and park in one of the lower lots if you plan to walk the paved shoreline trail. Continue to the upper parking lot if you plan to hike the interior trails or if the lower lots are full.

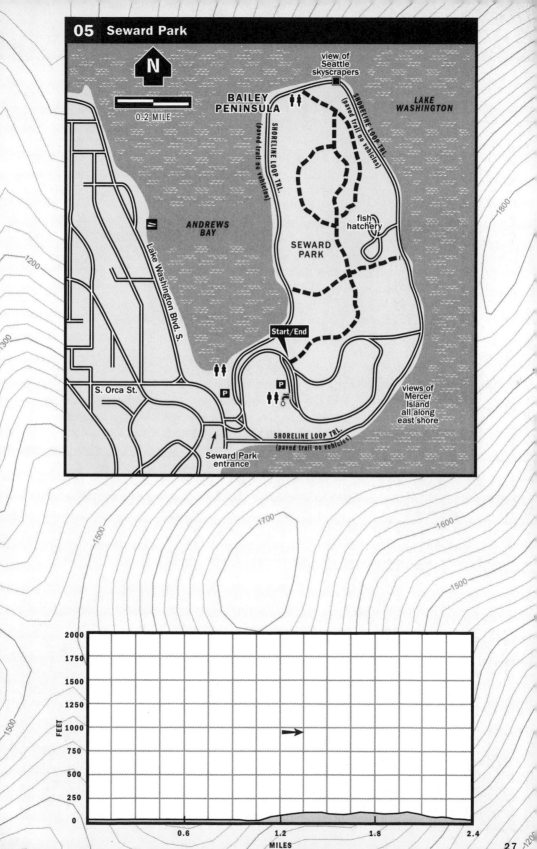

N

0.2 MILE

view of
Seattle
skyscrapers

BAILEY
PENINSULA

LAKE
WASHINGTON

SHORELINE LOOP TRL.
(paved trail no vehicles)

SHORELINE LOOP TRL.
(paved trail no vehicles)

ANDREWS
BAY

fish
hatchery

SEWARD
PARK

Lake Washington Blvd. S.

Start/End

S. Orca St.

P

P

views of
Mercer
Island
all along
east shore

SHORELINE LOOP TRL.
(paved trail no vehicles)

Seward Park
entrance

2000
1750
1500
1250
1000
750
500
250
0

FEET

0.6   1.2   1.8   2.4

MILES

conspiracy organized by John Wilkes Booth. On April 14, 1865, the same night Booth shot Lincoln, a man named Lewis Powell stabbed Seward in the throat in an attempt to kill him as well. Despite suffering very serious wounds, Seward survived the attack and continued to serve in his post as Secretary of State under Andrew Johnson. During Johnson's administration, Seward became well-known for his pivotal role in the purchase of Alaska from Russia in the spring of 1867. At the time, Alaska was generally considered a frozen wasteland and the transaction was mocked as "Seward's Folly," a monumental waste of taxpayer money.

Today, it's hard to see how the acquisition of Alaska for the paltry sum of $7.2 million could be viewed as anything but one of the greatest bargains in U.S. history. Seward obtained 360 million acres of land for 2 cents an acre, substantially less than Thomas Jefferson had paid for his celebrated Louisiana Purchase six decades before. Seward's $7.2 million outlay in 1867 would be the equivalent of approximately $90 million in 2006, an amount that Alaskan oil revenue alone repays approximately every three days. And this says nothing for the vast value of the other natural resources the state is famous for—including gold, which was first discovered in the Klondike in the late 1800s.

Most historians credit the ensuing Alaska gold rush for the establishment of Seattle as a major city, the last outpost of civilization for thousands of would-be prospectors on their way to the Yukon. It's safe to say that without Alaska, Seattle would be a very different place today. For that reason, Seward's name was worthy of being attached to a 300-acre park along the western shore of Lake Washington.

Ironically, although Seward indirectly spurred Seattle's urban expansion, his namesake park is one of the few places remaining in the city that development has never reached. It's hard to imagine from most parts of Seattle now, but there was a time when the entire area was covered in a thick forest—and Seward Park is one of the last remaining stands.

A 2.4-mile Shoreline Trail, following a paved road now closed to motor vehicles, loops around the perimeter of the park along the edge of Lake Washington. This route is very popular and provides views of the lake and the surrounding communities. Particularly interesting are some of the palatial houses visible on Mercer Island to the east; it wouldn't take many of these estates to top the $7.2 million price tag of Seward's entire Alaska purchase. Also, looking northward offers a view of some of the tallest skyscrapers downtown rising above the Mount Baker and Beacon Hill neighborhoods and the I-90 Bridge spanning the lake.

A fish hatchery on the eastern side of the park was constructed by the Works Progress Administration (WPA) during the New Deal to raise trout for stocking local lakes, including Lake Washington. The vision was for Seward Park to become a fisherman's paradise, but the reality has not quite lived up to those expectations. The fishery is not generally open to the public, but a new education center is slated to be completed sometime in 2007.

For most hikers, the primary attraction at Seward Park is its forest, which exhibits all of the required characteristics of old-growth—standing snags, a layered canopy, fallen nurse logs, and some very large trees, among others. Although lacking any truly gigantic specimens, Seward Park harbors some trees that are up to 200 years old and contains one of the largest madrones in the state. Along with

Young hiker looking toward the
Seattle skyline from Seward Park

madrones, the lowland forest contains a mix of western red cedars, Douglas firs, western hemlocks, and big leaf maples. The maples are marked for their ability to host epiphytes (plants that grow on other plants) such as licorice ferns, mosses, and lichens. Unfortunately, English ivy, a foreign, invasive plant that chokes out endemic species, grows here as well. Volunteer groups are working in conjunction with park administration to eradicate the plant in an attempt to restore the natural ecosystem.

The best way to see the Seward Park is to find your own way around. The central spine of the park is laced with a series of dirt paths, seven separate segments (totaling 2.2 miles) linked on all sides to the Shoreline Trail. By following a mix of the interior trails and the Shoreline, this network can lead you to all corners of the park and its varied attractions. Thanks to the general topography and short distances involved, navigation is simple even for first-time visitors.

▶ NEARBY ACTIVITIES

Try the Columbia City Ale House for a posthike beer or meal. Part of the revitalization of the historic Columbia City community, this cozy neighborhood pub offers a wide variety of excellent local brews and often features special seasonal varieties. The Ale House, located at 4914 Rainier Avenue S, can be reached from Seward Park by following S Orcas Street until it intersects with Rainier Avenue and then turning right (north). For more information, call (206) 723-5123.

WASHINGTON PARK ARBORETUM AND FOSTER ISLAND TRAIL

KEY AT-A-GLANCE INFORMATION

LENGTH: 3.5 miles (1.5-mile loop in Arboretum; plus optional 2-mile round-trip out-and-back on Foster Island Trail)

CONFIGURATION: Loop with many options

DIFFICULTY: Easy

SCENERY: Incredible display of plant life from around the world, island shoreline trails, territorial views across Union Bay, bird-watching and other wildlife watching

EXPOSURE: Mostly shaded

TRAFFIC: Heavy

TRAIL SURFACE: Dirt, gravel, small amount of boardwalk

HIKING TIME: 1–3 hours

ACCESS: Hikable year-round; no fee for parking or park access

MAPS: USGS Seattle North

FACILITIES: Restrooms and water at the visitor center

Washington Park Arboretum and Foster Island Trail

Latitude: North 47d38.382m

Longitude: West 122d17.668m

IN BRIEF

A few Seattle parks provide a glimpse of the way it was by harboring the last stands of the thick forest that once covered the region. The Washington Park Arboretum is a similar sanctuary, instead featuring exotic plant life from around the world. Rather than a trip back in time, the Arboretum allows visitors to take a walk to all corners of the Earth via a peaceful system of trails through its carefully manicured gardens and groves.

DESCRIPTION

Any hike at the Washington Park Arboretum should begin at the visitor center, where plenty of good information on the park is available through a collection of maps, pamphlets, and handouts. An attached store sells general-interest books on botany, nature, and wildlife, and its helpful staff can assist by answering any questions. The center also occasionally hosts gala events and receptions in the great hall and under the trellis on the patio outside. For anyone seeking a more personal educational experience, the visitor center also offers free guided walks; call (206) 543-8801 for the schedule.

The Arboretum claims to have more than 40,000 plants from 4,600 different species, 139 listed as endangered. Chances are, if something can grow in the climate and soil at Washington Park, a sample will be on display. Many are grouped into named collections, including lindens,

DIRECTIONS

From I-5 north of downtown Seattle, go east on WA 520. Take the first exit off WA 520, Montlake Boulevard. Go straight across Montlake Boulevard onto Lake Washington Boulevard E. In about 0.5 miles, turn left onto Foster Island Road, then turn right onto Arboretum Drive E. The parking area at the visitor center is immediately on the left.

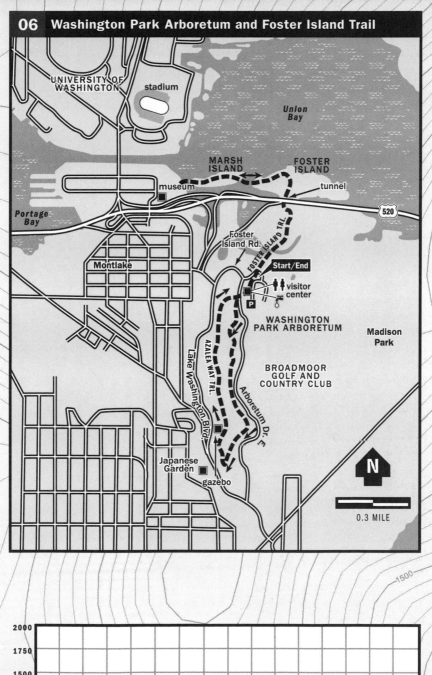

UNIVERSITY OF WASHINGTON

stadium

Union Bay

MARSH ISLAND

FOSTER ISLAND

tunnel

museum

520

Portage Bay

Foster Island Rd.

FOSTER ISLAND TRL.

Montlake

Start/End

visitor center

P

WASHINGTON PARK ARBORETUM

Madison Park

AZALEA WAY TRL.

BROADMOOR GOLF AND COUNTRY CLUB

Lake Washington Blvd.

Arboretum Dr. E.

Japanese Garden

gazebo

N

0.3 MILE

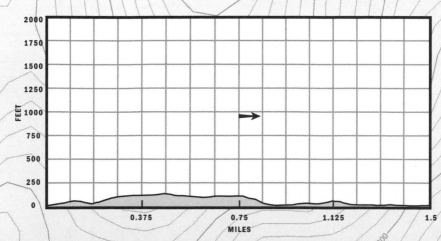

camellias, magnolias, Asiatic maples, larches, and numerous others. Several specific exhibits highlight individual classes or geographic areas, such as a rhododendron grove and the New Zealand high country.

Multiple species are identified with signs, listing both common and scientific names. Trees range from the very familiar *Pseudotsuga menziesii,* or Douglas fir, icon of the Pacific Northwest, to the extremely rare *Franklinia alatamaha,* or Franklinia, originally from the state of Georgia and thought to be extinct in the wild since about 1800.

The Arboretum is carefully landscaped with ponds, a gazebo, and plenty of places to stop and reflect. A mix of scents and fragrances fill the air. And although the park is particularly popular during the spring bloom, the wide range of species means that something is at its peak virtually every month out of the year.

Laid out linearly along a north-south axis, the Arboretum is generally bounded on the east by Arboretum Drive E and on the west by Lake Washington Boulevard E, though some sections spill over the road on either side. In between, a maze of connecting trails wind their way through the heart of the park, allowing visitors to explore the various groves and gardens.

This kind of design does not lend itself well to a single recommended route, however. The best way to see the majority of the Arboretum's displays is to form an elongated loop by traveling south on the trails generally paralleling Arboretum Drive E, then returning on Azalea Way, a broad, grassy path that forms the spine of the park. Side trips to individual areas of particular interest can easily be added to this general framework to suit personal tastes.

FOSTER ISLAND TRAIL

A second hiking option—commonly known as the Foster Island Trail, or the Arboretum Waterfront Trail—leads northeast from the visitor center parking lot. Although passing through what is technically part of the Arboretum, this route explores the marshlands along Lake Washington's western shore and has an entirely different look and feel than the carefully arranged plant collections in the park's main section.

The trail begins as a dirt and gravel road and soon reaches a bridge that crosses a lake inlet to reach Foster Island. Pass through the Arboretum's last identified grove of trees and then duck underneath WA 520 through a tunnel, with the traffic humming overhead. Enter a grassy area on the far side, then turn left where the trail narrows into the reeds.

A wooden observation platform is on the right, looking out over the Montlake ship canal, Union Bay, and Webster Point at the tip of the Laurelhurst neighborhood across the water. The University of Washington, with its distinctive winged stadium rising unmistakably above the lake, occupies most of the land to the left. At any time of year a steady parade of boats will be passing by. And if the Huskies are in action, an entire armada of loyal supporters unfailingly anchors in the bay.

However, the chief sightseeing attraction here is not the cityscape but the natural environment. Foster Island is an excellent bird-watching site, with flocks of ducks and other waterfowl swimming on the lake and congregating among the reeds.

The trail continues on an extensive boardwalk system of wood, metal, and concrete, occasionally crossing out over the water. The lake is very shallow in this area,

Foster Island Overlook and
Husky Stadium

and it is possible to see the bottom in several places. The boardwalk eventually ends on Marsh Island, where the trail returns to dirt and enters a tangled thicket of mud and stunted trees. Additional opportunities abound for observing the island's wildlife, including beavers, whose teeth marks are visible on some of the stumps

At the far end of Marsh Island, the trail crosses back to the mainland on a bridge and reaches its western terminus in the parking lot for the Museum of History and Industry (MOHAI), a total of about 1 mile from the Arboretum's visitor center. From here, it is possible to complete a loop back to the starting point by walking along Lake Washington Boulevard E. This busy road is not well-suited for foot traffic, though; the safer and more scenic option is to return the way you came.

▶ NEARBY ACTIVITIES

The Washington Park Arboretum also maintains an excellent 3.5-acre Japanese garden, which includes a traditional teahouse. The garden, located at 1075 Lake Washington Boulevard E, is adjacent to the southern end of the Arboretum's main grounds and charges an admission fee. For more information, call (206) 684-4725 or visit the garden's Web site at **www.ci.seattle.wa.us/parks/parkspaces/japanesegarden.htm**.

WOODLAND PARK AND GREEN LAKE PARK

KEY AT-A-GLANCE INFORMATION

LENGTH: 1.33 miles around the perimeter (many more trails in the park interior; side trip options around Woodland Park Zoo, the rose garden, and the Green Lake multi-use trail)

CONFIGURATION: Loop with many different options

DIFFICULTY: Easy

SCENERY: Wildlife (millions of rabbits), Woodland Zoo animals; views of Green Lake and Seattle neighborhoods

EXPOSURE: Wooded park with many shady areas

TRAFFIC: Popular on sunny days

TRAIL SURFACE: Mixture of gravel, dirt, and paved

HIKING TIME: 1–2 hours or longer with side trips

ACCESS: Hikable year-round during daylight hours; rose garden, 7 a.m.–dusk; no fee for parking

MAPS: None needed, though trails meander throughout the park, USGS Seattle North

FACILITIES: Restrooms across the street at Green Lake; water near tennis courts

Woodland Park and Green Lake Park

Latitude: North 47d40.205m

Longitude: West 122d20.583m

IN BRIEF

No one will mistake Woodland Park or Green Lake Park for wilderness, but their central location and convenient access from so many neighborhoods make this outdoor complex the signature recreation area for many Seattle residents.

DESCRIPTION

It is estimated that as many as 10,000 people visit Green Lake Park daily during the summer. And if you show up in midafternoon, you might think they all arrived just before you did. Woodland Park does not see quite the same crowds, but it is still sure to be busy, with its playing fields occupied and in use.

If it's solitude you seek, your best bet is to arrive at the break of dawn—or head somewhere else. However, a rewarding walk can be found here if you're willing to share the trail; special attractions like the zoo and the rose garden add a unique flavor. Woodland is also a good place to bring your pet, as a special off-leash play area allows dogs to run free in a controlled space, a relative rarity for Seattle.

Woodland Park virtually defines a multiuse facility. Tennis courts, soccer fields, softball fields, and a running track are all immediately accessible, and walkers, runners, and bicyclists utilize the area. Further reaches of the park offer more

DIRECTIONS

From I-5 north of downtown Seattle, take Exit 169, NE 50th Street, and go west. Continue over a hill to a five-way intersection at the bottom, and go right on E Green Lake Way N. In a short distance, go left at the fork in the road onto W Green Lake Way N. Take the first left into the parking lot next to the tennis courts near the sign for Woodland Park. There is additional parking along W Green Lake Way N.

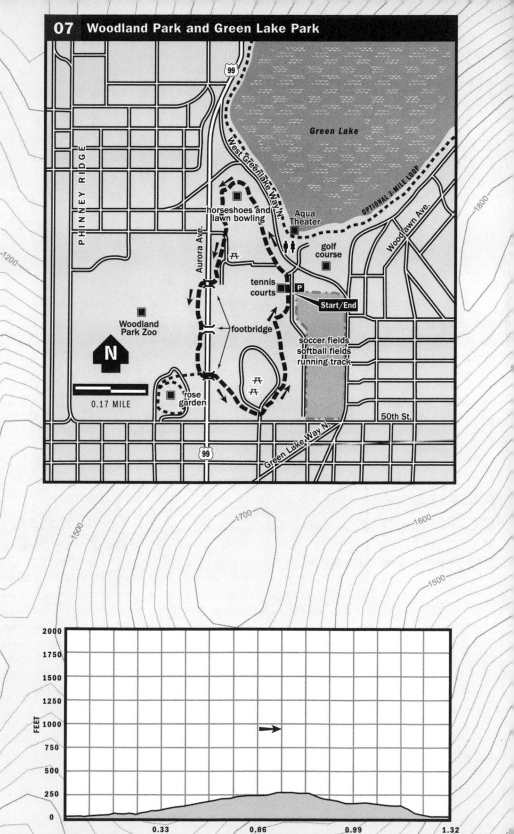

Green Lake

99

West Greenlake Way N.

OPTIONAL 3-MILE LOOP

Woodlawn Ave.

horseshoes and
lawn bowling

Aqua
Theater

golf
course

PHINNEY RIDGE

Aurora Ave.

tennis
courts

P

Start/End

Woodland
Park Zoo

footbridge

soccer fields
softball fields
running track

N

0.17 MILE

rose
garden

50th St.

99

Green Lake Way N.

1200

1300

1500

1700

1600

1800

1500

1500

300

MILES			
0.33	0.66	0.99	1.32

FEET

2000
1750
1500
1250
1000
750
500
250
0

Red rose at Woodland Park Rose
Garden

unusual playfields, including a series of horseshoe pits and a lawn bowling pitch.

Start your hike on the northern side of the tennis courts by heading up the park road and then veering to the right, next to the off-leash dog run. Pick any trail, and continue up a hill through a small wooded area until another parking lot and Green Lake are visible through the trees to the north.

As you advance up the hill, watch for rabbits; scores of these small mammals in all sizes and colors can be seen throughout the park. For most visitors, this is the most exotic wildlife they will encounter. But bald eagles have been spotted in the trees here, so keep your eyes peeled.

Emerge from the woods to find a fenced-in activity area for horseshoe tossing and a green for lawn bowling. Circling the playfields, you will soon be standing above the busy traffic on Aurora Avenue N and facing a residential area on Phinney Ridge. Cut back to the left along Aurora Avenue to pass through some nicely shaded picnic areas.

Three bridges link the eastern and western sections of the park, divided when Aurora Avenue was built in the 1930s. Cross the northernmost bridge, the first one you will reach. At the far end a high fence topped with barbed wire marks the edge of the Woodland Park Zoo.

A trail circles the perimeter of the zoo; turn left and head south along the fence. With a little imagination, the traffic below sounds like a rushing river. Commingled, the noises and the scents from the animals in the zoo can make this area seem like the true outdoors.

Pass the second bridge, continue to the third, then enter an arched tunnel on the right. Go across a parking lot, climb a small rise, then bend around to the left to find the entrance to the Woodland Park Rose Garden behind some heavy wrought-iron gates. The garden is free to the public and open year-round from 7 a.m. to dusk, although the best time to visit is surely at the height of the spring bloom.

The garden displays a vast collection of roses in all colors and sizes, interspersed with a lily pond, some hedges, and a gazebo. Many of the flowers—with names like "Love and Peace" and "Fragrant Cloud"—have won awards, and several hybrids bloom in shades you never imagined. This is a great area for photography, especially for capturing close-up views.

Return the way you came, and cross back on the third bridge to the eastern side of the park into more fields and picnic areas. Continue west to the edge of a short ridge, then descend through a wooded ravine to return to the parking lot where you began. There are many interconnected trails in this section of the park to extend your exploration, if time allows.

To visit Green Lake Park, cross W Green Lake Way N and find either of two obvious loop trails. The paved inner loop is more developed, more traveled, and posted at 2.8 miles in length. The outer loop is a dirt path that follows closer to the perimeter of the park rather than the lakeshore and is slightly longer at 3.2 miles.

Either path will lead you around the lake and back, providing a tour of Green Lake's various attractions, including basketball courts, tennis courts, a pitch-and-putt golf course, open fields, playgrounds, two fishing piers, and a boathouse. Rowing shells, kayaks, and canoes are frequently seen on the water, and various paddleboats are available for rental in the vicinity of the main north parking lot.

A sandy beach area might look inviting in the heat, but swimming in the lake is not recommended. The indoor Evans Swimming Pool, at the northern end of the park, is a better bet. Or head to the popular wading and splash pool about a quarter mile farther around to the west.

Although it is more of an annoyance than a hazard for swimmers, the lake suffers from milfoil infestation. This invasive aquatic plant apparently spread here via boat trailers, just as it has at many other freshwater lakes in the Pacific Northwest. Eurasian water milfoil (*Myriophyllum spicatum*) was first found in the Seattle area in the 1960s, and has been steadily expanding its range ever since. It is now considered the most problematic plant in Washington State.

Ironically for such a pest, milfoil is quite attractive and can easily be identified by its feathery leaves and threadlike composition in areas where it reaches the surface of the lake.

▶ NEARBY ACTIVITIES

The surrounding Green Lake and Wallingford neighborhoods offer countless opportunities for a posthike meal or drink. In particular, look along N 45th Street, a few blocks south of Woodland Park or along the northern and eastern corners of Green Lake Park. Many establishments along E Green Lake Way N offer outdoor seating and allow for excellent people-watching in the park. The Woodland Park Zoo also makes a great trip, especially with children. Try visiting midweek to avoid the crowds. For more information, visit **www.zoo.org**.

BLAKE ISLAND STATE PARK

KEY AT-A-GLANCE INFORMATION

LENGTH: 3 miles around the perimeter (many side trip options)

CONFIGURATION: Loop

DIFFICULTY: Easy

HIGHLIGHTS: Plant life, wildlife, beaches, local history, Tillicum Village and lodge, kayaking; views across Puget Sound

EXPOSURE: Mostly shaded

TRAFFIC: Moderate (low in off-season)

TRAIL SURFACE: Dirt

HIKING TIME: 2–3 hours

ACCESS: Hikable year-round (a few private boat tours scheduled in winter months); no hiking fees; moorage fees at Tillicum Village marina

MAPS: Park maps posted at Tillicum Village; USGS Seattle South

FACILITIES: Restrooms, water, picnic areas, gift shop at Tillicum Village

Blake Island State Park

Latitude: North 47d32.499m

Longitude: West 122d29.01m

▶ IN BRIEF

Located in clear view of the Space Needle and just 8 miles from downtown Seattle, Blake Island is nonetheless a remote destination that's only accessible to those who can cross its moat of Puget Sound waters. Anyone making the journey, however, will be richly rewarded with the opportunity to explore the island's history, wildlife, and natural setting. Blake Island State Park is so close to the city, yet so far away.

▶ DESCRIPTION

Although there are multiple places to moor a private boat around Blake Island's shoreline and you can pull up almost anywhere if arriving by sea kayak, the best landing spot is the marina at Tillicum Village. Located on a prominent point on the island's northeast corner, the village commands a view of most of the Seattle skyline to the

▶ DIRECTIONS

See Tillicum Village Web site (**www.tillicum village.com**) for information on camping, moorage for private boats, and public-tour-boat schedules. However, a great way to reach Blake Island is by sea kayak; the three closest launch points are at the Fauntelroy ferry dock (or Lincoln Park) in West Seattle, the Vashon Island ferry dock, and the Southworth ferry dock (see Washington State Ferries Web site for schedules and driving directions: **www.wsdot.wa.gov/ ferries**). The shortest open-water crossing is the Southworth route, at about 1 mile. The park also has a sandy beach launch point at the end of a dead-end street adjacent to the north side of the ferry dock. No matter how you reach the island, the loop trail can be accessed from any of the three camping areas (see map); But the recommend starting point is at Tillicum Village.

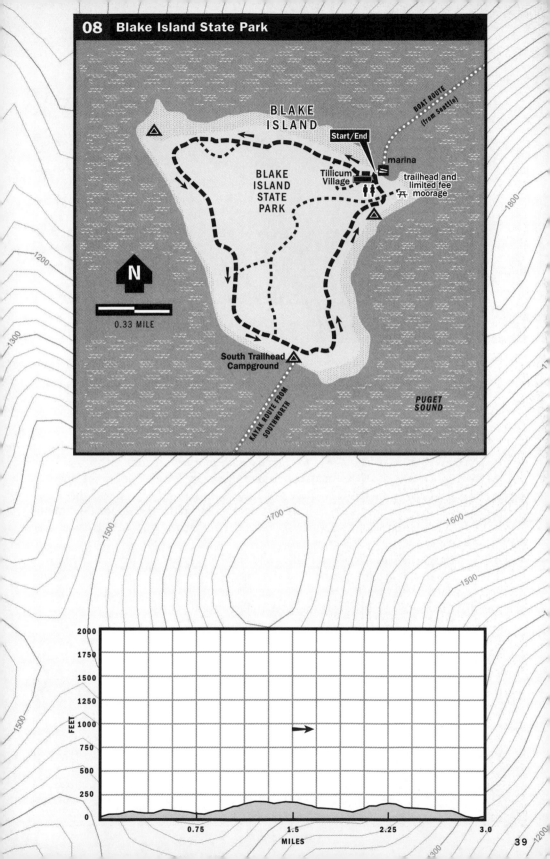

BLAKE ISLAND

BLAKE ISLAND STATE PARK

BOAT ROUTE (from Seattle)

Start/End

marina

Tillicum Village

trailhead and limited fee moorage

N

0.33 MILE

South Trailhead Campground

KAYAK ROUTE FROM SOUTHWORTH

PUGET SOUND

1200
1300
1500
1700
1600
1500
1800

FEET

2000
1750
1500
1250
1000
750
500
250
0

0.75   1.5   2.25   3.0

MILES

Sea kayaks on Blake Island shore

east, Bainbridge Island to the north, and Vashon Island to the south. On a clear day, look for many of the Cascade Mountain range's peaks above the city, including Mount Rainier. From this sea-level vantage point, the massive ice-clad volcano shows its entire vertical relief, rising 14,411 feet into the sky.

Tillicum Village has been the focal point for visitors to the island since its official opening in July 1962, aimed to coincide with the Seattle World's Fair. The large crowds at the fair site never materialized on the island, however, starting a series of rocky financial years for the village's managers and investors. Further problems plagued the development through its first decade, including the seasonal nature of the business, struggles with the Seattle Chamber of Commerce, and the power that private tour companies had over access via their boats.

Nonetheless, despite massive debt and cash-flow problems, founder Bill Hewitt refused to file for bankruptcy, believing he owed it to the family and friends who had backed him financially to make the project successful. His persistence paid off in the end: Tillicum Village eventually turned a profit and still operates under the guidance of the Hewitt family today.

The heart of Tillicum Village is a massive wooden longhouse, modeled on the traditional style of the Northwest Coast Native American tribes. Inside the structure, salmon is cooked on cedar stakes over an alder wood fire and served to guests in the dining area while they watch *Dance on the Wind,* an interpretive stage show. Totem poles and murals decorate the interior and exterior of the building, and Native American artists can sometimes be observed at work inside. The entire development does not reflect the culture of any one tribe in particular, but instead incorporates influences from groups ranging geographically from the Chinooks of northern Oregon to the Kwakwaka'wakws of British Columbia and the Tlingits of southeastern Alaska.

The attractions of the village were sufficient for President Bill Clinton to select the site to host the historic Asia Pacific Economic Cooperation meeting in November 1993, where world leaders from around the Pacific Rim met to discuss their mutual future economic development while enjoying the traditional hospitality of their hosts.

The story of Blake Island predates Tillicum Village by centuries, though. The island was once the ancestral camping ground of the Suquamish tribe, and local legend holds that the great Chief Seattle was born there. Captain George Vancouver was the first European explorer to visit the area in 1792, a trip that resulted in many prominent geographic landmarks throughout the Pacific Northwest being named after members of his crew. However, Blake Island was not named until 1841, in honor of George Smith Blake, who was head of the U.S. Coast Guard survey at the time.

William Trimble purchased the island around 1900 and turned it into a private estate. For many decades afterward, the land passed in and out of the hands of various owners with mixed property claims, until it was acquired by the state in 1959 and reborn as Blake Island State Park. By chance, the competing legal interests kept the southern end of the island from ever being logged, leaving an impressive stand of old-growth forest for current visitors to enjoy.

To explore the island for yourself, find the trailhead on the northwest side of the village, just past the visitor center, and begin a counterclockwise loop. A network of trails laces the center of the island. But the perimeter trail makes a great hike that quite literally reaches every corner of the park, including its three campsites: one adjacent to Tillicum Village, one on the westernmost point, and the last on the southernmost point, facing Vashon Island.

The trail is a reclaimed dirt road, making it wide and easy to follow. Wooden benches offer periodic vantage points for viewing the water. And early on, some interpretive signs identify various plant species along the way.

The lowland growth here shares some similarities with forests at higher elevations in the Cascades, including a large number of Douglas firs, hemlocks, and cedars. Other species here, however, are unique to the coastal environment, including the majestic red-barked madrones, which are particularly prevalent along the shoreline; look for an exceptional grove of these trees adjacent to the southern campground.

Because this is an island, you only need to follow the shoreline to complete the loop and end up back where you started, regardless of the various junctions you might encounter along the way. For most of its length, the trail stays above the waterline and occasionally turns in toward the island's interior. On the western side, it climbs to near the island's highest point, at approximately 225 feet.

Watch out for wildlife along the way, including deer, elk, and raccoons. Eagles, osprey, and owls are just a few of the bird species that can be spotted in the trees overhead. And marine life, abundant in the surrounding waters, includes seal pups that sometimes rest on the beaches.

There are many options to extend or shorten your hike by using the various trails through the island's interior. You also may choose to relax at a picnic table at one of the campsites, or enjoy the volleyball pits, playgrounds, or other recreational facilities available at Tillicum.

Ornate longhouse doors
at Tillicum Village

Private-tour operators offer boat trips from downtown Seattle to Tillicum Village throughout the year. Package deals typically include a buffet featuring traditional Native American–style baked salmon, the *Dance on the Wind* stage show, and some free time to explore on your own. For more information, visit **www.tillicumvillage.com** or call (206) 933-8600.

BELLEVUE AND
THE EASTSIDE

MERCER SLOUGH AND BELLEFIELDS NATURE PARKS

 KEY AT-A-GLANCE INFORMATION

LENGTH: 2.1 miles (side trip options)

CONFIGURATION: Figure 8 loop

DIFFICULTY: Easy

SCENERY: Wetlands, slough, wildlife, blueberry farm, native flora and fauna

EXPOSURE: Mostly open, some shady areas

TRAFFIC: Popular on sunny days

TRAIL SURFACE: Mixture of gravel, boardwalk, dirt, and wood-chip

HIKING TIME: 1–2 hours

ACCESS: Hikable year-round; no fees for parking or park access

MAPS: See map at trailhead or pick up pamphlet in Winter House Visitor Center, USGS Bellevue South

FACILITIES: Restrooms and water at visitor center

Mercer Slough and Bellefields Nature Parks

Latitude: North 47d35.477m

Longitude: West 122d11.523m

▶ IN BRIEF

This Bellevue Parks and Community Services Department gem offers easy access to a vast array of native plants and wildlife, just minutes from downtown. The vestigial wetlands provide a window into life here prior to modern development. And the interesting site history and working blueberry farm ensure that everyone will find something they'll enjoy.

▶ DESCRIPTION

Surrounded by high-rises, rampant suburbs, and two interstate highways, the Mercer Slough Nature Park is a true ecological oasis in the heart of Bellevue. Encompassing more than 320 acres of wetlands and several miles of hiking trails, the location offers a great quick escape for nature-lovers of all kinds.

But don't be fooled; the slough's easy access does not compromise its natural setting. Mercer is the largest urban wetland in King County, and it contains an incredible range of wildlife despite its relatively small size. Mink, otter, beaver, and even coyote call the park home, along with more than 100 different species of birds, making it one of the most diverse ecosystems in the Puget Sound region.

Before beginning your hike, be sure to stop by the visitor center in the Winters House at the northern end of the parking lot. Listed on the National Register of Historic Places, the Spanish-styled house was built by Frederick and Cecelia

▶ DIRECTIONS

From Interstate 5 just south of downtown Seattle, go east on Interstate 90. Take Exit 9, Bellevue Way SE, and go north. Soon you will pass a boat launch, the South Bellevue Park and Ride, and the Overlake Blueberry Farm. Just past the farm, look for the blue Winters House sign on the right and park in the adjacent lot.

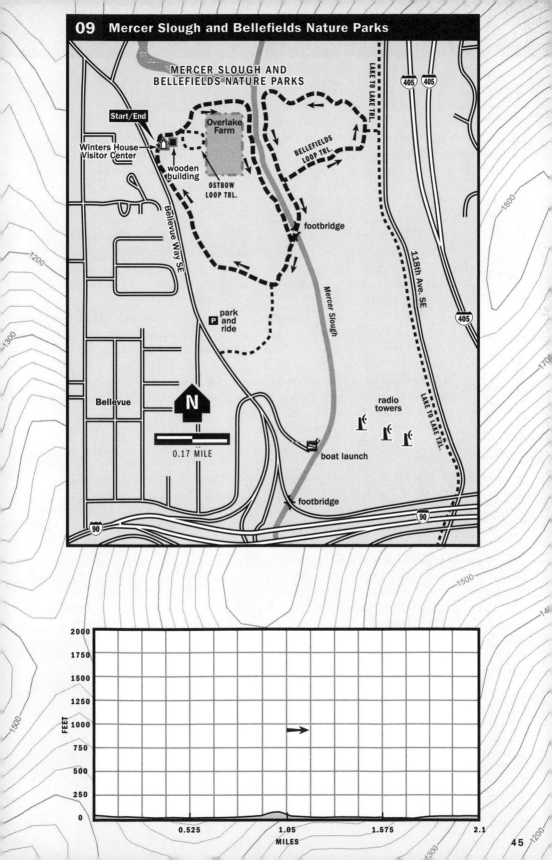

MERCER SLOUGH AND
BELLEFIELDS NATURE PARKS

Start/End

Winters House
Visitor Center

wooden
building

Overlake
Farm

OSTBOW
LOOP TRL.

BELLEFIELDS
LOOP TRL.

footbridge

Bellevue Way SE

Mercer Slough

LAKE TO LAKE TRL.

405   405

118th Ave. SE

405

park
and
ride
P

Bellevue

N

0.17 MILE

radio
towers

LAKE TO LAKE TRL.

boat launch

footbridge

90   I-90

1800

1200

1300

1700

1500

1500

1400

1300   1200

FEET

2000
1750
1500
1250
1000
750
500
250
0

0.525   1.05   1.575   2.1
MILES

Winters in 1929 with funds earned from their on-site nursery. Initially specializing in greenhouse-raised azaleas, daffodils, and irises, the Winters attained success in bulb farming after the spread of an infectious blight led to a quarantine on imports.

The estate was purchased in 1943 by Austrian immigrants Anna and Frank Riepel; Mrs. Riepel resided in the house until 1983, when it began to fall into disrepair. Five years later, the city of Bellevue purchased the property and restored it to its current condition. In addition to serving as the park's visitor center, the Winters House also is home to the Bellevue Historical Society and serves as a gathering place for meetings, receptions, and banquets.

The hike begins on the eastern side of the parking lot; look for a display board featuring park information and an excellent map. Head north on the gravel path to the start of the Heritage Trail boardwalk. The trail is well marked, but note that on many signs decimal points are missing from the stated distances—0.3 miles looks like 3 miles, for instance.

As you enter the wetlands, the ruins of an old wooden building appear on the right. The structure is falling apart and sinking into the ground, being reclaimed by the mud. Although you are only a stone's throw from Bellevue Way SE, the sounds of birds singing and winging through the willows begin to overtake the dull roar of traffic.

In less than 100 yards, the Ostbow Loop both starts and ends on the right. Endre Ostbow grew rhododendrons here on land purchased from the Riepels, and the side loop that now bears his name winds through many of these plants still thriving in the bog. Whether you explore this spur or not, at the second intersection follow the main trail to the left, heading north.

The boardwalk passes under a living arch of dogwood branches before bending through a cattail marsh and reaching an abrupt end. A fence separates the neatly planted rows of Overlake Farm blueberry bushes on the right from the wood-chip trail and chaos of natural growth on the left. Like Ostbow's surviving rhododendrons, the blueberry farm connects the developed Bellevue of today with its agricultural roots of the past. Continue along the fence to where a riot of wild blackberry bushes lines the main channel of the slough.

Cross the footbridge over the dark, slow-moving water, watching for kayakers and canoers paddling by. The high-rises of downtown Bellevue are visible just to the north, a reminder of the development that lays siege to this last natural refuge.

Great blue herons often fly overhead or stand in the rushes on the banks here. Despite their striking size and color, these birds can be surprisingly well camouflaged in the reeds. Other bird species you might spot include ruddy ducks, wigeons, buffleheads, hooded mergansers, and mallards. And if you are here during the fall run (September–December), you may catch sight of chinook and coho salmon swimming upstream to spawn.

The boardwalk resumes on the eastern side of the bridge, reaching a T-shaped junction with the Bellefields Loop. Follow the wood-chip-lined trail to the right (east) into shrubs and meadows. Several interpretive displays around the loop provide valuable natural and historical information about the area.

In less than a quarter mile, a group of benches marks a gravel path that enters from the right. Continue on the main trail to the left, past a stand of large western red cedars. These massive trees mark the original eastern shore of Lake Washington, which receded after the construction of the ship canal in 1917. Stay to the left again and cross Trail Creek, bypassing the short hill to the right leading to the Bellefields trailhead on 118th Avenue SE.

On the far side of the stream, the trail splits and you can veer right over a small rise or head left to stay along the lower path. Skunk cabbage lines both trails here; the sight of the plant's yellow flowers helps to offset its thick, unpleasant odor during the spring and summer bloom. Either direction will take you to the next junction, where the trails meet again. From there, continue westward through scrub to reach the edge of the slough, passing viewpoints that offer continued chances to spot wildlife. Returning to the boardwalk, you will complete the Bellefields Loop and arrive back at the footbridge you crossed earlier.

After crossing, stay to the left and continue on the boardwalk. As you navigate the wetlands, be sure to watch for tulips in the thicket. It is amazing that these flowers can capture enough sunlight in the heavy tangle of reeds and brushes to grow. Enjoy the small miracle of these beautiful blooms if you should be lucky enough to see one.

Before long, a gravel path branches to the right. Leave the boardwalk and follow this path back along the Overlake Farm building and then finally to the Winters House parking lot, where you began.

Note that there are many options for lengthening your hike. A paved biking and running trail circumnavigates the entire park perimeter and joins with the Lake-to-Lake Trail, which connects Lake Sammamish to Lake Washington.

▶ NEARBY ACTIVITIES

Canoe and kayak lessons and rentals are available at Enatai Beach Park Boathouse, just to the south on Lake Washington; call (425) 637-8838 for more information. Contact the Mercer Slough Environmental Education Center near the Bellefields trailhead for educational and informational programs; call (425) 452-2752, or visit the Mercer Slough Nature Park Web site at **www.cityofbellevue.org**.

SAINT EDWARD STATE PARK

KEY AT-A-GLANCE INFORMATION

LENGTH: 2.5 miles (round-trip)

CONFIGURATION: Loop

DIFFICULTY: Moderate

SCENERY: Lake Washington shoreline and area; views across the lake; a grotto

EXPOSURE: Mostly shaded

TRAFFIC: Moderate to heavy

TRAIL SURFACE: Dirt

HIKING TIME: 2–3 hours

ACCESS: Hikable year-round; Washington State Park Pass required for parking, daily passes available at trailhead

MAPS: USGS Seattle North

FACILITIES: Restroom and water available near the swimming pool near the parking area; a great park with large play structures for small children

Saint Edward State Park

Latitude: North 47d43.99m

Longitude: West 122d15.327m

▶ IN BRIEF

This former Catholic seminary sits on a high, forested bluff above the northern end of Lake Washington, providing access to one of the last stretches of undeveloped land on the waterfront via an excellent trail system.

▶ DESCRIPTION

Many people primarily know Saint Edward State Park as the host of the annual Summer Brewfest, during which thirsty crowds fill the expansive lawn and eagerly sample the showcased hand-crafted beers." The popular event, held each year on Father's Day, also features live music, food and craft booths, and even a raucous keg-toss competition.

Yet most of the time Saint Edward is quiet and calm, closer to the contemplative retreat likely envisioned when the seminary was founded by the Sulpician Order in the early 1930s. Named for Edward the Confessor, the second-to-last Anglo-Saxon king of England and founder of Westminster Abbey, the impressive facility was run by the Seattle Archdiocese until it was donated to the state of Washington in 1977 and turned into a park.

The seminary was built in a Tuscan architectural style, complete with arches and a bell tower,

▶ DIRECTIONS

From I-5 just north of downtown Seattle, go east on WA 520. After crossing Lake Washington, go north on I-405 and take Exit 20A, NE 116th Street. Continue on 116th Street, which becomes NE Juanita Drive then turns north and changes its name to Juanita Drive NE. Watch for the park entrance on the left (west) side of Juanita Drive NE, which is also the entrance to Bastyr University. After entering the park, stay to the right and park in the main parking lot near the swimming pool building and seminary.

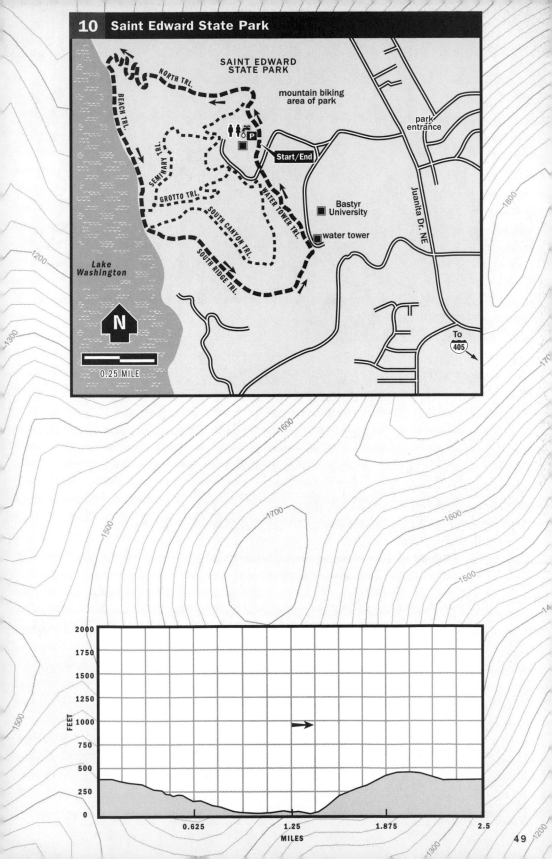

SAINT EDWARD
STATE PARK

mountain biking
area of park

NORTH TRL.

BEACH TRL.

SEMINARY TRL.

GROTTO TRL.

SOUTH CANYON TRL.

SOUTH RIDGE TRL.

WATER TOWER TRL.

P

Start/End

park
entrance

Juanita Dr. NE

Bastyr
University

water tower

Lake
Washington

N

0.25 MILE

To
405

1200

1300

1500

1600

1700

1500

1600

1700

1500

1400

1800

1700

1200

2000
1750
1500
1250
1000
750
500
250
0

FEET

0.625   1.25   1.875   2.5

MILES

Fern fronds unfurling at Saint
Edward State Park

giving the structure a distinctly European flair. The occasional cricket or soccer game on the grass only heightens the atmosphere, extending a general sense of peace that pervades the park. The serenity may reach its apex at the Grotto, an outdoor sanctuary and shrine on the southwest corner of the lawn. This same tranquility is evident throughout Saint Edward's trail network as well.

A counterclockwise loop around the park perimeter is provided by linking the North, Beach, South Ridge, and Water Tower trails, designated almost entirely as "hiking-only." Although Saint Edward is popular with local mountain bikers, who call it Saint Eddy, they tend to stay in the northeast corner of the park near the main entrance and have limited access to Lake Washington and the bluffs, where most of this loop occurs.

Find the trailhead by heading north from the parking lot, past the park office, some storage sheds, and another small parking area. The park's office building also houses a gymnasium (one of many fine recreation facilities available at Saint Edward), in addition to a popular indoor pool and an engaging playground for young children. Park maps can prove helpful in finding the way, and are usually available at a display board near the picnic area.

The North Trail (identified as the Perimeter Trail) begins by ducking into the trees and then bending to the left, following a ridge downhill. A narrow ravine to the right houses a small creek that tumbles toward the lake.

The descent steepens as you get closer to the water, employing some easy switchbacks to lessen the drop. The forest is a mix of typical Pacific Northwest lowland species, including Douglas firs, western hemlocks, and big leaf maples, with a carpet of sword ferns and other ground cover underneath. Gaps in the canopy provide views of the water and the houses of Lake City on the opposite side, a little more than a mile away.

After dropping about 100 feet, the North Trail ends on the lakeshore at a junction with the Beach Trail. Turn left and head south along the bank, where several distinctive red-barked Pacific madrones hang out over the water. Boats frequently pass by, along with float planes from the Kenmore Air Harbor, 2 miles north at the mouth of the Sammamish River.

A thick tangle of plants prohibits easy access to the water until you reach a beachfront clearing with a swimming area along some rocks, where kayakers frequently stop to rest. The wide Seminary Trail enters the clearing from the left; this is the only beach access available to mountain bikers. For hikers seeking a shorter loop, it is possible to return to the main lawn by heading directly up the hill. Just past two lavatories, the Grotto Trail branches off the Seminary Trail to the right, providing another path to the top. At 0.4 miles long, the narrow Grotto Trail is closed to mountain bikes and may be a more rewarding hike than the Seminary Trail.

To resume the Perimeter Loop, continue on the Beach Trail. Bypass the first left to the South Canyon Trail and stay right to join the South Ridge Trail, which quickly climbs above the lake. This trail is surprisingly demanding, running through a series of short ups and downs while ascending a high crest between the South Canyon on the left and a shallower ravine to the right.

Emerge from the woods below a water tower overlooking Bastyr University, a leading center for study of the natural-health sciences. Bastyr now leases the Saint Thomas Seminary, added to the Saint Edward Seminary in 1958 and still owned by the Seattle Archdiocese. The Water Tower Trail starts here, heading immediately left from the wooden gate at the end of the South Ridge Trail and running through the trees along the Bastyr parking lot and access road.

The Plateau Trail enters from the right, open to mountain bikers who may share the broad Water Tower Trail with you the rest of the way. Only about a quarter mile remains until you exit the forest next to the playground and cross the grass to return to your vehicle.

O. O. DENNY COUNTY PARK LOOP

KEY AT-A-GLANCE INFORMATION

LENGTH: 1.2 miles (round-trip)

CONFIGURATION: Loop

DIFFICULTY: Easy

SCENERY: Old-growth trees (including a 600-year-old Douglas fir), salmon-spawning creek, historic structures; views of Lake Washington

EXPOSURE: Shaded

TRAFFIC: Low

TRAIL SURFACE: Dirt, gravel

HIKING TIME: 1–2 hours

ACCESS: Hikable year-round; no fees for parking or park access

MAPS: USGS Bellevue North

FACILITIES: Restroom and water at lakefront picnic area

O.O. Denny County Park Loop

Latitude: North 47d42.569m

Longitude: West 122d14.993m

▶ IN BRIEF

At O. O. Denny Park, nothing is as it seems. What looks like a small, lakefront green space in the city of Kirkland is actually a narrow slice of deep forest owned by the city of Seattle. Some of the largest trees in the city stand here, including the broken-off trunk of a 600-year-old Douglas fir, reportedly the largest tree in King County until high winds felled it in the early 1990s. An easy trail loops through the narrow creek valley.

▶ DESCRIPTION

O. O. Denny Park is largely known for its beach— if it is known at all. With an open picnic area right on Lake Washington, families arrive on hot summer weekends to relax, play, and have barbecues on the grass. A large wooden shelter is often reserved for formal occasions and large gatherings, and a quarter mile of access to the water provides good views of the opposite shore, including the enormous National Oceanic and Atmospheric Administration (NOAA) installation at Sand Point to the south.

Yet even residents of the quiet Juanita neighborhood that surrounds the park seem largely unaware of the astonishing forest that lies along the Denny Creek ravine, across the road from the

▶ DIRECTIONS

From I-5 just north of downtown Seattle, go east on WA 520. After crossing Lake Washington, go north on I-405 and take Exit 20A, NE 116th Street. Continue on NE 116th Street, which becomes NE Juanita Drive then turns north and changes to Juanita Drive NE. Turn left onto 76th Place NE, which becomes Holmes Point Drive NE. Continue more than 1 mile from Juanita Drive NE, and look for the trailhead parking lot across the road from the O. O. Denny Park lakefront picnic area.

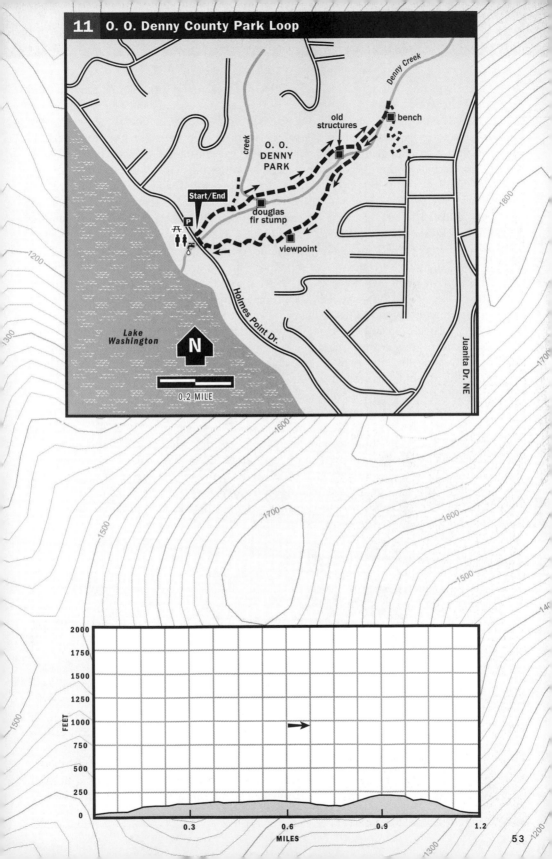

11 O. O. Denny County Park Loop

Denny Creek

old
structures

bench

O. O.
DENNY
PARK

creek

Start/End

douglas
fir stump

viewpoint

P

Holmes Point Dr.

Juanita Dr. NE

Lake
Washington

N

0.2 MILE

1200

1300

1500

1600

1700

1800

1700

1600

1500

1400

2000
1750
1500
1250
1000
750
500
250
0

FEET

0.3   0.6   0.9   1.2
MILES

lake. On some of the busiest days, relatively few visitors venture out on the trails and into the woods, missing out on some of the park's most outstanding features.

The trail begins uphill into the trees from the northern side of the parking lot. Within a few hundred yards, a small network of side trails branches to the left to explore a grove of giant western red cedars. These substantial trees are just the beginning of some of the exemplary specimens representing many of the signature species of the Pacific Northwest that can be found in the park. Along with the red cedars, various Douglas firs, grand firs, black cottonwoods, and western hemlocks all stand more than 150 feet tall, some even rise more than 200 feet, placing them among the largest known samples of their kind anywhere in Seattle.

Denny Creek appears down the slope to the right, bubbling through the underbrush. The trail is frequently wet and muddy and in near-constant shade from the tall trees above, but thoughtfully placed blocks of wood and stone set into the ground keep hikers' feet above the worst of it. The ravine is surprisingly deep, more than 100 feet to the rim, retaining the park's seclusion by keeping nearby development out of sight.

A large Douglas fir lays across the route, spanning the creek and reaching far up the bank on the far side. The trail cuts through the trunk near the roots, providing a good look at the interior of the tree and a chance to count its many rings. It is also possible to climb up around the end to inspect the tree's massive exposed root system and speculate on its demise, likely during a heavy storm.

But even that fallen tree cannot prepare you for what you will find just up the trail—the giant trunk of what was once the largest Douglas fir anywhere in King County. The word stump cannot adequately describe what is left of this incredible tree, which still stands more than 60 feet tall and has a base circumference that easily tops 25 feet. Even its bark is impressive, deep and rugged like an inscription from the ages, a testimony to its six centuries of survival and growth. This tree once towered far above the ravine and everything else around it, a condition that unfortunately exposed it to the wild wind that finally brought it down.

Beyond the fallen Douglas fir, an open clearing in a natural amphitheater with a few ruined buildings gives a glimpse into some local history. The park is named for Orion O. Denny, second son of Seattle founders Arthur and Mary Denny, who once owned a country estate on the property. Named *Klahanie,* an adaptation of a Chinook tribal word meaning "the outdoors," the estate was deeded to the city as a public park in Denny's memory by his third wife around the time of World War I. This site was accessible via a gravel road on the far side of the creek, the beginning of the hike's return loop.

This trail continues up the ravine another quarter mile, adding an out-and-back tail to the loop. The route crosses the creek and climbs a few wooden stairs to reach a bench on the southern side of the ravine. Some short switchbacks continue up the slope, eventually ending at the side of a street in the Finn Hill community. A better option is to descend back along the creek to reach an interesting exposed clay wall in the side of the bank, an optimal turnaround point just around the next corner.

Return to the gravel road and cross the creek on a footbridge. Local volunteers undertook an extensive habitat-rehabilitation project here in 2002, adding boulder weirs and step pools as part of a man-made fish ladder to help with salmon recovery.

Clusters of snake grass and sword ferns run along the creek, along with salmonberry, blackberry, salal, and big leaf maples.

The wide trail climbs toward the top of the ravine, where it ends on a residential street. A view opens out to the south through the trees, encompassing Lake Washington and the eastern end of the WA 520 bridge. After enjoying the view, follow a singletrack trail along the creek to return to Holmes Drive NE, just south of where your vehicle is parked.

▶ NEARBY ACTIVITIES

Kirkland's Juanita Bay Park lies just a few miles southeast of O. O. Denny Park and is particularly noted for its bird-watching opportunities. More than 150 different species have been spotted at Juanita Bay, ranging from bald eagles to hairy woodpeckers. To reach Juanita Bay, turn right (south) on Juanita Drive NE from Holmes Drive NE and then right again on 98th Avenue NE for about a half mile to reach the entrance. For more information or to join one of the highly recommended public tours offered by volunteers from the East Lake Washington Audubon Society, check the park's Web site at **www.ci.kirkland.wa.us/depart/parks/tours.htm** or call (425) 587-3312.

REDMOND WATERSHED PARK AND PRESERVE

KEY AT-A-GLANCE INFORMATION

LENGTH: 4.6 miles (round-trip)

CONFIGURATION: Loop with side trip options

DIFFICULTY: Easy to moderate

SCENERY: Wetlands, plant life, well-maintained hiking trails, and optional interpretive trails

EXPOSURE: Mostly shaded

TRAFFIC: Medium to high

TRAIL SURFACE: Mixture of dirt and gravel

HIKING TIME: 2–3 hours

ACCESS: Hikable year-round; no fees for parking or park access

MAPS: USGS Bellevue North

FACILITIES: Restroom at trailhead; no drinking water available

SPECIAL COMMENTS: Two additional short loops, both natural interpretive trails, are available as hiking options from the parking lot: the Tree Frog Loop Trail runs for 0.3 miles from the eastern side, and the 0.6-mile Trout Loop Trail starts on the western side. It is also possible to string together any number of shorter or longer trips through the preserve on any trail combination of your choosing.

Redmond Watershed Park and Preserve

Latitude: North 47d41.788m

Longitude: West 122d03.054m

IN BRIEF

Well maintained in trails and facilities and yet well protected from encroaching development, the Redmond Watershed Preserve offers a worthwhile natural experience right on the city's doorstep. A wide network of multiple-use trails explores the reaches of the preserve, providing good hiking opportunities in a surprisingly scenic environment.

DESCRIPTION

The city of Redmond purchased some land from the Weyerhauser Corporation in 1926, hoping to use it as a source of water. At the time, the property, in what was then essentially the wilderness, must have seemed a long way outside the city. Although the site never panned out as a suitable watershed (the water was not of sufficient quality), as the city spread eastward the value of the land became apparent in other ways. What was once a distant piece of backwoods has now become a great outdoor-recreation site right in Redmond's backyard, and the watershed preserve has, in fact, turned into a forest and wetlands preserve instead.

Nonetheless, the setting is not entirely pristine, as open corridors for overhead power lines and a buried gas pipeline stand as reminders that the area was born to serve the urban population. But even these pieces of civilization are well integrated into the trail system: the two corridors together form the park's backbone and link the preserve to the extended Tolt Pipeline Trail, popular with mountain bikers who follow the path on long-distance rides.

DIRECTIONS

From I-5 in Seattle, take Exit 168B onto WA 520 E. Stay on WA 520 to the end in Redmond, and continue straight onto Avondale Road. After just more than 1 mile, turn right onto Novelty Hill Road. Continue 2.3 miles to the park entrance on the left, across from 118th Avenue NE.

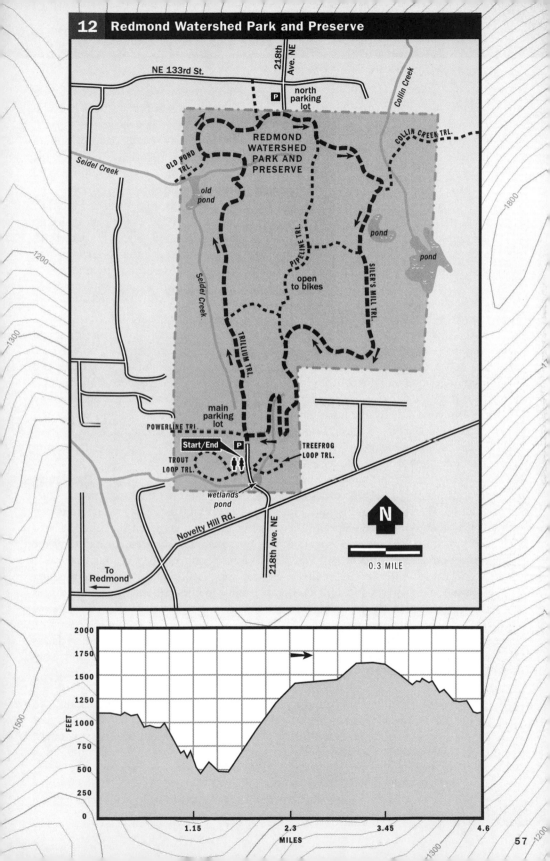

NE 133rd St.

218th Ave. NE

Collin Creek

P north parking lot

REDMOND WATERSHED PARK AND PRESERVE

OLD POND TRL.

COLLIN CREEK TRL.

Seidel Creek

old pond

pond

pond

PIPELINE TRL.

open to bikes

SILER'S MILL TRL.

Seidel Creek

TRILLIUM TRL.

main parking lot

POWERLINE TRL.

Start/End P

TROUT LOOP TRL.

TREEFROG LOOP TRL.

wetlands pond

Novelty Hill Rd.

218th Ave. NE

To Redmond

N

0.3 MILE

2000
1750
1500
1250
1000
750
500
250
0

FEET

1.15   2.3   3.45   4.6
MILES

Since 1994, great efforts have been put into upgrading the preserve's recreation facilities, enhancing everything from parking lot bathrooms to bridges, benches, and signs on the trails. The new sign system is now so thorough and the routes so well-marked you couldn't get lost if you wanted to. Yet amazingly, despite its proximity to the ever-growing suburbs of Redmond and the good natural experience available, the preserve still seems underused. The city estimates that only about 25,000 people visit the watershed each year—half as many as climb Mount Si.

A grand tour of the park, linking several different trails in an extended 4.6-mile loop, presents the best hiking option. Start at the northern end of the parking lot on the signed Trillium Connector Trail, which heads into the woods on a wide gravel surface. After 0.2 miles, go straight across a four-way junction with the Power Line Trail to join the Trillium Trail, open to hikers and equestrians but not mountain bikers.

The Trillium Trail runs through a forest of second-growth Douglas firs and western hemlocks as it rolls over a few gentle ups-and-downs. Visible in a depression on the left is the main fork of Seidel Creek, which flows through ferns in the understory. At 0.6 miles from the junction, bypass the Pipeline Connector Trail on the right and continue straight ahead, to the north. The surface underfoot changes from gravel to dirt and back again several times, but the trail remains broad and smooth. Cross two footbridges over side forks of Seidel Creek, flowing down the slope from the right.

After the two creek crossings, bend around to the left and reach a junction with the Old Pond Trail, which leads for a quarter mile to an exit onto 209th Avenue. The small pond itself can be seen through the trees on the left, where the three forks of Seidel Creek run together. The marshy land around the pond provides habitat for animals like beavers, great blue herons, and other waterfowl.

Stay on the Trillium Trail by following a tight turn to the right. Then curve through the northwestern corner of the park for about a half mile to reach another junction. Go right on the Pipeline Trail (signed as Collin Creek Trail), which runs parallel to the northern boundary of the preserve. Pass two spurs on the left that head out into the local suburban neighborhood, then bend back toward the center of the park. After another quarter mile you'll reach a junction with the Collin Creek Trail.

Turn left onto the Collin Creek Trail for another 0.3 miles to reach a junction with the hikers-only Siler's Mill Trail on the right. Join the Siler's Mill Trail and pass through a wooden gate designed to keep out horses and mountain bikers. Despite the limited access, the trail remains just as wide as on the previous sections.

A pond becomes visible on the left, part of the park's most extensive wetlands ecosystem which is also the source of north-flowing Collin Creek. A second, substantially larger pond lies a quarter mile behind the first on the preserve boundary; it is neither visible nor accessible from here.

The Siler's Mill Trail offers the purest hiking experience in the park, thanks to its restricted access and views of the scenic wetlands. Stay left at a junction just past the first pond to remain on the trail through the rich forest for another 1.1 miles, then pass through another wooden gate and turn left to rejoin the Pipeline Trail, which is open to all users. Follow the pipeline to a major junction with the Power Line Trail and turn right underneath the humming wires. A final 0.7 miles returns you to the Trillium Connector Trail, where a left turn carries you back to the parking lot and your vehicle.

JOHN MACDONALD TOLT RIVER COUNTY PARK

▶ IN BRIEF

An unheralded King County property in the Snoqualmie Valley, John MacDonald Tolt River Park has good river access in a scenic setting. Hikers can climb to a high viewpoint or explore along the river on two moderate and pleasant trails.

▶ DESCRIPTION

John MacDonald, the visionary behind the King County park that now bears his name, organized the development of recreational facilities at the confluence of the Tolt and Snoqualmie rivers in 1976 as a bicentennial project. MacDonald was the chief of the Seattle Council of Boy Scouts at the time and hoped to build campsites in the spirit of another Boy Scout facility—West Seattle's Camp Long. The fruits of his efforts are still being felt today, as the park provides a number of good camping opportunities. Other pieces of inspired development include a restored picturesque red barn that now serves as a picnic shelter and an elegant suspension footbridge that links the park's eastern and western sides.

Naturally, the park is popular with campers. But mountain bikers also like to ride a network of trails on the high bluff to the west, where it is possible to connect with trails originating at Ames Lake, about a mile away. And hikers can

▶ DIRECTIONS

From I-5 south of downtown Seattle, go east on I-90. Take Exit 22 (Preston–Fall City), and turn left, crossing over I-90. At the T-shaped intersection, turn right onto Preston–Fall City Road SE and proceed on this winding road to Fall City. Cross the Snoqualmie River, then go left onto Fall City Carnation Road SE. Continue on this road to Carnation and turn left on NE 40th Street. Drive straight to the end of the road at the parking lot and trailhead.

ⓘ KEY AT-A-GLANCE INFORMATION

LENGTH: 2.3 miles (round-trip on Bluff Trail and 2-mile River Loop)

CONFIGURATION: Out-and-back and loop options

DIFFICULTY: Easy on River Trail, moderate on Bluff Trail

SCENERY: High bluff viewpoint over the Snoqualmie River Valley, quiet stretch of beach along the Snoqualmie River bank

EXPOSURE: Mostly shaded

TRAFFIC: Medium traffic (note that bikes may be seen on the trails)

TRAIL SURFACE: Mixture of dirt and gravel

HIKING TIME: 2–4 hours

ACCESS: Hikable year-round; no fees for parking or park access

MAPS: USGS Carnation

FACILITIES: Restrooms and water at trailhead

John MacDonald Tolt River County Park

Latitude: North 47d38.65m

Longitude: West 121d55.455m

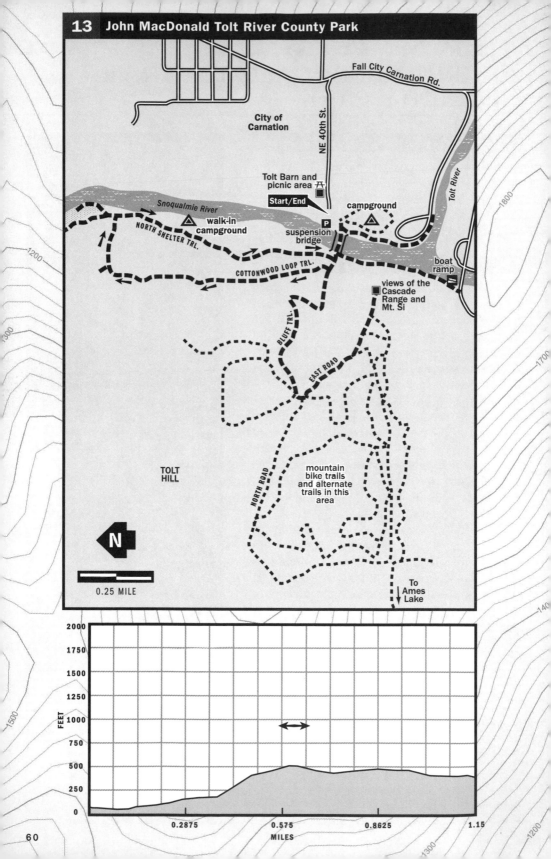

City of
Carnation

Fall City Carnation Rd.

NE 40th St.

Tolt River

Tolt Barn and
picnic area

Start/End

campground

Snoqualmie River

walk-in
campground

NORTH SHELTER TRL.

suspension
bridge

COTTONWOOD LOOP TRL.

boat
ramp

views of the
Cascade
Range and
Mt. Si

BLUFF TRL.

EAST ROAD

TOLT
HILL

NORTH ROAD

mountain
bike trails
and alternate
trails in this
area

To
Ames
Lake

N

0.25 MILE

FEET

2000
1750
1500
1250
1000
750
500
250
0

0.2875   0.575   0.8625   1.15

MILES

follow a good loop through the forest and along the river, or join the bikers on the bluff with an out-and-back trail to an impressive viewpoint.

For the loop hike, start across the suspension footbridge over the Snoqualmie River. Fishermen frequently ply the waters directly below from either shore. And swimmers collect on the beach just upstream to the left, where a sandy, alluvial bank sits at the Tolt confluence and provides good access to the shallow and easy rapids. Once across to the western side of the river, head up a gentle slope through a camping area and stay to the right. Look for a single-track heading past some picnic tables to enter the trees, the start of the Cottonwood Loop Trail.

The trail climbs for a short distance and then contours around to the north through a forest of alders, maples, cottonwoods, and ferns (typical for this area). Neither the river nor any of the development around the city of Carnation can be seen, providing a welcome sense of remoteness.

Snoqualmie Valley view from suspension bridge at Tolt Park

This stretch of trail might be the least-used anywhere in the park; campers tend to stick to the North Shelter Trail along the river bank, and most mountain bikers prefer to stay on the bluff far above to the left. The relative seclusion here makes this a good place to spot the deer that frequent the area.

Continue for 0.75 miles through the trees and then descend around a steep and sharp corner to reach an unmarked junction, where a poorly defined trail leads across a creek to the left. Stay to the right, still heading downhill, and you'll come to an abandoned dirt road. If you are attempting this loop in the opposite direction, this junction can be tricky to find because it is unsigned and difficult to spot.

Turn left on the road, which soon fades to a true trail, and approach the edge of the Snoqualmie River to reach a Y-shaped junction. Both forks are worth exploring—the left branch runs along the bank until it dead-ends in a clearing with a Private Property sign stuck to a fence at the northern end the park boundary; the right fork leads out onto a sandy and pebbly beach on the water's edge, one of the best places to enjoy the river. A bend to the south keeps most of the park out of sight. And a gravel island is exposed just downstream at low water, when it is also possible to make your way along the bank in either direction.

Return to the trail, heading back the way you came. Follow the road southward, parallel to the river, to reach a grassy clearing, site of the North Shelter Campground. There is room for multiple tents here, centered on the shelter structure itself, and the spot makes a great place to spend a night or two in the woods. From the campground, the road follows the river back upstream to the suspension footbridge where you began. Along the way, multiple short out-and-back footpaths lead to the sandy river bank on the left, providing access to the water. The total distance around the loop is about 2 miles.

The hike to the high viewpoint on the bluff also starts from the western side of the suspension footbridge. Follow the gravel surface from the end of the bridge up the hill, to the left of the previously described loop. The wide trail bends to the right past some camping shelters and narrows considerably, changing to dirt. For the next half mile, climb steeply through several turns up the side of the ridge. This is the only access to the upper part of the park, so expect to share the route with mountain bikers going in either direction.

A yellow sign on the left marks a transition to private property. Thanks to a generous easement from Port Blakely Tree Farms, the area beyond is open to public access for recreational use.

At the top of the bluff, known as Tolt Hill, a mess of poorly marked jeep roads and informal trails winds through the trees. Although the area only covers a few hundred acres, it is easy to lose your way in the complicated maze of options. Luckily, the viewpoint is easy to find.

Crest the ridge of the bluff, and you'll reach a major intersection. Although not indicated on any sign, the road you have been following is the North Road; the one you want to take is the East Road, around a sharp turn to the left. After a quick quarter mile uphill on the East Road, watch carefully for a junction with a single-track on the left side. A soup-can lid hammered into a tree may identify the trail as "Bob's Run," a helpful flourish provided by the mountain bikers who frequent the area, but the small metal circle is not easy to spot. If you come to a more obvious route heading to the right, you have gone a little too far.

Follow the narrow trail through a dense forest of low conifers and then a lighter forest of taller deciduous trees. Turn left at a junction (the right turn would take you back to the East Road), then descend to another junction. Stay to the left once again and emerge at the viewpoint, a total of about a quarter mile from the road.

This high overlook stands 300 feet straight above the river. Although the view to the north is blocked by trees, sweeping vistas are available to the east and southeast, from the farms and development around Carnation to the Cascade Mountains' front range and the distinctive rocky western face of Mount Si, about 15 miles away. Be sure to stay away from the edge, as the sandy cliff below is unstable and prone to slides.

Return the way you came, a round-trip of about 2.3 miles.

COAL CREEK PARK

▶ IN BRIEF

It might be hard to believe, but this modest park helped build Seattle. Supplying coal to a rapidly expanding population across the lake, the Newcastle mine that used to operate here fueled the region's explosive growth at the end of the 19th century. Today, the park still serves the city, but as a refuge from the urban sprawl it once spawned, with a trail through a narrow creek ravine leading to two waterfalls and several excellent historical sites.

▶ DESCRIPTION

The trail through Coal Creek Park is surely one of the most surprising hikes anywhere around Puget Sound. Featuring several waterfalls, a small canyon, and an environment typical of the Cascade foothills, the park stretches the boundary between the suburbs of Bellevue and the natural areas of the Issaquah Alps, a green finger pointing from the foot of Cougar Mountain through the rows of houses along Lake Washington's eastern shore.

The greater Seattle area is blessed with many excellent urban hikes, each offering a quick escape from the local neighborhood. What makes Coal Creek Park so unusual, though, is not that it is an undeveloped island in a sea of civilization but that only a century ago it was just the opposite. In the late 1800s, when virgin forest still

▶ DIRECTIONS

From I-5 south of downtown Seattle, go east on I-90. Immediately after crossing Mercer Island and Lake Washington, take the I-405 S exit and stay in the right-hand lane. Then take the first exit—Exit 10, Coal Creek Parkway. At the end of the exit, turn left and go underneath I-405. Continue on this winding road past the Factory Mall area. At about 1.3 miles from I-405, look for the trailhead parking area on the left (east) side of the road at the bottom of Coal Creek Canyon.

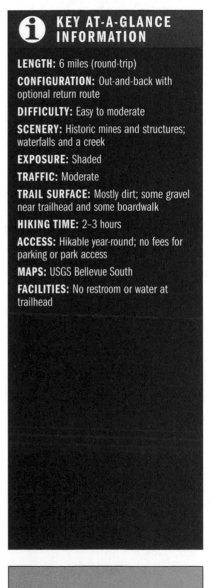

❶ KEY AT-A-GLANCE INFORMATION

LENGTH: 6 miles (round-trip)

CONFIGURATION: Out-and-back with optional return route

DIFFICULTY: Easy to moderate

SCENERY: Historic mines and structures; waterfalls and a creek

EXPOSURE: Shaded

TRAFFIC: Moderate

TRAIL SURFACE: Mostly dirt; some gravel near trailhead and some boardwalk

HIKING TIME: 2–3 hours

ACCESS: Hikable year-round; no fees for parking or park access

MAPS: USGS Bellevue South

FACILITIES: No restroom or water at trailhead

Coal Creek Park

Latitude: North 47d33.25m

Longitude: West 122d09.983m

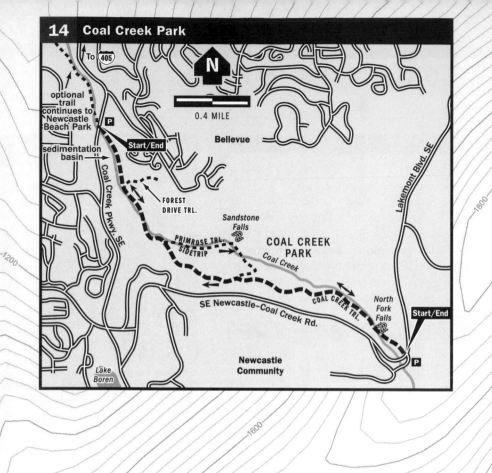

To (405)

optional
trail
continues to
Newcastle
Beach Park

P

Start/End

sedimentation
basin

N

0.4 MILE

Bellevue

Coal Creek Pkwy. SE

FOREST
DRIVE TRL.

Sandstone
Falls

PRIMROSE TRL.
SIDETRIP

**COAL CREEK
PARK**

Coal Creek

COAL CREEK TRL.

SE Newcastle–Coal Creek Rd.

North
Fork
Falls

Start/End

P

**Newcastle
Community**

Lake
Boren

Lakemont Blvd. SE

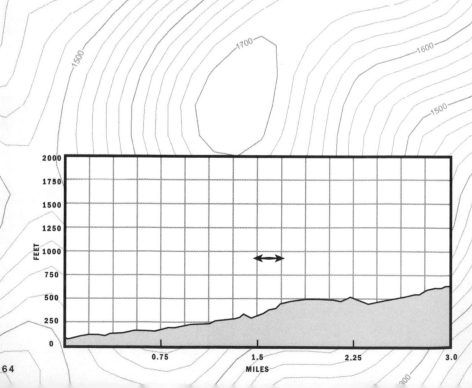

reached all the way to the shores of Elliot Bay and today's Eastside was mostly untracked wilderness, the park was the site of the Newcastle coal mine—a substantial industrial operation that, if it were still standing, would overwhelm even the busy neighborhoods that currently surround it. As you hike the trail, watch for remaining vestiges of the mining days, clues to the story of Newcastle coal. Yet the most compelling story in the park is undoubtedly the extent to which nature has reclaimed the land. Most of the time, it's difficult to imagine that any human development ever took place here at all.

The western trailhead begins at the parking lot, near the chain-link fence protecting the Coal Creek Parkway Sedimentation Basin. Built in 1986, the basin is designed to keep the creek channel clear by capturing sediment carried by the water before it can continue downstream; it also provides habitat for fish in several man-made pools and ponds, harboring a variety of trout and salmon species.

The trail narrows to a single-track as the canyon deepens along the northern side of the creek, crossing several side streams running down from the ridge. Although the Coal Creek watershed only drains the western side of Cougar Mountain, which rarely carries a snowpack, the water is usually high enough to cover the sound of the traffic from above.

After a half mile, the Forest Drive Trail enters from the steep slope on the left. Continue past this intersection for another half mile through a mix of brush and trees until you reach a signed junction with the Primrose Trail (numbered N11), allowing you to visit Sandstone Falls and complete a short loop with the main Coal Creek Trail (N1) on the return. Strangely, the trails are not named in an intuitive way and would make more sense if the titles were switched; it is the Primrose Trail which closely follows the creek, not the Coal Creek Trail.

Follow the Primrose Trail along the creek to a site with a few sandstone boulders, a relatively uncommon geologic formation for this area where rocks of volcanic origin are much more common. Reach Sandstone Falls after 0.4 miles, where a side creek slides down over an exposed piece of the underlying sedimentary rock before joining the main channel. Although the 20-foot drop isn't much by high Cascade Mountain standards, it is certainly exceptional by Bellevue standards, especially during periods of peak flow.

The canyon reaches its deepest point just past the falls, and the sides begin to steepen. Watch for some remnants of the old mining operation along the southern side of the creek, including rusty iron cart wheels and a cable partially buried in the dirt.

The trail climbs out of the inner canyon to rejoin the Coal Creek Trail, some 0.8 miles from the previous junction. Turn left and pass below a ridge, notable for the multitude of ferns which seemingly pour down from the top, to the right. The trees soon give way to a small open area at a retired gravel pit, with views of some radio towers and large houses on the western slope of Cougar Mountain. A glance back the way you came might provide a glimpse of the northern end of the Olympic Mountain Range and the prominent Columbia Tower in downtown Seattle, more easily seen in winter when the trees are bare.

Join a dirt road through the clearing, then return to the trail on the far side at a sign for Red Town Trailhead. Just beyond the bottom of some boardwalk stairs, look

Hiker peering into an old coal mine shaft

for a concrete slab off to the right, the base of the old locomotive turntable. Surprisingly, the concrete looks as if it was poured yesterday, without significant weathering, yet all other evidence that a busy rail line once ran here has essentially disappeared, swallowed by the woods.

Beyond the turntable, two waterfalls mark the last quarter mile of the trail. Coal Creek pours over a short man-made drop of beams and planks—all that is left of a substantial wooden housing that once enclosed the entire flow—in the creek bed. Mere steps above it, North Fork Falls tumble down a striking slab of red rock on the left, similar in height to Sandstone Falls but much more impressive, with a greater volume of water.

The trail splits nearby, creating a very short loop; be sure to explore both sides. On the north, a rich vein of coal (all that remains of an old mine shaft) is exposed and open for inspection. The opposite side features a fascinating information kiosk on the Newcastle operation from 1867 to 1929. It is almost impossible to imagine that at one time a large hotel stood nearby, locomotives steamed through, and crowds of physical laborers toiled on the very spot you now stand. Several old photographs tell the story, though, revealing the magnitude of the development needed to recover, process, and transport the coal.

Red Town trailhead is just up a short hill, the turnaround point for this hike. Head back the way you came, remembering to stay on the main Coal Creek Trail at the junction for the Primrose Trail to complete the central loop.

Many options are available if you wish to continue farther. Red Town is also one of the most popular places for access to Cougar Mountain, just across the road from the end of the Coal Creek Trail. From the western trailhead where you began, look for a sign to the Lower Coal Creek Trail on the opposite side of Coal Creek Parkway SE. The linear park continues down the canyon as far as Newcastle Beach Park via the Lake Washington Trail, 2.3 miles one way.

COUGAR MOUNTAIN REGIONAL WILDLAND PARK: LICORICE FERN TRAIL

IN BRIEF

Thanks to a hidden trailhead in a residential neighborhood, few outsiders ever venture up the quiet creek valley of the Licorice Fern Trail, and even most long-time visitors to Cougar Mountain have probably never experienced its beauty or solitude. The intrepid few who do, however, will find both surprising seclusion in a corner of one of the busiest parks in the Puget Sound region and good access to a peaceful waterfall and a modest viewpoint.

DESCRIPTION

Without a doubt, the most difficult part of hiking the Licorice Fern Trail is finding the trailhead. There are no clues to its existence beyond the "blink and you've missed it" sign along the road. And although the official park map dutifully shows the trail in one corner, many other maps do not indicate that this is part of the Cougar Mountain complex at all. Even if you spot the small post emblazoned with a hiking symbol, you might not believe that this—the head of an apparent driveway through a private garden—could be the right place. But this is indeed the correct trailhead, and once you've gone through the difficulty of finding it, your troubles can be put behind you to begin this tranquil hike.

DIRECTIONS

From I-5 south of downtown Seattle, go east on I-90. Take Exit 15 and drive south on WA 900, which begins as 17th Avenue NW and then becomes Renton-Issaquah Road SE. After driving 4 miles, turn right onto SE May Valley Road. After just more than 1 mile, make a hard right onto SE 112th Street. Immediately after the road bends to the left and becomes 169th Avenue SE, look for a hiker sign marking the driveway easement to the trailhead on the right. Park along 169th Avenue SE away from the residential driveways.

KEY AT-A-GLANCE INFORMATION

LENGTH: 4.5 miles (round-trip)

CONFIGURATION: Out-and-back

DIFFICULTY: Moderate

SCENERY: Streamside trail with lush vegetation and licorice ferns, cascading mossy waterfall, a modest viewpoint

EXPOSURE: Shaded

TRAFFIC: Low

TRAIL SURFACE: Dirt

HIKING TIME: 2–3 hours

ACCESS: Hikable year-round; no fee for parking or park access

MAPS: Green Trails–Cougar Mountain/ Squak Mountain 203S; USGS Bellevue South

FACILITIES: None at trailhead

Cougar Mountain Regional Wildland Park: Licorice Fern Trail

Latitude: North 47d30.183m

Longitude: West 122d06.691m

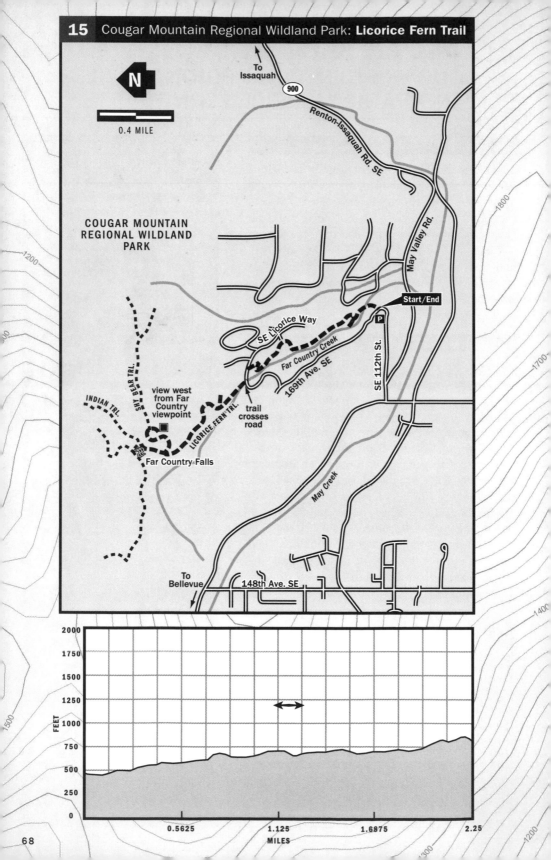

Undergrowth along the Licorice
Fern Trail

Taking care to respect the private property on either side, start down the drive-way directly toward the woods. Avoid the left turn up the hill, which leads to a nearby residence. Instead, continue straight ahead to reach a second, more visible sign indicating Licorice Fern Trail at the edge of the trees, the start of the actual trail.

Head down the hill on a series of switchbacks and wooden stairs to reach Far Country Creek, then cross the small stream and begin climbing up the bank on the other side. A giant downed log covered in moss and ferns lies over the trail and creates an interesting natural bridge. Children probably will have free passage, but most adults will be compelled to duck underneath.

The single-track trail is often soft and muddy. But despite the minimal foot traffic, it is well-maintained, evidence that it is indeed part of the larger Cougar Mountain Regional Wildland Park, no matter how much of a secret it might seem to be. Although development encroaches on all sides, the surprisingly steep valley walls shield Far Country Creek and its ecosystem from the surrounding threats. This natural protection was not enough to keep it from being logged some time in the past, however, as shown by several large stumps along the way. Various species of ferns grow thickly on the either side of the stream, appearing to spill down the sides of the gulch and giving the trail its name.

After 0.8 miles and a modest climb of 200 feet, emerge from the trees at SE Licorice Way, a paved road. The trail resumes at a series of wooden posts and a sign on the far side, then runs along the road for a few hundred yards before turning back into the woods. Be careful when crossing SE Licorice Way, which carries local residential vehicle traffic.

Quickly descend the western side of the creek and then climb back up the eastern bank to follow a fence line practically in the backyards of some of the park's neighbors, one of the few places where civilization manages to intrude on the trail's natural setting. Just past the houses, stay left at a junction to join the Indian Trail.

The Indian Trail drops sharply and then enters an airy flat area filled with young maples and an understory of ferns. After a quarter mile, reach a signed junction—S1 Far Country Trail—which leads to the right. Before following this route up the hill, it is worth staying on the Indian Trail for another 0.2 miles to visit the small Far Country Falls. Look for an informal track leading off the trail to the left to reach the top of the cascade, where the creek tumbles down through a series of mossy rocks. Although the side trip is unsigned, the noise from the falling water makes it easy to find.

Return to the previous junction and climb about 100 feet on the Far Country Trail to reach a signed, three-way intersection. Turn left for the shortcut to Far Country Lookout. The viewpoint is another 0.1 miles, where a wooden bench and a narrow gap in the trees provides a glimpse to the west of some suburban areas around Lake Washington, part of the lake itself, and the Olympic Mountains in the distance. Although the Far Country Lookout falls far short of spectacular, it makes a suitable resting spot and turnaround point for the hike. For a little variation, it is possible to complete a quick loop by following the trail through the lookout then staying right at the next junction with the Shy Bear Trail, soon returning downhill to the beginning of the shortcut.

Although a few hikers from the crowded Red Town trailhead occasionally access this section of Cougar Mountain, you are likely to have the lookout to yourself and enjoy just as much solitude here as offered by the Indian and Licorice Fern trails on the approach. Return to the trailhead the same way you came.

▶ NEARBY ACTIVITIES

If you didn't see any wildlife on the Licorice Fern Trail, the Cougar Mountain Zoo provides a fail-safe second chance. Dedicated to endangered species, the zoo has some exceptional educational exhibits that children are sure to love. To reach the zoo, take WA 900 (Renton-Issaquah Road SE) northeast from the turnoff to the trailhead, then turn left onto Newport Way in Issaquah. After just more than a mile, turn left onto SE 54th Street; the zoo is another quarter mile up the road at 19525 SE 54th Street. For more information, visit the zoo's Web site at **www.cougar mountainzoo.org** or call (425) 391-5508.

COUGAR MOUNTAIN REGIONAL WILDLAND PARK: WILDERNESS CREEK AND WILDERNESS PEAK LOOP

▶ IN BRIEF

Cougar Mountain receives many visitors, but most are concentrated at the busy Red Town trailhead, far from the mountain's high point at Wilderness Peak. The quiet Wilderness Creek Trail climbs to the park's little-known summit via an appealing valley, passing several viewpoints along the way.

▶ DESCRIPTION

Unlike its higher neighbors in the Issaquah Alps, Cougar Mountain has a flat, marshy area as its heart. Where both Squak and Tiger mountains have a clearly discernible central crest, Cougar is more like a plateau, climbing on all sides to reach a broad, even middle. With this unusual topography, the true summit is difficult to discern from a wide range of similar high points among the trees.

Aided both by its drive-up approach and its name, which recalls the mountain's history as a military installation, Anti-Aircraft Peak attracts a lot of attention. However, at 1,483 feet it is only the second-highest point on Cougar Mountain, more than 100 feet lower than 1,595-foot Wilderness Peak, about a mile away to the south.

The hike to Wilderness Peak starts from the northwest end of the small parking lot, signed as E6 Wilderness Creek Trail. Note that the letter E indicates that this trail is in the eastern section of the park, a naming convention used throughout Cougar Mountain; other trails can also be preceded by N, W, or S for the remaining compass directions, or C for trails in the center.

▶ DIRECTIONS

From I-5 south of downtown Seattle, go east on I-90. Take Exit 15 and drive south on WA 900, which begins as 17th Avenue NW and then becomes Renton-Issaquah Road SE. About 3.3 miles from I-90 and just after SE 95th Street is the entrance to a parking lot for the Wilderness Creek trailhead on the right.

KEY AT-A-GLANCE INFORMATION

LENGTH: 3.5 miles (round-trip) plus a 0.6-mile side trip

CONFIGURATION: Loop

DIFFICULTY: Moderate

SCENERY: several modest viewpoints and cascading Wilderness Creek

EXPOSURE: Mostly shaded

TRAFFIC: Low to moderate

TRAIL SURFACE: Dirt

HIKING TIME: 2–3 hours

ACCESS: Hikable year-round; no fee for parking or park access. No parking or access fees required.

MAPS: Green Trails—Cougar Mountain/Squak Mountain 203S; USGS Bellevue South

FACILITIES: Restroom at trailhead; no drinking water available

Cougar Mountain Regional Wildland Park: Wilderness Creek and Wilderness Peak Loop

Latitude: North 47d30.612m

Longitude: West 122d05.227m

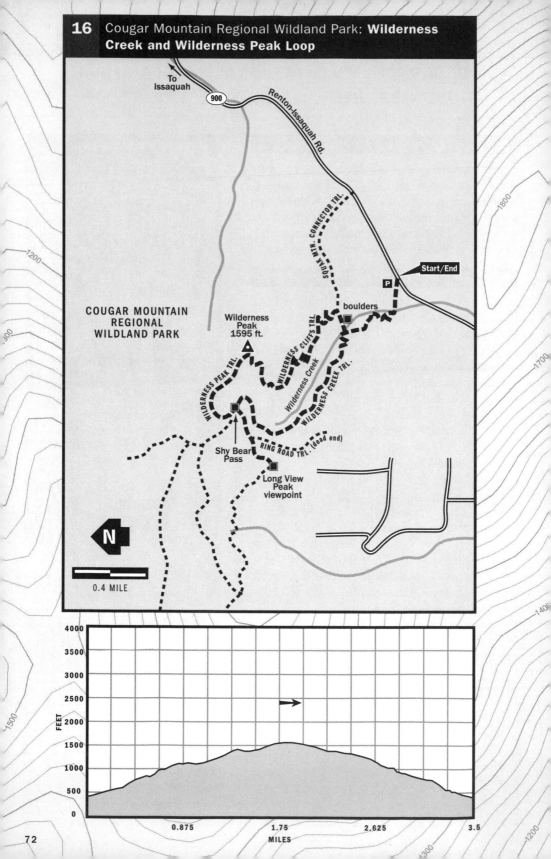

To Issaquah

900

Renton-Issaquah Rd

SQUAK MTN. CONNECTOR TRL.

Start/End

P

boulders

COUGAR MOUNTAIN REGIONAL WILDLAND PARK

Wilderness Peak 1595 ft.

WILDERNESS CLIFFS TRL.

Wilderness Creek

WILDERNESS CREEK TRL.

WILDERNESS PEAK TRL.

Shy Bear Pass

RING ROAD TRL. (dead end)

Long View Peak viewpoint

N

0.4 MILE

FEET

4000
3500
3000
2500
2000
1500
1000
500
0

0.875   1.75   2.625   3.5

MILES

Just past the trailhead, a footbridge crosses Wilderness Creek as it splashes down through mossy boulders and logs. The trail then climbs on the southern side of the creek through some short switchbacks, generally with the water flowing within earshot as it heads up the ridge.

Cross back over the creek on a second bridge after about a half-mile to reach the first junction, and stay to your left; the right-hand option, signed as Wilderness Creek Trail, serves as the end of the loop on the descent.

Some glacial erratics, not surprisingly known as "The Boulders," soon appear on the right. The big rocks continue intermittently up the slope, inviting speculation on both the massive forces required to deposit them here and the power of erosion that may eventually grind them to dust.

Cross the creek several more times as the trail ascends to a flatter marshy area. Carefully laid wooden planks wind between some more erratics, keeping hikers above the mud and away from both stinging nettles and thorny devil's club, with some particularly nasty specimens reaching more than ten feet high. Past the marsh, the trail starts climbing again through a forest of tall Douglas firs and eventually reaches an important intersection at Shy Bear Pass, elevation approximately 1,350 feet, where several S and E trails converge.

The signed trail to Long View Peak heads left, allowing a 0.6-mile out-and-back side trip to a nearby viewpoint. The overlook is far short of spectacular and typical for Cougar Mountain, with intervening trees and a relatively narrow angle of view; nonetheless, it makes an interesting diversion. To reach the viewpoint, stay on the S4 Long View Peak Trail past a junction with the S5 Ring Road Trail, then turn left onto an unsigned spur where the S3 Deceiver Trial branches to the right. The spur goes up and over a small rise to reach the viewpoint, which looks out over a slice of South Seattle and Puget Sound.

Return to Shy Bear Pass and follow the signed E4 Wilderness Peak Trail on a gentle uphill single-track to where it crests after about 0.3 miles. Drop down slightly and go past the right turn onto the E5 Wilderness Cliffs Trail. The high point is only another 0.1 mile, where the trail dead-ends at a bench in a circular grove of tall trees. Lacking a view or even a single exposed rock, Wilderness Peak hardly passes for a summit, by most definitions of the word. But the spot beneath the trees is pleasant and peaceful, like a quiet chapel in the woods.

Return to the previous intersection and turn left to start descending the Wilderness Cliffs Trail. The route drops gradually at first, but soon becomes steeper and enters some switchbacks beneath the high Douglas firs. Two viewpoints look out over the May Creek Valley through gaps in the trees—the first just off to the right and the second farther down to the left—although neither provides what could be described as an all-encompassing vista. Wilderness Creek can be heard in the ravine below, too far down to be visible.

The signed Squak Mountain Connector Trail eventually branches off to the left. Stay to the right for another 400 feet to return to the Wilderness Creek Trail at the junction you encountered earlier, closing the loop. From here, continue down the same way you originally came up.

▶ NEARBY ACTIVITIES

The kid-friendly Issaquah Salmon Hatchery provides a window into efforts to restore coho and chinook salmon to the Issaquah Creek Watershed. The return of the fish to spawn each fall is surely the yearly highlight, but there is always something of interest going on here. To reach the hatchery, follow WA 900 (Renton-Issaquah Road SE) northeast from the trailhead, then turn right onto Newport Way NW in Issaquah. Take Newport Way into downtown, then turn left onto W Sunset Way. The hatchery is located at 125 W Sunset Way, on the right-hand side of the road. For more information, visit the Friends of the Issaquah Salmon Hatchery Web site at **www. issaquahfish.org** or call (425) 427-0259.

SQUAK MOUNTAIN STATE PARK: DOUBLE PEAK LOOP

▶ IN BRIEF

The Double Peak Loop hike quickly escapes the lower section of Squak Mountain State Park (which is open to horses) to explore a dense forest and the historic ruins of the Bullitt family settlement, passing two good viewpoints that rival any in the Issaquah region along the way. Plus, you just might have the trail to yourself.

▶ DESCRIPTION

Cougar and Tiger mountains draw most of the attention in the Issaquah Alps, leaving central Squak Mountain relatively underused. Whether hikers stay away because of Squak's limited size, reputation as an equestrian center, or for some other reason, their loss can be your gain.

Because Squak Mountain's trail network is complex and can be confusing, the best place to start this hike is at the kiosk on the eastern side of the parking lot where free copies of a park map are available. The trail itself starts on the opposite side of the parking lot and quickly reaches the gravel South Access Road. Across the road, a gate through a double split-rail fence leads to the Thomas Interpretive Trail, a short loop through a lush lowland forest of ferns and moss-covered big leaf maples. Children will love this quick side trip, complete with interpretive displays that detail the story of a field mouse that learns about the forest and its wildlife denizens, including a

ⓘ KEY AT-A-GLANCE INFORMATION

LENGTH: 6.8 miles (round-trip)

CONFIGURATION: Loop

DIFFICULTY: Moderate

SCENERY: Historic Bullitt family fireplace and home site; views south toward Mount Rainier and northwest to the Seattle skyline

EXPOSURE: Mostly shaded

TRAFFIC: Low to medium

TRAIL SURFACE: Dirt

HIKING TIME: 3–6 hours

ACCESS: Hikable year-round; Washington State Park Pass required for parking, daily passes available at trailhead

MAPS: Green Trails–Cougar Mountain/ Squak Mountain 203S; USGS Bellevue South, Maple Valley

FACILITIES: Restroom at trailhead, no drinking water available

▶ DIRECTIONS

From I-5 south of downtown Seattle, go east on I-90. Take Exit 15 and drive south on WA 900, which begins as 17th Avenue NW then becomes Renton-Issaquah Road SE. After driving 4 miles, turn left onto SE May Valley Road. Continue another 2.5 miles to the Squak Mountain State Park parking area on the left just past the gated South Access Road.

Squak Mountain State Park: Double Peak Loop

Latitude: North 47d28.906m

Longitude: West 122d03.236m

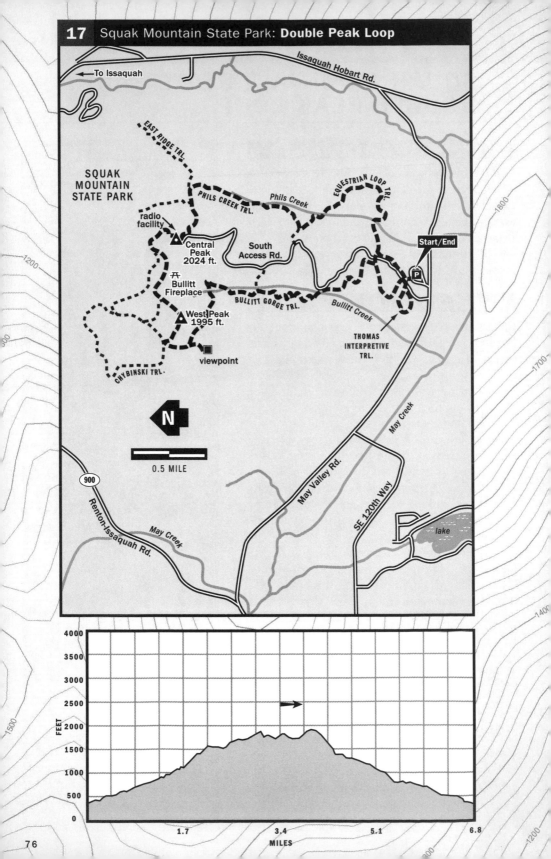

Seattle skyline from Squak
Mountain

crow and a bear. They can also count the rings on several fallen logs and search for
the unusual "Pretzel Tree," with two entwined trunks.

After completing the Thomas Loop, continue uphill on the South Access Road
for about 20 yards and look for a trail heading into the woods on the left. Follow this
trail for a quarter mile or so through a carpet of triangular oak ferns until it reaches
an unsigned junction with the Lower Bullitt Gorge Trail, also known as Mad Mountain Beaver Way. Turn left and head uphill on a soft surface of mud, both natural and
horse-made.

Bullitt Creek soon becomes audible in a shallow gully to the left, which the trail
approaches and then crosses on a footbridge. Various side branches head off into the
underbrush along the creek and another leads out to the right to meet the road, creating the possibility of some confusion. Be sure to continue uphill on the main Bullitt Gorge Trail.

Climb for another half mile through some giant stumps, many charred and pep-
pered with woodpecker holes and resembling the old volcanic plugs typically found
in the southern Cascade Mountains. Another unsigned junction marks the beginning
of the hikers-only trail, which narrows and heads left. (Equestrians have to turn right
on the wider trail, crossing Bullitt Creek.)

The primitive trail climbs steeply at first, then levels out to reach a T-junction.
Take the signed Perimeter Loop Trail to the left, which bends around the southern
side of Squak Mountain on a gradual climb and then shifts back to the north.

The trail comes to its high point at about 1,750 feet and then starts to descend.
At the crest, look carefully for a faint path heading downhill to the left, which leads
100 yards to a small clearing with an excellent view. The spur receives minimal use,
so it may be overgrown or difficult to find, but it is well worth the effort. The viewpoint provides a wide-ranging perspective over nearby neighborhoods and hills all
the way to Mount Rainier. This is the best vista available anywhere on Squak's slopes,

making the viewpoint a great place to stop and spend some time, especially since it faces south and gets plenty of sun.

The Perimeter Loop Trail ends at a T-junction with the Chybinski Trail. However, the correct route to follow is on a tricky and very sharp turn to the right at the same intersection, identified with a sign to West Peak. This indistinct trail, which climbs to the western summit at an elevation of just less than 2,000 feet, is steep and usually muddy.

The top of West Peak is in a grove of tall trees with no view to speak of. Just on the far side, a rapidly deteriorating cabin marks a now-abandoned communication installation. Look for the continuation of the West Peak Trail (on the southeast corner of the structure), where it heads downhill through a pleasant forest of cedars and Douglas firs. The footing is soft and forgiving, thanks to a blanket of fallen needles and decaying wood.

Drop into a narrow saddle, then climb steeply back up the other side to reach a T-junction with the May Valley Trail. Take the unsigned fork to the left and arrive at yet another T-junction with the broad but unsigned Bullitt Fireplace Trail. Turn right and moments later arrive at the stone chimney that marks the ruins of the original homestead that once stood here. A picnic table on the old concrete floor provides a good place to stop and rest.

The Bullitt family donated the original parcel of land that created the public park at Squak Mountain, one of the many ways the Bullitts have made their mark on the Puget Sound region over the years. The prominent clan includes Dorothy S. Bullitt, the founder of King Broadcasting; Stim Bullitt, a real estate developer whose Harbor Properties helped revitalize downtown Seattle; Harriet Bullitt, the founder of *Pacific Northwest* magazine; and Dorothy C. Bullitt, an attorney and author who helped write *Addicted to Danger,* the best-selling memoir of noted Seattle mountaineer and adventurer Jim Wickwire.

Continue east from the Bullitt fireplace and follow a short descent to an intersection. Take the signed Central Peak Trail uphill to the right for a quarter mile, pass through a steel gate, and emerge at 2,024 feet beneath the towers of the Squak Mountain Microwave Installation on the summit. An unexpected view of downtown Seattle is available to the northwest, a line of sight that is the likely reason for the working radio facility.

Around the far side of the buildings, start downhill on the gravel South Access Road for a few hundred feet and turn left on the signed Summit Trail. Pass through a gate and begin a quick descent into the woods, which continue for 0.4 miles to a junction with Phil's Creek Trail. Turn right and reach another intersection with the East Ridge Trail, only 0.1 mile farther along. Stay on the Phil's Creek Trail, once again, to the right.

The next section of trail apparently receives minimal use and may be overgrown and lined with stinging nettles, so hiking in long pants might be a good idea. Cross through a gate to return to the lower mountain where horses are allowed, and head a quarter mile downhill on the Phil's Creek Trail to a left turn onto the signed Equestrian Loop Trail. Expect mud underfoot as you cross Phil's Creek.

The Equestrian Loop Trail descends for another half mile through a forest of mossy big leaf maples, eventually doubling back to the west and passing a number of intersections before rejoining the South Access Road. Head downhill on the gravel, pass through a private traffic gate, and watch for the short return trail to the parking lot on the left.

▶ NEARBY ACTIVITIES

The Issaquah Depot Museum, one of two Issaquah historical museums, provides a good look into how the early fortunes of the town went hand-in-hand with the development of the railroad. The restored depot building houses a series of interesting exhibits, including an impressive mural by local artist Bill Haddon. To reach the museum, head east on SE May Valley Road and then turn left onto Issaquah-Hobart Road, which becomes Front Street in Issaquah. In the heart of downtown, turn right onto E Sunset Way and look for the museum next to the train tracks on the left at 50 Rainier Boulevard N. For more information, contact the Issaquah Historical Society on the Web at **www.issaquahhistory.org** or call (425) 392-3500.

TIGER MOUNTAIN STATE FOREST: CHIRICO TRAIL

ℹ KEY AT-A-GLANCE INFORMATION

LENGTH: 4 miles (round-trip)

CONFIGURATION: Out-and-back

DIFFICULTY: Moderate

SCENERY: Two separate viewpoints (one north, one south), possible paraglider watching

EXPOSURE: Mostly shaded

TRAFFIC: Crowded; get an early start

TRAIL SURFACE: Dirt

HIKING TIME: 2–3 hours

ACCESS: Hikable year-round; no fee for parking or park access

MAPS: Green Trails—Tiger Mountain 204S; USGS Maple Valley

FACILITIES: Restroom at trailhead; no drinking water available

Tiger Mountain State Forest: Chirico Trail

Latitude: North 47d30.022m

Longitude: West 122d01.298m

▶ IN BRIEF

The Chirico Trail provides the shortest and easiest hike to two of the finest vistas anywhere in the Issaquah Alps, including spectacular Poo Poo Point. If the wind is right, you may share the trail with paragliders who launch from the top and fill the sky with their colorful sails, an unforgettable sight.

▶ DESCRIPTION

Although the Issaquah Alps look like a set of Cascade Mountain foothills, they are in fact part of a separate range, born long before their more famous counterparts were ever thrust up toward the sky. In contrast with the brash, young Cascades, which still show the sharp peaks and jagged spires of adolescence, the inexorable efforts of erosion have tamed and polished the geography of the Alps over the eons. Like the Appalachian Mountains of the eastern United States, the Issaquah Alps show their advanced age with low summits and gentle grades.

Sprawling Tiger Mountain is no exception, with no dominant high point and a series of indistinct bumps spaced along a lengthy ridge passing for summits. At the extreme western end, however, an unusually steep drop-off at Poo Poo Point provides good views and a great place to launch a paraglider. Unfortunately, access to the area was difficult for many years, requiring either an endless drive on the gated West Side Road or the carrying of bulky equipment up one of the long approach trails from the north.

▶ DIRECTIONS

From I-5 south of downtown Seattle, go east on I-90. Take Exit 17 and turn right onto Front Street in Issaquah. After passing through Issaquah, Front Street curves and becomes Issaquah-Hobart Road. The parking lot is on the left (east) side of Issaquah-Hobart Road, just past SE 111th Street. The trailhead is on the far side of the grassy paraglider-landing field.

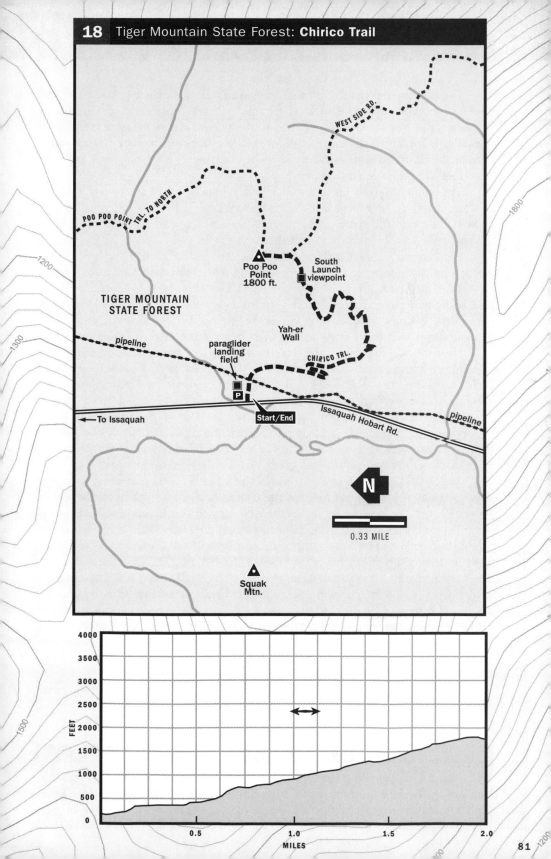

The Chirico Trail changed all that, providing a back entrance to Poo Poo Point. The trail owes its existence to local paragliders who petitioned the Washington Department of Natural Resources (DNR) to develop an access trail straight up from the valley to the west. Issaquah paragliding guide and instructor Marc Chirico spearheaded the effort, bringing together scores of contributors and volunteers to realize his vision; the trail was named in his honor.

The trailhead reveals the area's paragliding roots. The hike starts on the far side of a flat, grassy meadow, which is the traditional landing field, complete with a circular bull's-eye in the center for a target. A stream frequently referred to as Hang Glider Creek runs along the field's northern edge.

Climbing more than 1,500 feet in less than 2 miles, the Chirico Trail is one of the steepest on Tiger Mountain. It begins by heading south, traversing the foot of the Yaher Wall for the first half mile while gaining 500 feet. The trail is like a climber's way trail, with exposed roots and rocks, not surprising since its original intended users were paragliders seeking to reach the top as quickly as possible. The forest is pleasant, scenic, and damp, with heavy moss draping over the trees and mud collecting underfoot.

Near the 700-foot mark, the trail runs through a switchback and then turns right (east), escaping the sound of the traffic from the valley below. Soon after, the forest begins to thin, and occasional viewpoints open to the south through the scrubby trees as you continue to mount the ridge.

A grassy clearing just off to the right marks the beginning of the South Launch Viewpoint. Continue on the trail uphill to reach the top of the clearing, where the best views can be found. Watch out for a series of informal paths, mostly cutting switchbacks or heading out into the grass, skirting the edge of the trees.

The South Launch Viewpoint sits at about 1,600 feet and provides a great vista over the landscape to the south, from the community of Mirrormont all the way to Mount Rainier. The lack of trees makes the view panoramic and uninterrupted.

The trail heads back into the spongy forest on the eastern side, to the left of two double-track jeep roads. After another quarter mile you will emerge at Poo Poo Point, home to a second clearing that is the North Launch Viewpoint, elevation 1,800 feet. The view here is even more spectacular than it is on the other side, encompassing the eastern face of Squak Mountain, the Sammamish Plateau, downtown Bellevue, and even the top of the Space Needle through a saddle high on Cougar Mountain to the west. Look for a display board which provides a helpful reference to the landmarks below.

When the wind is rising suitably out of the valley, typically in the afternoon, scores of paragliders use Poo Poo Point to soar into the sky. Many are able to rise far above the take-off site before eventually descending to the landing field at the bottom.

Unfortunately, the descent for most hikers will be much less exhilarating, requiring a hike back down the trail. It is also possible to head down the Poo Poo Point Trail, if you have prepared a shuttle at one of Tiger Mountain's busy northern trailheads.

▶ NEARBY ACTIVITIES

Stan's Bar-B-Q at 58 Front Street N is a local favorite, showcasing Stan's signature Kansas City flavor. To get there, follow Issaquah-Hobart Road into downtown Issaquah until it becomes Front Street. Stan's is on the right, just past the Sunset Way intersection. For more information, visit **www.stansbarbq.com** or call (425) 392-4551.

TIGER MOUNTAIN STATE FOREST: POO POO POINT TRAIL

▶ IN BRIEF

Poo Poo Point is much nicer than it sounds. Perched on the western end of Tiger Mountain, it provides one of the best views anywhere in the Issaquah Alps, even though it is more than 1,000 feet below the true summit. The Poo Poo Point Trail climbs to the viewpoint through some of the best forest anywhere on West Tiger Mountain and avoids most of the crowds that congregate on the mountain's northern side.

▶ DESCRIPTION

Tiger Mountain's best feature might also be its worst: more trails mean more options, but confusing routes and the occasional lost hiker frequently come along with them—the downside to the maze of good trails available on Tiger's slopes. Hiking anywhere in the area generally requires careful consultation of the directions and the map, and the Poo Poo Point Trail is no exception. However, that rarely dissuades the crowds who enjoy the easy drive from Seattle, less than 30 miles away on I-90.

Starting the hike to Poo Poo Point from the Sunset Way trailhead avoids most of the people who flock to the better-developed High Point trailhead a few miles to the east. Although the early section of the hike can be confusing, the lesser traffic makes it worthwhile—and this approach is no harder to follow than any of the others, some of which require navigating through the center of the Tradition Plateau.

The trail starts steeply up the hillside from the parking lot, presenting one of the most

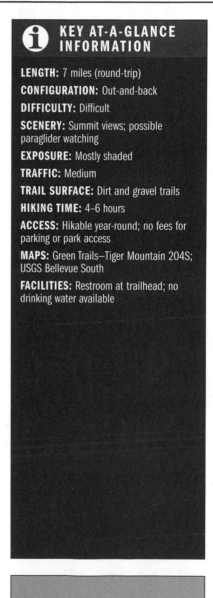

ⓘ KEY AT-A-GLANCE INFORMATION

LENGTH: 7 miles (round-trip)

CONFIGURATION: Out-and-back

DIFFICULTY: Difficult

SCENERY: Summit views; possible paraglider watching

EXPOSURE: Mostly shaded

TRAFFIC: Medium

TRAIL SURFACE: Dirt and gravel trails

HIKING TIME: 4–6 hours

ACCESS: Hikable year-round; no fees for parking or park access

MAPS: Green Trails–Tiger Mountain 204S; USGS Bellevue South

FACILITIES: Restroom at trailhead; no drinking water available

▶ DIRECTIONS

From I-5 south of downtown Seattle, go east on I-90. Take Exit 17, and turn right onto Front Street in Issaquah. At a stoplight in the Issaquah city center, turn left onto Sunset Way. The gravel parking lot is located on the right side of Sunset Way just before the road ascends to enter I-90.

Tiger Mountain State Forest:
Poo Poo Point Trail

Latitude: North 47d31.796m

Longitude: West 122d01.519m

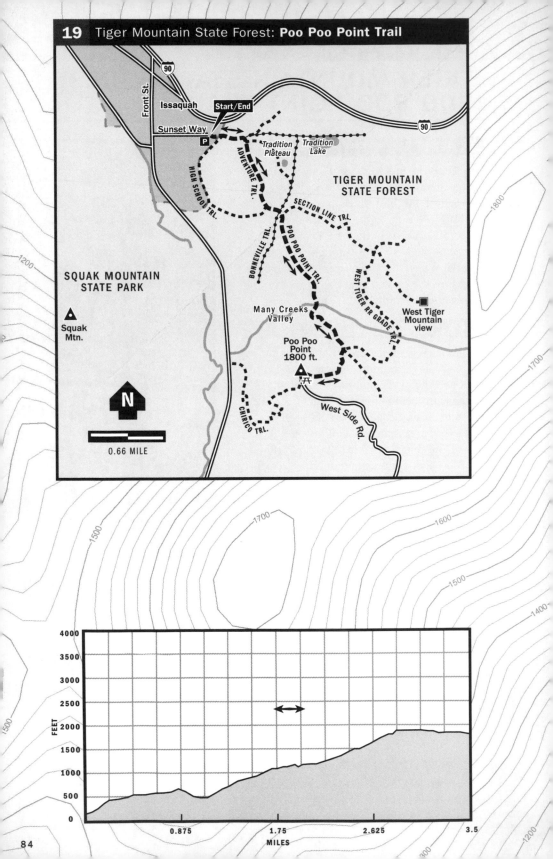

Front St.

Issaquah

90

Start/End

Sunset Way

P

Tradition Plateau

Tradition Lake

ADVENTURE TRL.

HIGH SCHOOL TRL.

TIGER MOUNTAIN STATE FOREST

SECTION LINE TRL.

BONNEVILLE TRL.

POO POO POINT TRL.

WEST TIGER RR GRADE TRL.

West Tiger Mountain view

SQUAK MOUNTAIN STATE PARK

Squak Mtn.

Many Creeks Valley

Poo Poo Point 1800 ft.

CHIRICO TRL.

West Side Rd.

N

0.66 MILE

1800

1700

1200

1700

1600

1500

1500

1400

1200

1300

FEET

4000
3500
3000
2500
2000
1500
1000
500
0

0.875   1.75   2.625   3.5

MILES

demanding sections of the entire hike in the first quarter mile. Follow the dirt path up the slope and turn left at an unsigned T-junction where the trail first meets a set of power lines, running in from the right. After the turn you will be directly above the eastbound lanes of I-90, visible through the trees.

Take the next right at another unsigned junction, climbing some steps and then following a ridgeline as it heads uphill to the east. The trail emerges under the power lines again at the top of the hill, some 300 feet above the trailhead where you started.

From here the route is easier to find, heading east directly under the power lines on a gravel road. Known as the Puget Power Line Trail, the road leads through a dense field of Scotch broom. The bright, eye-catching yellow flowers of this plant, common in the Pacific Northwest, belie its status as an invasive weed species native to Europe and Africa and originally imported as an ornamental. The Puget Power Line Trail links many of the most popular routes on Tiger Mountain, so you are likely to see other hikers.

The 0.4 miles to the next junction are flat and easy. Head through a wooden split-rail gate on the right, signed for the Wetlands Trail. Almost immediately, the trail forks underneath the power lines; stay right, following a sign to the Adventure Trail. The brush soon gives way to the trees at the edge of the forest.

The Adventure Trail is a dirt single-track, negotiating a number of quick ups and downs and short turns while gradually climbing to a high point at around 650 feet. It descends again on the far side to reach a T-junction at a wooden gate with the unmarked High School Trail, which has a wide gravel surface.

Pass through the gate and turn left, starting a very gradual ascent through some stately birches. After crossing a creek, emerge from the trees to reach another set of power lines and the Bonneville Trail. You have now traveled about 1.5 miles total from the trailhead and about 0.2 miles from the end of the Adventure Trail.

Stay left and head uphill under the power lines on the gravel of the Bonneville Trail. This is a particularly confusing intersection, so make sure to watch carefully for an unsigned dirt trail to the right, just before you reach the first metal tower.

Follow the worn trail as it crosses under the power lines and through a row of trees to reach a second clearing, where a gas pipeline runs underground. Stay right at a signed fork for the Poo Poo Point Trail.

Starting at about 550 feet, this trail does most of the heavy lifting on the hike, reaching almost 2,000 feet at its highest point. Thankfully, the next junction is 2.8 miles farther up the mountain, leaving hikers free to stop worrying about navigation and enjoy the beauty of the natural surroundings. Even though the Poo Poo Point Trail is open to equestrians, both horse and human visitors tend to be much rarer here than farther down.

The trail climbs steadily over the next mile into the Many Creeks Valley. The valley is blessed with some of the nicest forest anywhere on Tiger Mountain, including some particularly large cedars that have successfully managed to avoid the axe and the saw over the years. When sunlight filters through the canopy, the woods here can feel like deep wilderness far from civilization.

Cross three separate creeks (for whom the valley is no doubt named), going over the last on a substantial wooden footbridge with handrails. After the bridge, the trail steepens through a series of switchbacks. Mature trees tower overhead, with many decaying logs hosting thick ferns and moss underneath.

The climb abruptly levels off at a final junction, where the West Tiger Railroad Grade Trail and One View Trail intersect the Poo Poo Point Trail. Although the junction is signed, there is no sign to Poo Poo Point. Take a hard right, shown as the continuation of the West Tiger Railroad Grade.

The trail has a net elevation loss over the last half mile, dropping from its high point with an altitude of more than 1,900 feet at the junction to about 1,800 at Poo Poo Point, but there are several short climbs and drops as the route curls around the northern side of the mountain. The trail finally emerges at a gravel parking lot, the end of the West Side Road.

The overlook is just up the short rise to the right, rewarding the long approach with a spectacular view to the northwest, rivaled by only a handful of others anywhere in the Issaquah Alps. Be sure to allow plenty of time to enjoy the setting and possibly observe the colorful paragliders who frequently use Poo Poo Point as an afternoon launch site when rising thermals are at their best. A picnic table above the parking lot makes a great place to relax and refuel before heading back down.

The directions should be easier on the descent, although it is still necessary to pay attention to the many turns, especially where there are no signs. It is also possible to head down the Chirico Trail to the west, if you have left a shuttle vehicle at the second trailhead along the Issaquah-Hobart Road.

▶ NEARBY ACTIVITIES

For a good northwestern microbrewed beer, head to the Issaquah Brewhouse at 35 Sunset Way. Follow Sunset Way west from the trailhead into downtown Issaquah to find the brewery on the left-hand side, just past the Front Street intersection. The brewhouse serves mostly handcrafted Rogue Ales, including unusual treats like Chocolate Stout, which can even be used to make hearty ice cream floats. For more information, check the brewery's Web site at **www.rogue.com/locations-issaquah. html** or call (425) 557-1911.

TIGER MOUNTAIN STATE FOREST:
WEST TIGER MOUNTAIN THREE LOOP

▶ IN BRIEF

Although Number Three is the lowest of West Tiger Mountain's triple summits, the view from the top is as good as from any of them. This fun loop takes a direct line to the popular peak, then descends a secluded route through the mountain's lush forests to explore some interesting natural features at Talus Rocks and Tradition Lake.

▶ DESCRIPTION

With more than 80 miles of trails spread over 13,500 acres of land, Tiger Mountain attracts outdoor enthusiasts of all kinds. It is also large and complicated enough that it is possible for visitors to get lost, so it's a good idea to bring a map.

While mountain bikers are mostly restricted to the trails and logging roads in the working forest of East Tiger, hikers tend to stay in the 4,500-acre Natural Resources Conservation Area on West Tiger. Most come to the busy High Point trailhead, bringing families, dogs, and anyone else they can find along with them. High Point provides access to a multitude of trails laid out on the nearby Tradition Plateau, where the linking of countless small segments allows for the creation of many easy loops. The climbs to any of West Tiger's numbered peaks attract plenty of traffic, as well, especially to West Tiger Three, the closest summit to the trailhead. However, it is possible to escape the crowds on this hike with an alternate route on the descent.

▶ DIRECTIONS

From I-5 south of downtown Seattle, go east on I-90. Take Exit 20, High Point, and turn right onto 276th Avenue SE. Immediately turn right again onto SE 79th Street and continue past the end of the paved road through a gate (closes at dusk). The West Tiger Mountain High Point trailhead parking area is located about a half mile up the gravel road from the gate.

ⓘ KEY AT-A-GLANCE INFORMATION

LENGTH: 5.1 miles (round-trip)

CONFIGURATION: Loop

DIFFICULTY: Moderate to difficult

SCENERY: Tradition Lake, summit views, huge boulders and caves at the Talus Rocks area, a section of seldom-used trail on popular Tiger Mountain

EXPOSURE: Mostly shaded

TRAFFIC: High on the way up, low on the way down

TRAIL SURFACE: Mostly dirt, a few sections of gravel

HIKING TIME: 3–4 hours

ACCESS: Hikable year-round; no fee for parking or park access

MAPS: Green Trails—Tiger Mountain 204S; USGS Fall City

FACILITIES: Restroom at trailhead, no drinking water available

Tiger Mountain State Forest:
West Tiger Mountain Three Loop

Latitude: North 47d31.767m

Longitude: West 121d59.676m

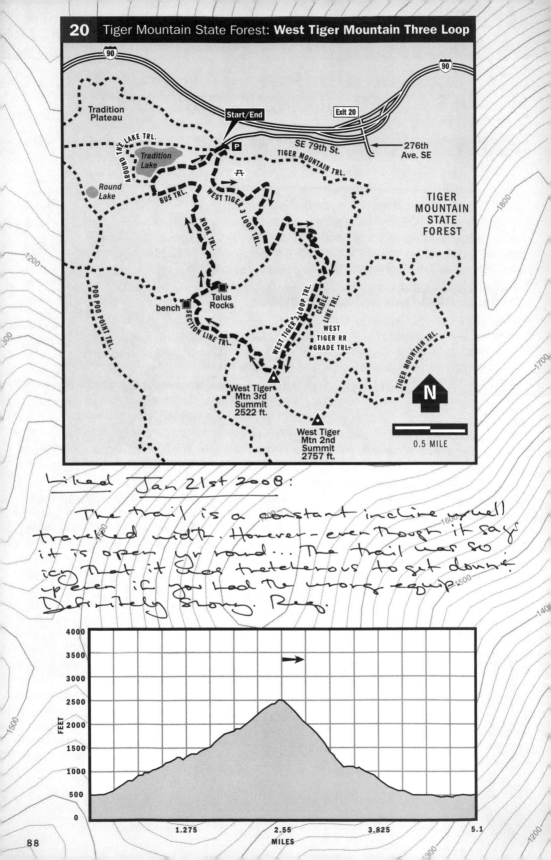

Liked Jan 21st 2008:

The trail is a constant incline up well traveled width. However - even though it says it is open yr round... The trail was so icy that it was tretcherous to get down. even if you had the wrong equip. Definitely snowy. Reg.

The start of the hike can be confusing, with a small maze of trails running between an educational shelter, a picnic area, a latrine, and an informational kiosk on the southern side of the parking lot. The true trailhead can be found by following various signs to The Trails below the power lines at the western end.

At a four-way intersection, head south through a wooden split-rail fence, signed as West Tiger Three Trail, and start hiking on a gravel surface lined with wooden planks. Moments later, head off the gravel to the left and pass through another gate to follow a muddy dirt track wide enough to be a reclaimed road, signed again for West Tiger Three Trail.

Stay straight at an intersection with the Tiger Mountain Trail (TMT) to continue on the West Tiger 3 Trail, which soon begins to climb in earnest. The footing becomes rougher, with many rounded stones set in the ground.

After about 0.8 miles from the trailhead, the trail crosses a creek and meets a junction with the Connector Trail, branching to the right. Stay left, continuing to climb through a bright green forest of ferns and moss. The forest is perpetually damp here, keeping the track muddy at all times. Even though the Issaquah Alps do not scrape as much rain from the clouds as the higher Cascades farther east, the western side of Tiger gets plenty of year-round precipitation, which falls almost exclusively as rain at this elevation.

Bend sharply around to the right just above 1,300 feet to mount a short ridge. The West Tiger Cable Line Trail comes up the steep slope from the left and runs with the main trail for a short distance before exiting again on the right. The Cable Line Trail runs straight up to the summit, forgoing switchbacks and crossing the West Tiger 3 Trail many times. It is possible to follow the unmaintained Cable Line, although it is considerably rougher and steeper than the main trail.

In the next mile, the trail swings through a series of switchbacks and enters a glade of tall evergreens. Tiger Mountain was once extensively logged for its western red cedars, so few remain on the lower-elevation slopes. Although this section has also been harvested in the past, it nonetheless gives a better idea of what the mountain's original forests once looked like. Enjoy the easier grade through the trees, the last significant break before the ascent resumes on the far side of the flats.

Cross a junction with the West Tiger Railroad Grade Trail and continue uphill, following a sign to West Tiger Three. After several more intersections with the Cable Line, the trail emerges from the trees on an open ridge with views out to the northeast, including I-90, Mount Si, and the nearby radio towers of West Tiger Two.

The summit lies just beyond at 2,522 feet, a clearing with a broad view over Tiger Mountain State Forest. To the south, Mount Rainier rises above the trees on the West Tiger Two ridgeline, and Squak and Cougar mountains can be seen in front of downtown Seattle and the Olympic Mountains to the west. For the ambitious, a trail continues from the far side of the clearing to climb the forested ridge to the other two West Tiger summits, each a few hundred feet higher.

To start the descent, head downhill on the unsigned Cable Line Trail, the widest route leaving the summit to the north, just west of the West Tiger Three Trail. After only about 50 yards on the rocky surface, the single-track Section Line Trail drops off to the left. The start of the trail is neither signed nor obvious, so be sure to look carefully. If there is snow on the ground, the trail may be particularly hard to find and follow at the top, so a better option may be to descend the way you came until you reach the junction with the West Tiger Railroad Grade, then head west (a left turn when traveling downhill) for a half mile until you reach the signed junction with the Section Line Trail.

The path drops steeply on a narrow and tricky surface of roots, mud, and fallen needles, but the quiet of the forest more than makes up for it. The sounds of birds singing are the rule here, rather than the loud voices and dogs barking typical at the summit.

After a drop of about 500 feet in 0.4 miles, reach a junction with the wide West Tiger Railroad Grade Trail, which provides an optional way to reach this point (as described above). Continue straight down the hill, signed as Section Line Trail, losing another 800 feet in a steep drop over the next half mile.

Take a sharp turn to the right at a wooden bench, signed as Nook Connector, and leave the Section Line Trail. The connector runs only about a quarter mile before meeting the Nook Trail.

A quick side trip to the right, signed as Talus Rocks Loop Trail, is well worth the minimal effort required. The loop's name does little to illuminate its destination; talus typically refers to a pile of small, loose rocks at the base of a cliff or steep slope, but this trail actually runs through a series of giant glacial erratic boulders. The rocks are covered in ferns and moss, with some shallow caves, alcoves, and overhangs underneath, all suitable for exploration. The trail itself travels an inventive route, climbing over some of the boulders and squeezing through small gaps between others.

Return to the previous junction and head downhill on the signed Nook Trail, which follows a gradual descent for about 0.8 miles before ending at a T-junction with the Bus Trail. Head left on the wide, gravel Bus Trail, likely joining other hikers already on it.

A flat quarter mile leads to the trail's namesake, an old, rusted-out bus frame laying on its side in the woods to the right and looking like a forgotten war-zone relic. Just past the bus, continue on the gravel trail (signed as Connector Trail) as it bends around to the right. After another 500 feet, turn right on the signed Around the Lake Trail.

The waters of Tradition Lake are visible through the trees, although it is difficult to actually reach the shore. Access used to be easier, but it was withdrawn in the early 1990s to protect nesting birds in the wetlands from being disturbed by frequent human traffic. The Around the Lake Trail is dead flat and circles around the lake heading east for about a half mile before returning you to the High Point trailhead, where you began.

▶ NEARBY ACTIVITIES

The Gilman Town Hall Museum provides a good look into pioneer life in Issaquah, dating back to when the settlement was known as Gilman. The restored building looks as if it was lifted straight off a Western movie set, and the original concrete jailhouse out back is complete with iron bars on the windows. To reach the museum, head west on I-90 to Exit 18 and follow E Sunset Way into Issaquah. The museum is at 165 SE Andrews Street, one block south of Sunset Way between First and Second avenues. For more information, contact the Issaquah Historical Society on the Web at **www.issaquahhistory.org** or call (425) 392-3500.

CEDAR RIVER TRAIL: LANDSBURG PARK TO BIG BEND NATURAL AREA

▶ IN BRIEF

The Cedar River Trail runs between Renton and Landsburg, mostly through housing developments and suburban sprawl. This hike starts at the far eastern end of this rail-trail, however, where wild salmon still spawn and the river maintains a measure of its natural state, inviting lazy wandering and exploration along the bank.

▶ DESCRIPTION

Even though much of the development in South King County was fueled by Seattle's recent high-tech boom, it was the far-less-glamorous business of extractive mining that first put the region on the map. A century before Microsoft arrived in Redmond or Amazon had shipped a single book, nascent communities were growing along the Cedar River corridor, served by the Columbia and Puget Sound Railway. The trains that once hauled coal from the local mines to the ocean are now gone, but the old right-of-way still remains, linking a number of towns between Maple Valley and Renton along the Cedar River Trail.

The least-developed part of the 16-mile route is at its far eastern end, around the quiet community of Landsburg. Although the town might seem awfully close to the sprawl around Kent and Auburn, it actually has a few surprises.

▶ DIRECTIONS

From I-5 south of downtown Seattle, go east on I-90. Take Exit 17, and turn right onto Front Street in Issaquah. After passing through Issaquah, Front Street curves and becomes Issaquah-Hobart Road. Continue on this road as it changes names and eventually becomes 276th Avenue SE. About 12 miles from Issaquah, the road descends to cross the Cedar River. The gravel parking area and trailhead are located on the right, just before the bridge over the river.

ℹ KEY AT-A-GLANCE INFORMATION

LENGTH: 3 miles (round-trip)

CONFIGURATION: Out-and-back

DIFFICULTY: Easy

SCENERY: A rail-trail and dirt hiking trails along the banks of the Cedar River, a bridge overlook

EXPOSURE: Mostly shaded

TRAFFIC: High on rail-trail, lower on dirt hiking trails

TRAIL SURFACE: Gravel (on rail-trail) and dirt

HIKING TIME: 1–2 hours

ACCESS: Hikable year-round; no fees for parking or park access

MAPS: USGS Hobart

FACILITIES: No facilities at trailhead; restrooms and water at Landsburg Park

Cedar River Trail: Landsburg Park to Big Bend Natural Area

Latitude: North 47d22.517m

Longitude: West 121d58.286m

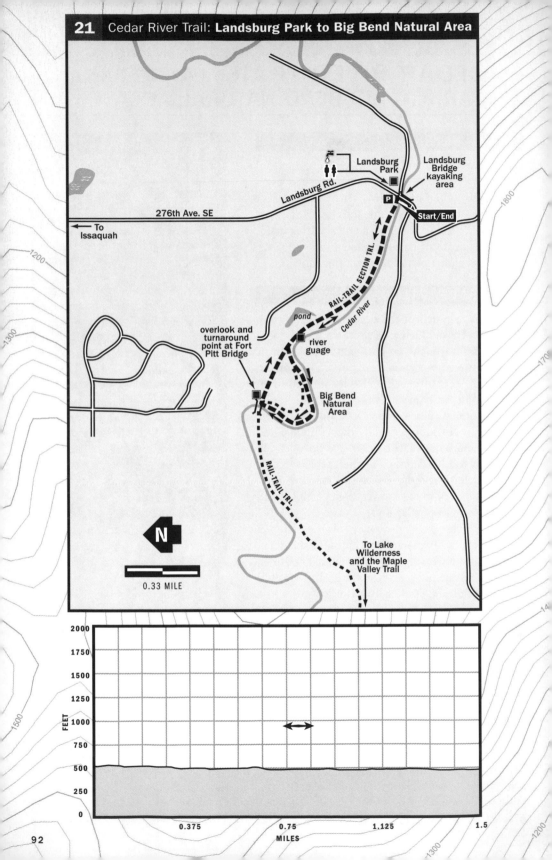

Landsburg Park

Landsburg Bridge kayaking area

Landsburg Rd.

276th Ave. SE

← To Issaquah

RAIL-TRAIL SECTION TRL.

Cedar River

P

Start/End

pond

river guage

overlook and turnaround point at Fort Pitt Bridge

Big Bend Natural Area

RAIL-TRAIL TRL.

To Lake Wilderness and the Maple Valley Trail

N

0.33 MILE

FEET

2000
1750
1500
1250
1000
750
500
250
0

0.375   0.75   1.125   1.5

MILES

Fort Pitt Bridge on the Cedar River Trail

As far east as the central Issaquah Alps and gateway to the protected Cedar River Watershed, a source of Seattle's water, the Landsburg trailhead provides access to a worthy natural experience in a riparian environment.

The Cedar River Trail attracts users of all types on its entire length, and the Landsburg segment is no exception. However, the first 6 miles westbound are surfaced with gravel, which tends to attract slightly more rugged visitors than the final 10 miles to Renton, which are sealed and paved. Expect mountain bikers at Landsburg but not road bikers, who mostly avoid this area in favor of the pavement.

Some of the other trail users might provide a little entertainment, too. Look for a white-water slalom course set up immediately upstream of the parking lot on the rapids directly underneath the Landsburg Road Bridge. If the flow is right, expert canoeists and kayakers will be running the gates, a compelling display of skill that few people ever get to witness in person.

But no matter how impressive the sight of kayakers paddling on the rapids, nothing can compare to the sight of salmon swimming upstream. During the fall run in October and November, upwards of 60,000 salmon return here from the ocean to spawn in the crystal-clear water. Most are sockeye, but coho and chinook are present as well; in the best years the total fish count can reach 300,000 or more. If you arrive in season, walk across Landsburg Road from the trailhead to visit Landsburg Park, the best place to observe one of nature's grandest and most mysterious spectacles.

Neither kayakers nor salmon would favor the Cedar River here if the waterway didn't maintain a strong element of its natural, untamed state. The same qualities that bring paddlers and fish also make it good for hikers.

Two protected tracts of land designed to preserve the river environment lie just west of the trailhead—the Landsburg Reach and Big Bend Natural Areas. Begin walking west on the wide and flat surface and immediately enter Landsburg Reach. Although a wooded rise on the left quickly hides the river from view, the rapids can still be heard churning through the rocks below. A number of boot-beaten tracks without any specific destination other than the river's edge branch off from the gravel to reach the water. Often used by fishermen and swimmers, they invite curious hikers to investigate as well. It is difficult to proceed directly along the river bank, though, so it will usually be necessary to return to the main rail-trail after each short detour.

However, a better opportunity for escaping the gravel can be found toward the end of the first half mile. After passing a pond in the forest to the right, watch for a USGS gauging station just off to the left. The station is a distinctive green cylinder made out of sheet metal; it's just large enough for a person to stand inside and has a cone-shaped cap on top.

From the gauge, a dirt trail continues parallel to the water downstream and enters the Big Bend Natural Area. The river forms a broad oxbow in this section as it curves away to the left, diverging from the old rail bed behind a rocky ridge.

The trail winds its way along the river, sometimes at the water's edge, sometimes beneath the mix of second-growth coniferous and deciduous trees. There is no official route and the trail is not maintained, so expect several informal spurs leading to and fro and occasionally going nowhere at all. Boulders, deep pools, sandy beaches, and an impressive high-sediment cliff on the opposite bank are some of the things to see along the way, inviting casual meandering. The Cedar River Corridor is much better suited to hikers who like to relax, move slowly, and study the small details of their surroundings than it is to those in a hurry. Families with small children will find much of interest here; the serious, ultrafit adventurer, not so much.

The Fort Pitt Bridge comes up all too soon, where the single-track rejoins the gravel and the rail-trail crosses the river on a rust-colored trestle. The straight-line distance back to Landsburg is only about 1.1 miles from the bridge, and it is possible to complete the obvious loop by returning on the Cedar River Trail. However, you also can create an alternate sort-of-loop by simply picking a different return path through the network of trails along the water. This will extend the total distance of the hike as well, since it is closer to 1.5 miles back to the beginning around the river bend.

Another way to extend the hike is by continuing west on the abandoned rail line for whatever distance you choose and then returning the same way. Yet by the time you cross the bridge, the wildest and most accessible portion of the river will already be behind you, as the valley inevitably runs into more developed areas.

Instead, a better bet might be to bring a mountain bike and make the most of the wide, flat surface. For a gentle, recommended ride, follow the Cedar River Trail through several named communities and across a few more bridges nearly identical to the Fort Pitt. About 6 miles from the Landsburg trailhead, join the signed Maple Valley Trail (once known as the Lake Wilderness Trail) by making a sharp left turn up a short but steep hill. If you reach the paved portion of the Cedar River Trail, you have just missed the junction and need to backtrack slightly.

After the initial hill, the Maple Valley Trail is flat and graveled as it continues through quiet suburban communities for a few more miles to Lake Wilderness. The lake makes a good turnaround point, with a community park and a grand old lodge on the northern shore.

INTERSTATE 90 AND THE SNOQUALMIE PASS AREA

SNOQUALMIE FALLS VIEWPOINT VIA PRESTON-SNOQUALMIE RAIL-TRAIL

KEY AT-A-GLANCE INFORMATION

LENGTH: 3.6 miles (round-trip)

CONFIGURATION: Out-and-back

DIFFICULTY: Easy

SCENERY: Views of Snoqualmie Falls and the Snoqualmie River Valley

EXPOSURE: Mostly shaded

TRAFFIC: Low to moderate

TRAIL SURFACE: Paved

HIKING TIME: 1–2 hours

ACCESS: Hikable year-round; no fees for parking or park access

MAPS: USGS Snoqualmie

FACILITIES: Restroom at trailhead; no drinking water available

Snoqualmie Falls Viewpoint via
Preston-Snoqualmie Rail-Trail

Latitude: North 47d33.049m

Longitude: West 121d53.252m

IN BRIEF

Despite its proximity to Snoqualmie Falls, one of Washington State's biggest tourist attractions, this converted rail-trail gets limited attention. Yet it is well worth the easy hike, ending at an overlook with a view of the falls that most people never see.

DESCRIPTION

Several de facto global yardsticks exist for the outdoors that all other similar locations are measured up against. For mountains the model is obvious—one need only look at how many places with a nearby hill or two claim to be "Little Switzerland" or the "Switzerland of America." In the case of waterfalls, the benchmark is Niagara.

Spectacular Snoqualmie Falls can hold its own against the standard. Plunging 268 feet, Snoqualmie is one of the highest falls in Washington State and more than 100 feet taller than the 167-foot Canadian Horseshoe Falls, the largest vertical drop at Niagara.

Snoqualmie is no match for Niagara when it comes to water volume, however. Although the flow over Snoqualmie Falls fluctuates heavily depending on the season, normal flow is between 10,000 and 15,000 gallons per second, a mere drop in the bucket compared with the 750,000 gallons per second seen at Niagara on a typical

DIRECTIONS

From Interstate 5 south of downtown Seattle, go east on Interstate 90. Take Exit 22, Preston Fall City, and turn left, crossing over I-90. At the T-shaped intersection, turn right onto Preston Fall City Road SE and proceed on this winding road for almost 4 miles to Lake Alice Road SE (SE 47th Street). After turning right onto Lake Alice Road SE, continue about 1 mile to the Preston-Snoqualmie Trail intersection and the parking area on the right side of the road.

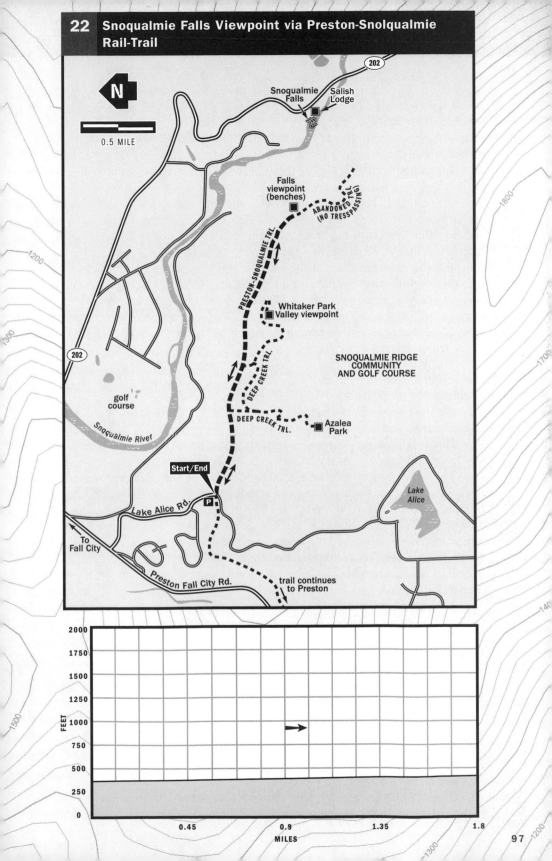

N

0.5 MILE

202

Snoqualmie Falls

Salish Lodge

Falls viewpoint (benches)

ABANDONED TRL. (NO TRESSPASSING)

PRESTON-SNOQUALMIE TRL.

Whitaker Park Valley viewpoint

DEEP CREEK TRL.

SNOQUALMIE RIDGE COMMUNITY AND GOLF COURSE

DEEP CREEK TRL.

Azalea Park

202

golf course

Snoqualmie River

Start/End

P

Lake Alice Rd.

Lake Alice

To Fall City

Preston Fall City Rd.

trail continues to Preston

FEET

2000
1750
1500
1250
1000
750
500
250
0

0.45   0.9   1.35   1.8

MILES

summer day. The difference is no surprise: Snoqualmie is only about 100 feet wide, and Niagara sprawls 3,660 feet across the American, Bridal Veil, and Horseshoe Falls together. There is also a huge difference in the amount of electric power generated at each site. Snoqualmie currently produces about 42,000 kilowatts, enough to serve the local area. But Niagara's seven separate stations made up of 64 generators produce 4.6 million kilowatts, making it one of the most important sources of electricity for much of the eastern U.S. and Canada.

Interestingly, both Snoqualmie and Niagara feature historically significant power plants introduced in the 1890s. The Adams Hydroelectric Station came online at Niagara in 1896 with the first significant commercial use of AC (alternating current) power in the world, solving the problem of long-distance electricity transmission. Bringing together some of the most important scientists and inventors of the age, the revolutionary design came from Nikolas Tesla and George Westinghouse, beating out competing ideas from William Kelvin and Thomas Edison. At Snoqualmie, an 1899 power plant commissioned by Charles Baker became the first in the world to house all of its generators completely underground (in a chamber carved out of the dark volcanic rock).

Thankfully, Snoqualmie's 1.5 million visitors are no match for the 12 million that descend upon Niagara each year. Nonetheless, crowds at Snoqualmie Falls can be substantial on virtually any weekend, especially during the high tourist season in summer. Most people come to stroll the grounds of the Salish Lodge, look at the falls from the rim, and browse the souvenir shops. Very few make it to the Preston-Snoqualmie Trail on the southern side of the river, however, which makes it a great way to get a unique look at the falls away from the crowds.

The route was originally developed in 1890 by the Seattle, Lakeshore, and Eastern Railroad. But the tragic collapse of a wooden trestle over the Raging River in 1900 precipitated a transfer of ownership in 1901 to the Northern Pacific Railroad, which became the Burlington Northern in 1970. Service ended in 1974, and the right-of-way was later purchased by King County for transition into its current form, joining a host of other famous rail-trails around Puget Sound first pioneered by the Seattle, Lakeshore, and Eastern line, including the Seattle Waterfront Pathway and the Burke-Gilman Trail.

Now paved and open to foot traffic and bicycles, the Preston-Snoqualmie Trail could not be easier to follow. Flat, straight, and wide enough to be a road, the path has only two junctions, both unsigned connectors to the Deep Creek Trail from the Snoqualmie Ridge development up the slope to the right. In either case, simply stay on the paved main trail to continue to the overlook.

Periodic views open to the left, looking out over the farmland of the Snoqualmie River Valley to the north and the Cascade Mountain peaks beyond. A few benches along the way make good rest points, although you are unlikely to need it on this gentle and forgiving trail. A mixed forest of second-growth evergreens lines the path, with some blackberry bushes along the way, hopefully providing fruit in summer. Depending on the water level, you may be able to hear the thundering falls a long way before you reach the viewpoint.

After 1.8 miles, the trail dead-ends at a fence, near which are a few benches and a latrine. Gaze through the trees to see the mighty falls, along with Salish Lodge and the obvious infrastructure of the electricity transmission towers from the century-old power plant. Clouds of mist rise above the trees from the torrent, and the western face of Mount Si dominates the background. Many tourist brochures feature images of Snoqualmie Falls from this angle, showing the lodge and the falls together in the same frame, a virtual impossibility to visualize from the northern side. However, such photos tend to be aerial shots from a much higher viewpoint than is available here.

The return trip to the Lake Alice trailhead is the same as the approach. For anyone seeking a longer hike, the Preston-Snoqualmie Trail continues another 3.5 miles westward from the parking area to the small town of Preston. After 1 mile, an overlook surveys the former site of the trestle over the Raging River, although little visible evidence remains of the 1900 collapse.

▶ NEARBY ACTIVITIES

The crowds that collect at the Salish Lodge and Spa can't all be wrong. With elegant rooms, fine dining, and a luxurious spa, the upscale hotel provides a great mountain getaway and is certainly worth a visit. Whether stopping by for a quick meal or staying an entire weekend, there might be no better way to wind down than by enjoying some of the available amenities. And yes, a short, steep, and popular trail leads to the bottom of Snoqualmie Falls for a close-up view. The lodge is located on WA 202 adjacent to the northern side of the falls. For more information, call (800) 272-5474 or visit **www.salishlodge.com**.

RATTLESNAKE LEDGE AND RATTLESNAKE MOUNTAIN

KEY AT-A-GLANCE INFORMATION

LENGTH: 4 miles (round-trip to the Ledge); 8.8 miles (round-trip to East Peak)

CONFIGURATION: Out-and-back

DIFFICULTY: Moderate to difficult

SCENERY: Forest, views

EXPOSURE: Mostly shaded

TRAFFIC: High on trail to ledge; trail beyond sees fewer hikers

TRAIL SURFACE: Dirt

HIKING TIME: 2–6 hours (depending on how far you travel from the trailhead)

ACCESS: Hikable year-round, though Rattlesnake Mountain may be snow-covered in winter; no fees

MAPS: USGS North Bend Quad

FACILITIES: Restrooms near the Rattlesnake Lake parking area

Rattlesnake Ledge and
Rattlesnake Mountain

Latitude: North 47d26.159m

Longitude: West 121d46.071m

IN BRIEF

Long a popular outing for its proximity to Seattle and commanding views of the Snoqualmie Valley, Rattlesnake Ledge is a well-known hiker's destination. Far less traveled, however, are the trails that continue past the ledge up on to Rattlesnake Mountain and stretch almost 10 miles along its broad summit ridge. For two excellent trip options, either climb to Rattlesnake Ledge if you have just a few hours or head to the solitude of the East Peak and return for a full day's hike.

DESCRIPTION

In 1911, Seattle closed off the Cedar River Watershed to protect the city's primary source of drinking water, established some 20 years earlier in 1889. For almost a century since, careful stewardship of the pristine waters and surrounding land has left the area largely undisturbed, leaving a semiwilderness right on the doorstep of the now-developed town of North Bend. The elk that occasionally wander through residents' yards are a testament to the still untamed nature of the protected region.

The trails on Rattlesnake Mountain skirt the edge of the Cedar River Watershed and allow the public to get as close to the area as possible without special access. An education center lies along the southern side of Rattlesnake Lake on Cedar

DIRECTIONS

From I-5 just south of downtown Seattle, go east on I-90. Take Exit 32, 436th Avenue SE, and turn right (south). The road becomes Cedar Falls Road and winds for more than 2.5 miles to a large sign for Rattlesnake Lake; turn right off Cedar Falls Road here. Immediately make another right into a parking lot signed for Rattlesnake Ledge Trail Parking. If this lot is full, there are many more spaces in the southern lot next to the lake.

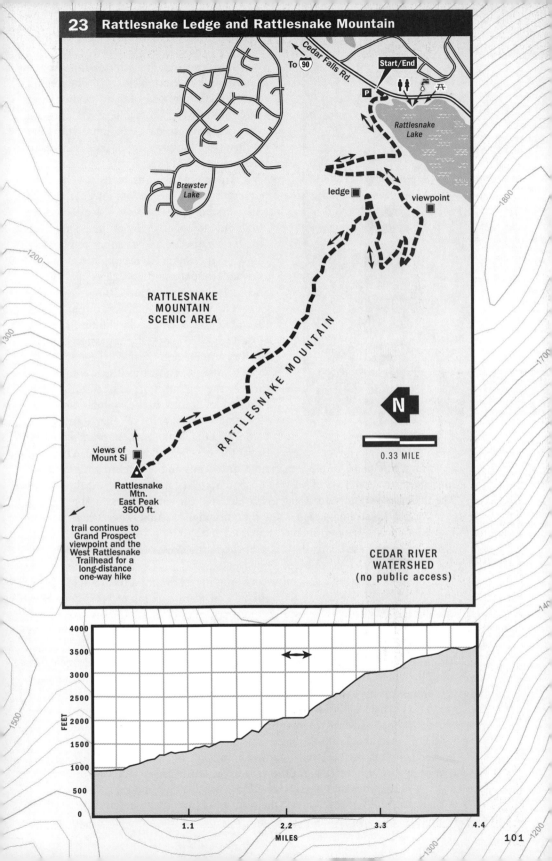

Cedar Falls Rd.

To 90

Start/End

P

Rattlesnake Lake

ledge

viewpoint

Brewster Lake

RATTLESNAKE MOUNTAIN SCENIC AREA

RATTLESNAKE MOUNTAIN

N

0.33 MILE

views of Mount Si

Rattlesnake Mtn. East Peak 3500 ft.

trail continues to Grand Prospect viewpoint and the West Rattlesnake Trailhead for a long-distance one-way hike

CEDAR RIVER WATERSHED (no public access)

FEET

4000
3500
3000
2500
2000
1500
1000
500
0

1.1   2.2   3.3   4.4

MILES

Rattlesnake Mountain from Rattlesnake Lake

Falls Road; it provides information on the natural and human history of the region along with an overview of many of the issues surrounding water storage and use and can easily be reached via a lakeshore trail that originates at the parking lot and is open to foot traffic and bicycles.

The ample parking area is well-developed and offers special lots for boat trailers and handicapped access. Many visitors come only to spend a day at the edge of the lake for a barbecue and swim, or to paddle a canoe on the water. No overnight camping is allowed, though, and the gates are closed and locked each night at 9:30.

The crowds of today are no anomaly; this area has seen regular human use for close to 10,000 years, starting when the first Native Americans arrived. Establishing routes around what was then a tall-grass prairie, they came from nearby settlements in search of berries, herbs, animals, and fish. Although the source of the Rattlesnake name remains unknown, it possibly dates back to these early inhabitants. The lake remains an important site for modern Native Americans and is stocked with rainbow trout for fisherman, under standard Washington State regulations.

The hikers-only trail starts as a gravel road from the southwest side of the parking lot; it's marked with a large sign. Note that although the trail is never hard to find or follow, the signage is often inconsistent and inaccurate. The information board and map by the lakeshore fail to show any of the Rattlesnake Mountain trails beyond the ledge, and distances tend to be underestimated.

Find the true trailhead a few minutes along the gravel road to the right. From this point, it is 2 miles one-way to Rattlesnake Ledge and a climb of 1,175 feet. Several signs here also give conflicting information, so look for the newest ones that show the correct distance. Similar signs along the way correctly mark each half mile to the ledge.

The trail starts on a gradual climb through a forest of moss-covered trees and ferns, with the occasional boulder or stump along the way. The Douglas firs are particularly impressive here, some reaching more than 100 feet tall with diameters of less than 4 feet. Their lack of low-level branches yields a pleasing display of strong vertical lines. The well-worn trail continues to gain altitude as it leads through a series of broad switchbacks up the slope.

Immediately before the 1-mile mark, a viewpoint opens out to the left, revealing views deep into the watershed protected area. Rattlesnake Lake and the education center appear to the southwest, with Mount Lindsay beyond.

A short downhill section follows, the only relief from the relentless climb which soon begins again. No Trespassing signs hang on some of the trees on the side of the trail to mark the watershed boundary. A few more long switchbacks lead to a junction that's signed and marked with a map.

The fork to the right leads to Rattlesnake Ledge, just a few steps away at an elevation of 2,080 feet. Even if you plan to head farther up the mountain, the ledge should not be missed. Considered the eastern terminus of the Issaquah Alps, the rocky ledge has a commanding view of almost 270 degrees, including the entire lower Snoqualmie Valley. Rattlesnake Lake and distant Chester Morse Lake sparkle below Cedar Butte and Mount Washington.

This is a great place to sun yourself on a rock and enjoy the view; arrive in the morning to take advantage of the southeastern-facing aspect. However, be careful of your footing, especially when hiking with children, as a deep chasm runs through the center of the ledge and cliffs drop off on all sides.

After visiting the ledge, return to the nearby junction. From here, you can descend the way you came or continue up the Rattlesnake Mountain summit ridge. The East Peak and Tower Viewpoint are another 2.4 miles distant and a climb of an additional 1,400 feet. For the truly fit or adventurous, the trail continues beyond the East Peak for another 2.7 miles to Grand Prospect Viewpoint and then goes 4.7 miles to the west Rattlesnake Mountain trailhead at the Old Snoqualmie Winery. With a shuttle, the entire ridge from the eastern trailhead at the lake to the western trailhead at the winery would make a fine long traverse of just less than 12 miles.

The climb up the ridge immediately becomes steeper, harder, and narrower; a true trail compared with the broad conduit from the lake. Underfoot, packed earth and mud give way to sections of exposed rocks and roots. Far fewer people venture this way, so with just a few steps you'll leave most of the crowd behind.

In less than a quarter mile, a spur leads to an obvious viewpoint to the right on a precipitous outcropping. The elevation here is close to 2,200 feet, providing a vantage downward to Rattlesnake Ledge just below.

Resume the uphill slog through a long tangle of salal. On a dewy morning, passage through this section can leave you soaked from the waist down, so be prepared for wetness. Persevere through the thick growth and enjoy the occasional view out to either side of the ridge. You will notice that the forest here is much less uniform than it is down below, with sudden changes in density and types of trees. Some areas are particularly damp and dark with thick decay underneath.

Ironically, although the upper section of Rattlesnake Mountain sees far fewer visitors than the area just above the lake, it nonetheless displays greater evidence of human activity. More than once you will encounter a network of dirt roads feeding some borrow pits (small, quarry-like excavations where material such as gravel is extracted for use as fill elsewhere) scattered along the ridge. However, the correct way is periodically marked with arrows, and a large wooden sign is at the most confusing intersection where you need to cross a road. Look for the trail to Snoqualmie Point, another name for the western trailhead, and enter a dark forest of short pines.

Almost immediately you will cross the road a second time and then emerge at the East Peak. A bench on the left below another trail sign (which understates the distance you have just traveled from the lake) marks the spot. Make a sharp turn to the right to reach two radio towers on the 3,500-foot summit. Unfortunately, tower access is prohibited, so you will have to enjoy the view from ground level only.

There is no single point here that provides an all-encompassing panorama, so explore the area to look through various gaps in the trees. An even larger tower facility can be seen to the northwest, marking Prospect Point farther along the ridge. A broad valley opens to the west and south, leading down to a corner of Puget Sound.

The best view, out to the north, is conveniently provided by a second wooden bench. The landmark Mount Si dominates the head of the valley, with some of the more-jagged Cascade Mountain peaks looming above the other end. In between, I-90 climbs toward Snoqualmie Pass. Traffic on the highway can be seen and heard, but it seems far away, some 2,700 feet below.

Enjoy the view from the bench, a great place for a snack and a drink of water. Relax here for a while before heading back down.

MOUNT SI TRAIL

▶ IN BRIEF

Just as no tourist can claim to have seen downtown Seattle without a visit to Pike Place Market, there is no such thing as a Seattle hiker who hasn't been to the top of Mount Si. Easy to reach, physically challenging, and capped by a commanding view, the mountain known simply as Si is like a city park crossed with a serious Cascade Mountain peak.

▶ DESCRIPTION

Mount Si is crowned by the Haystack, a rock outcropping boosting the summit elevation by about 200 feet and providing a significant visual landmark for much of the Puget Sound region. This landmark apparently works as a beacon, summoning people from all over western Washington on weekends year-round. No matter what season they come, the hikers who are drawn here keep the giant parking lot busy for most of the day, no easy feat given that Mount Si has room for at least 150 vehicles.

It's a safe bet that hikers do not come to Si to find solitude in the outdoors. Yet what they do find is a great hike, enjoyed by everyone from extended families with young children to mountaineers in training and hard-core trail runners chasing serious vertical gain.

The trailhead can be found past the last row of cars in the northeast corner of the parking lot,

❶ KEY AT-A-GLANCE INFORMATION

LENGTH: 8 miles (round-trip)

CONFIGURATION: Out-and-back

DIFFICULTY: Difficult hike, optional exposed-rock scramble

SCENERY: One of the best western views from the Cascade foothills to the Puget Sound lowlands, great rock scramble to summit of the Haystack

EXPOSURE: Mostly shaded; exposed in Haystack Basin and on the Haystack

TRAFFIC: Get an early start, or hike midweek for a less crowded trail and parking lot.

TRAIL SURFACE: Mostly dirt, boardwalk (at Snag Flat), gravel (near trailhead)

HIKING TIME: 4–7 hours

ACCESS: Hikable year-round (may be snowy or icy in winter); no fees for parking or park access

MAPS: Green Trails—Mount Si 206S; USGS Mount Si and Chester Morse Lake

FACILITIES: Restroom and water at trailhead

▶ DIRECTIONS

From I-5 south of downtown Seattle, go east on I-90. Take Exit 31, North Bend, and turn left (north) on Bendigo Boulevard S. In less than 1 mile turn right on E North Bend Way, then proceed a little more than 1 mile to Mount Si Road and turn left. Continue approximately 2.5 miles on this road to a well-signed parking lot on the left for the Mount Si trailhead.

Mount Si Trail

Latitude: North 47d29.228m

Longitude: West 121d43.383m

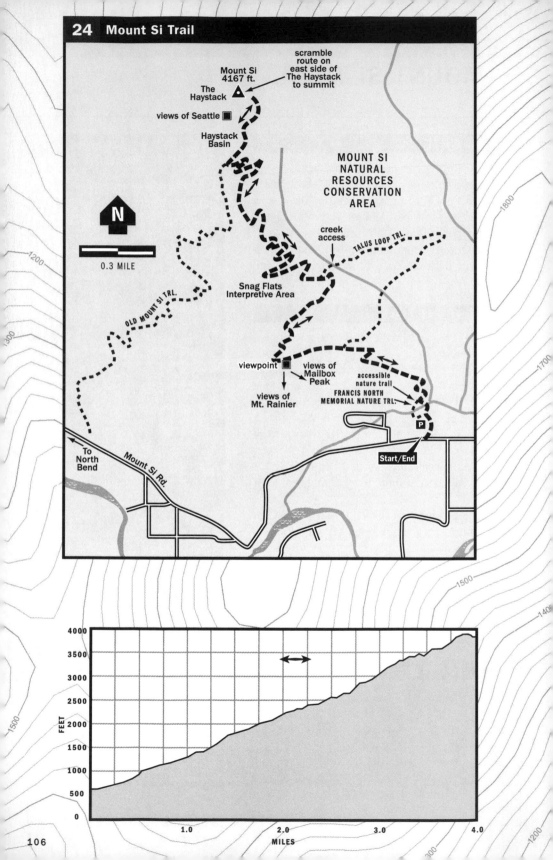

scramble route on east side of The Haystack to summit

Mount Si 4167 ft.

The Haystack

views of Seattle

Haystack Basin

MOUNT SI NATURAL RESOURCES CONSERVATION AREA

N

0.3 MILE

creek access

TALUS LOOP TRL.

OLD MOUNT SI TRL.

Snag Flats Interpretive Area

viewpoint

views of Mailbox Peak

accessible nature trail

FRANCIS NORTH MEMORIAL NATURE TRL.

views of Mt. Rainier

P

Start/End

To North Bend

Mount Si Rd.

FEET

4000
3500
3000
2500
2000
1500
1000
500
0

1.0   2.0   3.0   4.0

MILES

The western face of Mount Si

at an elevation of 500 feet. It is worth filling up with water from the public tap because there is no treated water available anywhere else along the way and the top is 4 miles up the trail—with a 3,500-foot climb.

Before the hike even starts, a wheelchair-accessible loop trail runs for a short 0.2 miles off the main trail, a memorial to Frances North. Look for a plaque detailing North's committed efforts toward the protection of Mount Si in the Washington State Legislature in the late 1970s. Thanks to her leadership, the region was declared a Natural Resources Conservation Area in 1987 and now includes almost 9,000 acres of land.

A bench at the end of the side loop provides a last chance for rest before the climb begins. Thanks to its popularity and continual labor from volunteers and maintenance crews, the trail is well-worn and well-maintained, with graded stairs and waterbars as it ascends through the woods. The uphill grade is steady and constant with long switchbacks, but never too steep.

The low-elevation forest is characterized by tall second-growth Douglas firs with high canopies, giving the understory an open, airy feeling. Watch for a small wooden sign marking the first half mile, elevation 1,120 feet. These signs are posted every half mile, although they can be hard to spot and do not always show the elevation.

Short of the 1-mile mark, the Talus Loop Trail branches to the right, heading uphill. The Talus Loop traverses several small creek valleys draining the southern side of the mountain and can provide an alternate route over the next mile, although adding slightly to the total distance. Along the main trail, look for a viewpoint over a cliff at a great resting spot after a long traverse to the west.

The Talus Loop Trail returns to the main Mount Si Trail at a signed junction just short of Snag Flats. Appropriately named, the flats is the only significant level section of the hike, making it a good spot for a rest. A short interpretive trail explores the area's namesake snags, describing the forest and its wildlife, on a boardwalk that keeps hikers above the frequently muddy ground. Pileated woodpeckers are common here; they hammer the decaying trees in search of insects.

The climb begins again in earnest on the far side of Snag Flats, rising through a series of switchbacks over the next 1.5 miles and gradually becoming rockier near the end. By the time the 3-mile mark is reached, the trees have become noticeably thinner and shorter, stunted by the harsher climate at the higher elevation.

A viewpoint finally opens out to the right after another half mile, revealing Mailbox Peak, the Snoqualmie River Valley, and Mount Rainier to the south. The trail then climbs through rocks and salal in its steepest section before emerging from the trees into a jumble of boulders.

It is not unusual to find scores of hikers relaxing here, enjoying the southern view and exposure to the sun that comes with it. The trail continues upward through the rocks, requiring an occasional moment of route-finding or scrambling. Concrete added in a few spots to create stairs and boot-polished stone to show the way make the going easy enough for everyone.

The trail branches at a sign, showing Snoqualmie Valley Viewpoint to the left and the Haystack Scramble to the right. For most Mount Si hikers, the effective summit is the wide bowl known as Haystack Basin to the left, whose views to the west and south are nothing short of spectacular. The name Snoqualmie Valley Viewpoint does not even begin to describe the view, which stretches far beyond the Snoqualmie River Valley to include downtown Seattle, Puget Sound, the Olympic Peninsula, and much of the southern Cascades, including Mount Rainier. It is worth poking around in the rocks to find an ideal spot to relax, as there is plenty of space to accommodate everyone.

The Haystack towers above the northern end of the basin, seemingly out of reach thanks to its sheer, daunting cliffs. However, experienced scramblers can reach the top via an easy Class 3 route on the rock's eastern face, starting from the end of the hiking trail. The ascent is not for beginners or children, but it has plenty of good, obvious holds, so qualified climbers should have no difficulty reaching the top. The view from Mount Si's true summit at 4,167 feet adds a northern aspect to what can be seen from the basin, including the high summits of Mount Baker and Glacier Peak. But adjacent Mount Teneriffe at 4,788 feet blocks sight lines to the northeast and keeps the view from being truly panoramic.

▶ NEARBY ACTIVITIES

Twedes Cafe, immortalized in David Lynch's television show *Twin Peaks* as the T-Mar Cafe where FBI Special Agent Dale Cooper came to get his cherry pie, lies on the southeast corner of the Bendigo Boulevard (WA 202) and North Bend Way intersection in the town of North Bend. The retro-1950's diner features 40 different burgers—and that's just for starters.

LITTLE SI TRAIL

▶ IN BRIEF

Long overshadowed both literally and figuratively by its big brother next door, Little Si is finally getting the attention it deserves. Although the peak was never unknown, the awkward parking and access kept it from true widespread popularity. Now that a new trailhead has finally been developed, Little Si is a worthwhile destination on its own and makes a great alternate when its hulking neighbor is too busy, too socked in, or too demanding.

❙ DESCRIPTION

From a distance, it can be hard to even identify Little Si as a separate peak from Mount Si proper. So complete is Mount Si's dominance over the area that the insignificant-seeming bump in front seems hardly worth noticing.

A closer view reveals that this is all a trick of perspective. The minor notch that separates the peaks is actually a deep cleft, and the tree-clad summit ridge of Little Si actually hides impressive cliff faces far more sought by climbers than any on the exposed rock of the bigger peak next-door. For hikers, the manageable distance married with a moderate elevation gain presents a solid challenge, although well short of extreme.

Little Si's attractiveness for rock climbers plays a big role in the tight trailhead parking, especially when the rock is dry. The good news is

❙ DIRECTIONS

From I-5 south of downtown, Seattle go east on I-90. Take Exit 31, North Bend, and proceed north on Bendigo Boulevard S. In less than 1 mile, turn right on E North Bend Way and proceed a little more than 1 mile to Mount Si Road and turn left. Just after crossing the river and rounding a bend to the right, look for the new trailhead parking area on the left signed for Little Si.

ⓘ KEY AT-A-GLANCE INFORMATION

LENGTH: 3.5 miles

CONFIGURATION: Out-and-back

DIFFICULTY: Moderate

SCENERY: An easier alternative to Mount Si with similar views of North Bend and the Snoqualmie River Valley

EXPOSURE: Mostly shaded

TRAFFIC: High on weekends

TRAIL SURFACE: Dirt with rocks and roots

HIKING TIME: 2–3 hours

ACCESS: Hikable year-round; no parking fees

MAPS: North Bend USGS Quad

FACILITIES: Restrooms at the trailhead

Little Si Trail

Latitude: North 47d29.193m

Longitude: West 121d45.186m

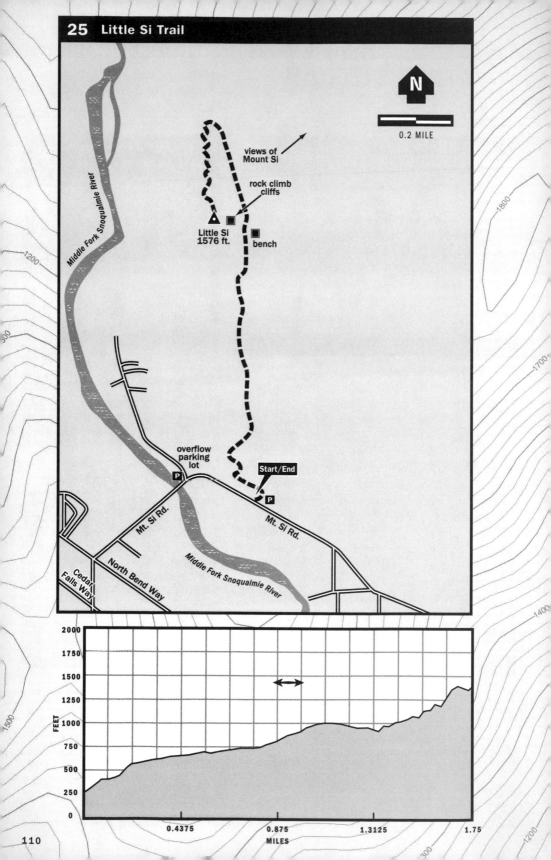

N

0.2 MILE

views of
Mount Si

rock climb
cliffs

Little Si
1576 ft.

bench

Middle Fork Snoqualmie River

overflow
parking
lot

P

Start/End

P

Mt. Si Rd.

Mt. Si Rd.

North Bend Way

Cedar Falls Way

Middle Fork Snoqualmie River

that this means even when the lot is full the trail itself will probably be less crowded than you might think. The bad news is that more often than not there will be a considerable volume of cars to contend with.

The new trailhead has space for more than 40 vehicles, but on some days you may need to head for the overflow parking in a gravel lot next to the bridge over the middle fork of the Snoqualmie River. Ironically, this lot served as the only parking for the old trailhead, which is now closed.

To reach the old trailhead, hikers were required to walk down a residential street, creating friction between hikers and residents and undoubtedly leading to the opening of the new trailhead. There are several upscale houses across the street from the new trailhead as well, but a set of gates will likely keep hikers and homeowners apart.

Start up the trail from the southeast corner of the parking lot, behind the toilets. Right away you face a tough incline on rocks and dirt. A glance back over your shoulder across the broad Snoqualmie River Valley reveals the long ridge of Rattlesnake Mountain, with pockets of radio towers marking its many peaks. The sun here can be brutal, thanks to thin growth and a south-facing slope. Luckily, a series of switchbacks soon lead into some shady trees and ferns where the trail levels out. The forest here is typical of the western Cascade foothills, with a primary mix of Douglas firs, alders, and maples.

The new trail is far better marked than the old one ever was, and already looks as worn. The two trails merge about a half mile from the start, although the old trail has been obscured and blocked off so well that it is easy to pass by without ever noticing it. A sign keeps you clearly on the right path, descending to a creek crossing just past the junction.

Views start to open through the trees onto the southwest face of Mount Si, with the summit of Little Si now to the left as the trail enters the gap between the peaks. An information board marks the first of many access points for rock climbers into the Mount Si Natural Resource Conservation Area, available for day-use only.

The canyon between the two Si's is defined on its western side by a long wall of rock below the Little Si summit ridge. It is this wall that attracts climbers who want to test their skills. Several vantage points offer the opportunity to stop and watch the climbers tackle the challenging routes and listen to their voices carry through the trees.

A memorial bench dedicated to Doug Hansen provides a place to sit along the way. Hansen was a popular Seattle-area mountaineer who honed his skills in the high Cascades and ended up being killed along with 11 others on Mount Everest in May 1996. Under the guidance of New Zealand guide Rob Hall, Hansen successfully reached the summit, but then died in a storm on the descent, events tragically immortalized in Jon Krakauer's *Into Thin Air*.

Past the bench the trail starts to climb again, now heavily shaded below the rock wall. Even on a hot summer day the temperatures are surprisingly cool here, where the sun never really penetrates. After reaching an old rockslide on the left, the trail enters a beautiful fern valley, a mix of dappled greens, sunlight, and shadow. Look for some of the ferns hanging off boulders along the wall and spreading like a carpet over the forest floor.

At the northern end of the valley, the path swings hard to the left and steeply uphill. Unfortunately, the bulk of the climbing on this trail occurs in the last third of its distance as the route exits the valley and mounts the summit ridge, doubling back in the direction you've already come. Prepare for a near-scramble through a few short sections.

When you finally reach the summit, you will feel like you have come a lot further than the stated 2.5 miles. Various ledges surround the high point; poke around for a while to find the one that suits you best. Don't miss the rocks slightly down the far side, which have some of the best views over North Bend and where mountain goats can occasionally be spotted. There are also several viewpoints just before the top looking over at Mount Si, clearly showing its much larger size. Stay back from the edge, and be careful not to knock anything off that could hit the rock climbers directly below. The return route is the way you came in.

▶ NEARBY ACTIVITIES

A factory-outlet mall in North Bend has a wide range of stores, including several that carry outdoor-related clothing and gear. This is a great place to find some bargains that just might make your next outdoor trip a little better. To find the outlet center, take Exit 31 from I-90 and head north for a quarter mile; the entrance is impossible to miss on the left. Call (425) 888-4505 for more information.

BARE MOUNTAIN

▶ IN BRIEF

Covering almost 400,000 acres between Snoqualmie Pass and Stevens Pass, the Alpine Lakes Wilderness attracts some 150,000 visitors each year. On a typical summer weekend when the hordes are camped at the Enchantment Lakes, Bare Mountain presents a great alternate escape. Tucked into a little-used corner of the wilderness area, this former fire-lookout site provides great high Cascade views, including three glaciated volcanoes.

▶ DESCRIPTION

According to the National Forest Service, more than half the population of Washington State lives within an hour's drive of the Alpine Lakes Wilderness. With its proximity to several urban centers and the undeniable attraction of its magnificent high-country, many of the most-popular sections of the wilderness can unfortunately no longer provide much isolation.

Bare Mountain, on the other hand, lies at the extreme western edge of the Alpine Lakes and

▶ DIRECTIONS

From I-5 south of downtown Seattle, go east on I-90. Take Exit 31, North Bend, and proceed north on Bendigo Boulevard S. In less than 1 mile, turn right on E North Bend Way and proceed just two blocks to Ballarat Avenue N and turn left. Stay on this winding road for about 4 miles to where the unsigned North Fork County Road branches off to the left going uphill. This road begins paved, then soon turns to gravel and winds past many gated spur roads along the North Fork Snoqualmie River Valley. At just less than 20 miles there is an intersection where the left branch quickly crosses Lennox Creek. Make this left then another quick right onto Lennox Creek Road (Forest Road 57). Proceed just more than 3 miles to the well-signed Bare Mountain trailhead.

ⓘ KEY AT-A-GLANCE INFORMATION

LENGTH: 7 miles (round-trip)

CONFIGURATION: Out-and-back

DIFFICULTY: Difficult (3,250-foot elevation gain)

SCENERY: Forested trails, old-growth forest, creek cascades, swimming hole, historic mines, views from summit

EXPOSURE: Last two-thirds is exposed

TRAFFIC: Low

TRAIL SURFACE: Dirt; watch for deep holes hidden by vegetation

HIKING TIME: 5–6 hours

ACCESS: Hikable late spring–early fall; no pass required for parking (self-issued wilderness permits at trailhead)

MAPS: Green Trails—Mount Si 174 and Skykomish 175; USGS—Mount Phelps and Grotto

FACILITIES: None

Bare Mountain Trail

Latitude: North 47d38.378m

Longitude: West 121d31.71m

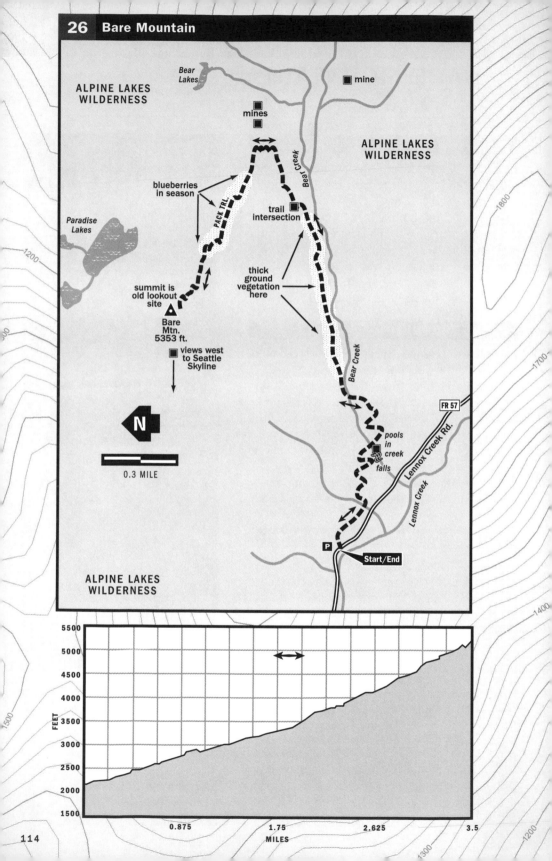

Bear Lakes

ALPINE LAKES WILDERNESS

mine

mines

ALPINE LAKES WILDERNESS

Bear Creek

blueberries in season

PACK TRL.

trail intersection

Paradise Lakes

thick ground vegetation here

summit is old lookout site

Bare Mtn. 5353 ft.

Bear Creek

views west to Seattle Skyline

N

0.3 MILE

FR 57

Lennox Creek Rd.

pools in creek

falls

Lennox Creek

ALPINE LAKES WILDERNESS

P

Start/End

is protected by a long gravel road through the north fork of the Snoqualmie River Valley. Although the drive is accessible to any vehicle during good weather, the time-consuming approach deters many potential visitors from making the trip. Take advantage of their reluctance and see what this challenging and rewarding hike has to offer, including solitude, wild huckleberries, and top-of-the world views.

Because Bare Mountain occupies a federally recognized wilderness, a permit is required between May 15 and October 31. Additional regulations also apply; for further information, call the North Bend Ranger District of the Mount Baker-Snoqualmie National Forest at (425) 888-1421. However, permits are free and can be self-issued at the trailhead, and the vast majority of users will not be affected by any of the other rules, so the process is simple and easy.

A board on the northern side of the road marks the beginning of the hike, signed Bare Mountain Trail 1037. Look for a host of relevant information posted here, including an area map, wilderness regulations, and notes from the rangers on local conditions.

The trail departs from behind the information board and immediately comes to the first of several creek crossings. These creeks drain the southern side of Prospectors Ridge and may run dry in the summer. Underfoot, the surface is lined with smooth, round rocks, more typical of a desert wash from the Southwest's Canyon Country than a trail in the western Cascades.

The path follows an old mining road, built to service several claims farther up the Bear Creek Valley. Owing to its original purpose, the trail is wide with a moderate grade, easing the long uphill grind. The steady climb is a constant reminder of the daily hardships faced by the region's early settlers and the lure of riches that brought them here.

After around 0.75 miles Bear Creek appears, flowing steeply down on the right. Note the different spellings of the creek and the mountain, which may be a testament to the illiteracy of the miners but is more likely the result of two separate derivations. Unlike many of the hikes along the I-90 corridor, there is no traffic noise here, only the sound of the rushing water.

The trail crosses the creek below a long slab waterfall, reminiscent of the exposed granite faces of Kings Canyon or Yosemite. Various bolted and decaying timbers are all that remain of a ruined bridge that once spanned the water here as part of the miner's road. Pick your way across the creek on a series of stepping stones and logs. A crystal-clear pool among the rocks allows for an icy dip on a hot day, probably best saved for the descent.

Near the 1-mile mark, the route crosses the creek again over a more recent and permanent bridge and then passes the official Alpine Lakes Wilderness boundary. On the far side, the trail surface changes to packed dirt and may be periodically muddy in areas even during the driest parts of the year due to the shade of several giant old-growth trees.

The ancient trees provide the last significant cover from the sun along the way, so appreciate it while it lasts. As the trail continues to climb eastward along Bear Creek, the path emerges into a vast field of bracken ferns crowding in from either side. Much of the thick growth reaches to chest or shoulder height, and the limited foot traffic on this hike does little to regularly beat it back.

Be careful through this section, as the ferns often hide the ground and the tread is highly uneven. Rocks, holes, and even streams can be hazardous and difficult to see. If the plants are wet, your legs soon will be, so hiking sticks, gaiters, and zip-off pants legs are recommended to ease you through. Keep your eyes peeled for hummingbirds that can occasionally be spotted flitting through the bushes here, although identifying a particular species is very difficult due to the birds' size and speed.

Near the head of the valley, the main trail makes a hairpin turn to the left and a spur continues through even thicker growth to the right. This side path dead-ends after another half mile at one of the old mines below the cliffs on the opposite side of Bear Creek, although the entrance can be difficult to find. Do not enter the dangerous shaft if you decide to explore among the rocks.

The junction with the side trail is beyond the halfway point of the 4.3-mile horizontal distance but only 1,300 vertical feet above the trailhead, with another 1,900 remaining to the summit. Needless to say, the bulk of the climbing occurs in the next part of the hike.

Start the long haul up a series of more than 50 switchbacks that leads to the top. For comparison, consider that the 14,494-foot summit of Mount Whitney in California can be reached via its famous 100 switchbacks. The trail ascends the southern side of Bare Mountain through limited cover, so the sun can be brutal during high summer when the path is dusty and dry. Look for wild huckleberry bushes as you near the crest of the ridge; the tart berries can provide refreshment from late July through mid-September. A few small streams flow down the slope and could prove useful water sources if properly treated.

Persevere through several false summits and finally scramble up the last few switchbacks to the rocky peak at 5,353 feet. It's easy to see why a fire lookout stood here until it was torn down in 1973—the view stretches far and wide to all points on the compass. The only evidence remaining of the lookout is a few twisted pieces of wood and metal, but the view is as good as ever.

On a clear day the high-rises of Seattle are just visible out to the west, dwarfed by the Olympic Mountains on the far side of Puget Sound. The familiar profiles of both the Brothers and Mount Constance are easily recognizable, some 80 miles away. Mount Baker and Glacier Peak poke above the northern Cascades, and Mount Rainier and the high crags of Summit Chief Mountain and Chimney Rock dominate the skyline to the south.

When you have had your fill of the commanding view, head back down the way you came. Use care on the descent, as the first few steps are slightly exposed and it may appear that a slip could plunge you into one of the Paradise Lakes that sparkle 1,300 feet below the northern side of the ridge. The section through the ferns is also trickier downhill, as your greater speed will make the hidden rocks and holes that much more treacherous.

TWIN FALLS NATURAL AREA AND OLALLIE STATE PARK

▶ IN BRIEF

Located well below 2,000 feet and just off I-90, Twin Falls makes a great year-round destination, especially when winter snows close many of the hikes farther up toward Snoqualmie Pass. This hike follows the rocky south fork of the Snoqualmie River and climbs to two significant waterfalls before connecting to a larger network of trails exploring Olallie State Park.

▶ DESCRIPTION

Mention Seattle and the first thing people think of is rain. The city is almost universally identified as one of the wettest places anywhere in the United States, despite the persistent efforts of the Washington State Tourism Department to dispel this image; travelers are invited to the Emerald City with the lure of only 36 inches of annual rainfall, less than such so-called dry places as New York (47 inches) or Atlanta (48 inches). And don't tell the sunbathers and scantily clad club-hoppers at famous South Beach, but the joke is on them: Miami receives 59 inches a year, some 50 percent more than Seattle.

The difference is that, where other cities receive most of their rain in concentrated downpours, Seattle usually sees mist and drizzle that lasts for days but doesn't add up to much, leaving endlessly cloudy skies for nine months out of the year—almost 300 days, on average—but limited total rainfall accumulations. Just 30 miles east, however, the region lives up to its reputation.

▶ KEY AT-A-GLANCE INFORMATION

LENGTH: 2.5 miles (round-trip) or longer

CONFIGURATION: Out-and-back

DIFFICULTY: Moderate

SCENERY: Waterfalls, old-growth trees, river viewpoints, riverside access

EXPOSURE: Shaded

TRAFFIC: Moderate to heavy; go midweek for less traffic

TRAIL SURFACE: Dirt (gravel on Iron Horse Trail)

HIKING TIME: 2–3 hours

ACCESS: Hikable year-round; Washington State Park Pass required for parking, daily passes available at trailhead

MAPS: Green Trails–Bandera 206; USGS Chester Morse Lake

FACILITIES: Restroom at trailhead

▶ DIRECTIONS

From I-5 south of downtown Seattle, go east on I-90. Take Exit 34, 468th Avenue SE, and turn right (south) onto 468th Avenue SE. In a short distance, turn left onto SE 159th Street. The parking lot for Twin Falls Natural Area and Olallie State Park is at the end of this road.

Twin Falls Natural Area and Olallie State Park

Latitude: North 47d27.157m

Longitude: West 121d42.316m

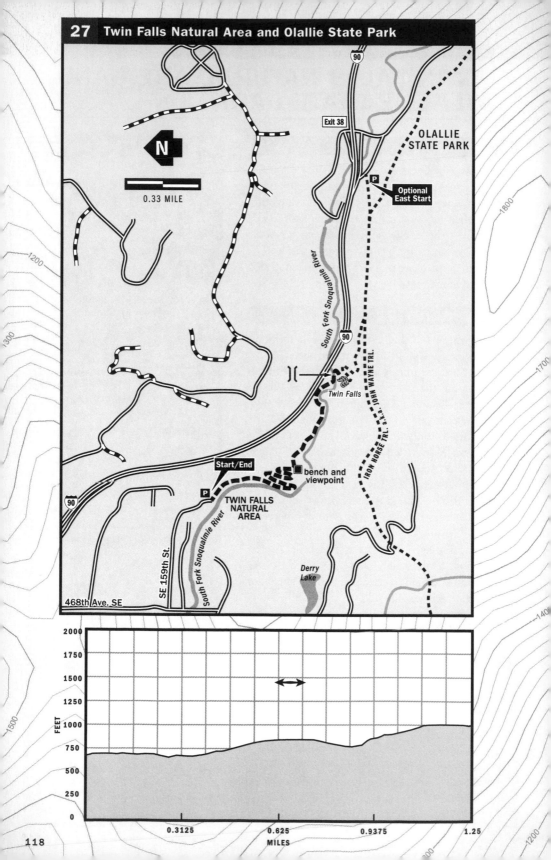

N

0.33 MILE

90

Exit 38

OLALLIE
STATE PARK

P

Optional
East Start

South Fork Snoqualmie River

90

Twin Falls

IRON HORSE TRL. a.k.a. JOHN WAYNE TRL.

Start/End

P

bench and
viewpoint

TWIN FALLS
NATURAL
AREA

South Fork Snoqualmie River

Derry
Lake

468th Ave. SE

SE 159th St.

2000
1750
1500
1250
1000
750
500
250
0

FEET

0.3125   0.625   0.9375   1.25
MILES

The lower western slope of the Cascades is probably the second wettest place in the state, trailing only the western side of the Olympic Peninsula. Although no match for the Hoh Rain Forest at 140 inches per year, the Twin Falls region gets more than 90 inches, 2.5 times as much as downtown Seattle. The heavy clouds from the Gulf of Alaska that sweep over the city, keeping it gray but relatively dry, get trapped by the mountains and dump their precipitation here.

However, the rain is not evenly distributed throughout the year, falling primarily in the winter and going through wide seasonal variations. In turn, the south fork of the Snoqualmie River rises and wanes as well, showing a remarkable range between the flow at low and high water.

According to the U.S. Geologic Survey gauge at Edgewick, the river in this area reached an all-time record-low flow on September 28, 2001—172 gallons of water per second. The record high occurred on November 24, 1990, at 80,790 gallons per second, a volume almost 470 times greater. Although this is a comparison between extreme values, yearly fluctuations also show amazing disparities. The flow on January 31, 2003, reached 44,359 gallons per second, 141 times the 314 gallons per second recorded on September 6 later that year. Even day-to-day readings can wildly oscillate; November 18, 2002 saw 1,571 gallons per second, a number that jumped to 14,288 the next day, and then fell back over the next week to less than 1,500. All of this occurs in a small drainage area of less than 65 square miles.

The character of Twin Falls is naturally dependent on the flow of the river. At high-water periods, typically in late winter and spring, expect to see a single thundering torrent. The low water of late summer and fall presents a much more peaceful display, as the falls split into several separate braids. This hike may well warrant several trips at different times of the year to appreciate the full range of experiences available.

The trail starts out winding along the bank of the river. When the flow is suitable, watch for whitewater kayakers who come here to hone their skills by "playboating" sometimes only a stone's throw from the parking lot. About a quarter mile along, some big boulders shelter several potential swimming holes. And another big boulder on the left side of the trail bears a remarkable resemblance to a man's face in profile.

Licorice and sword ferns testify to the volume of rain that falls here But the thick canopy created by the tall Douglas firs can keep the worst of it from reaching the ground, making this a better option than it would seem for hiking during the frequently questionable weather.

Climb through a few long switchbacks to arrive at a high point with a handrail and a bench. The bench faces out toward the lower falls, offering a view that's best in winter when the leaves have fallen from the nearby trees to provide a clear line of sight. Continue down the far side of the ridge and stay left at a junction to reach a giant old-growth fir that dwarfs the other trees around it. This is the first of several such trees, true forest outliers in terms of their monumental size, scattered along the trail.

Another short climb brings you to a set of wooden steps on the right, leading down to an overlook. A fenced platform provides a great straight-on view of the lower falls, where the river is channeled through a narrow gap in the basalt and then spills out over a rocky face, tumbling into a pool below.

Continue for another few hundred yards up the main trail to reach a boardwalk and bridge over the river. This bridge crosses just above the lower falls and provides a good view of the multiple stages of the upper falls, a series of plunge pools drop-ping through a narrow chasm. A curtain of mist billowing around the corner hints at the top level of the falls, which unfortunately are very difficult to observe from any-where on the trail.

The bridge makes a good end point, for a total of 2.5 miles round-trip when you reach the parking lot. For a longer hike, continue on the far side of the river for about a half mile to reach a junction with the gravel Iron Horse Trail. Although this section of the trail is pleasant and well-maintained, it rises far enough above the river gorge to be exposed to the sound of the traffic on I-90. It's so close, in fact, that occa-sional glimpses of asphalt and cars appear through the trees.

Adventurous hikers can continue eastward along the Iron Horse for several miles into the heart of Olallie State Park. This extended hike would make an excellent one-way journey with a shuttle; the eastern trailhead is at Exit 38, to the right off I-90.

MAILBOX PEAK

▶ IN BRIEF

Once reserved for the elite club of people who knew about it, the climb up Mailbox Peak is now open to anyone willing to pay the price in sweat and muscle to reach the top. In return for their efforts, hikers will be rewarded with a sea of wildflowers in season, 360-degree views of the western Cascades and Mount Rainier, and a great thigh-burning workout.

▶ DESCRIPTION

Mailbox Peak was unknown to the general public for a long time, as the trail and the mountain were traditionally unmarked on most maps. With a top elevation less than 5,000 feet, the summit was easily overlooked by most hikers, who instead headed to several more-famous destinations along the Snoqualmie River Valley.

Locals shared the peak with friends and family, eventually beating a trail up the mountain's western ridge. Mostly devoid of the smooth surface, measured grading, and other niceties typical of a well-maintained path, the steep ascent climbs more than 4,000 feet in about 3 miles. On

▶ DIRECTIONS

From I-5 south of downtown Seattle, go east on I-90. Take Exit 34, 486th Avenue SE, and turn left, (north) proceeding through the Edgewick "Truck Town" area. In less than 1 mile turn right on SE Middle Fork Road. Soon there is a Y in the road where the Middle Fork Road and Lake Dorothy Road meet. You can take either road since they meet up again in about a mile. After the two roads come back together, continue 0.3 mile on the Middle Fork Road to a parking area on the left and a side road turnout on the right with additional parking spots. Park wherever there is room off the sometimes-busy Middle Fork Road.

ⓘ KEY AT-A-GLANCE INFORMATION

LENGTH: 6 miles (round-trip)

CONFIGURATION: Out-and-back

DIFFICULTY: Difficult (more than a 4,000-foot elevation gain)

SCENERY: Forested trails, wildflowers along the summit ridge, views from the summit

EXPOSURE: Mostly shaded; final ridge walk and summit are exposed

TRAFFIC: High (get an early start to beat the heat and the crowds)

TRAIL SURFACE: Dirt; very steep in places

HIKING TIME: 5–8 hours

ACCESS: Hikable summer–fall; no passes or fees required

MAPS: Green Trails–Bandera 206; USGS–Chester Morse Lake

FACILITIES: None

Mailbox Peak

Latitude: North 47d28.058m

Longitude: West 121d40.494m

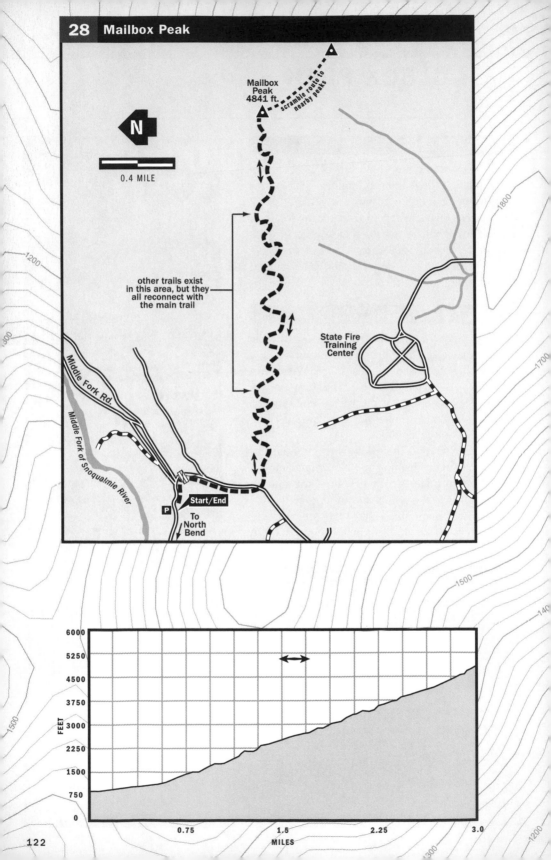

Mailbox
Peak
4841 ft.

scramble route to
nearby peaks

N

0.4 MILE

other trails exist
in this area, but they
all reconnect with
the main trail

State Fire
Training
Center

Middle Fork Rd.

Middle Fork of Snoqualmie River

Start/End

P

To
North
Bend

6000

5250

4500

3750

3000

2250

FEET

1500

750

0

0.75   1.5   2.25   3.0

MILES

Mount Rainier and beargrass from Mailbox Peak

this kind of incline, the horizontal distances are difficult to gauge and are largely irrelevant; only the vertical distance really counts.

The peak's name is derived from an actual mailbox that appeared on the summit in years past. Since then, the original has been replaced with a more-permanent structure, along with a box for *The Olympian* newspaper. A wide assortment of other interesting items have also come and gone over time, including a fire hydrant and an aluminum stepladder, but the Mailbox name has stuck.

Most of the summit's artifacts were likely hauled up and down by mountaineers in training, who use the brutal climb as off-season preparation for high volcano ascents. Although the twin challenges of high altitude and glacier travel can't easily be re-created here, a little extra weight (like a fire hydrant) carried in a backpack can help make up the difference. For the fit day-hiker, Mailbox offers the chance to experience a piece of the mountaineering spirit without the hassle and load of a 50-pound pack of gear.

However, nobody gets off completely scot-free. For this hike, everyone should still carry adequate supplies, including clothing, food, and water. The trail is particularly dry, with only one flowing stream available right at the beginning, so even with a filter or iodine you will be out of luck if you do not carry enough water to begin with. Regardless of the outside temperature you are guaranteed to sweat, so hydration is vitally important.

To begin the hike, cross the main road from the trailhead parking area and walk 40 yards up an unmarked gravel road. There is more parking available here, if needed, in front of a pair of heavy metal gates.

Skirt the gates and follow the old road up the hill to the right. Already the trail starts climbing, but this is nothing compared with what is to come. Pass a wide spur on the uphill side, now heavily overgrown as nature begins to reclaim it, and advance through scrub brush heading south.

After about a quarter mile, the gravel road enters a darker forest canopy after an apparent clear-cut. Look for the true trail on the left; if you reach the point where a creek crosses below the road you have gone too far. Much like the paraphernalia that periodically gathers on the summit, a toothbrush occasionally can be found on the ground here pointing out the trail at the junction, but it may or may not be present when you arrive.

The well-worn trail runs along the southern edge of the clear-cut slope, with some massive stumps left behind as evidence of the forest that stood before. Be careful of giant, thorny devil's club (*Oplopanax horridum*) along the way among some equally giant ferns. Devil's club has a long history as a useful medicinal plant, but because its spines can be very painful and difficult to extract from the skin, it is best avoided.

Soon you will be following the northern side of the creek that runs down to the road. Be aware that this is the last natural water available anywhere along the way, and it must be treated if you plan to drink it. However, this is a great place to stop for a rest and quick wash on the dusty descent.

Right after the creek, the real climb begins as the trail forgoes most of the usual switchbacks to mount straight up the demanding ridge. Thankfully, even on a hot summer day the forest of firs and maples offers a lot of shade, especially if you arrive in the morning when the sun is still hidden away on the eastern side of the mountain. Watch for banana slugs beneath your feet, no doubt also enjoying the cool cover of the forest.

With its history of informal maintenance and its route through a mix of Department of Natural Resources and Mount Baker-Snoqualmie National Forest lands, the main trail is plagued by ever-changing groups of social trails that lead off to one side or the other. In most cases, the trails rejoin the main way after a short diversion and pretty much every route here leads the same way: uphill to the summit.

Again and again the track tests the limits of how steep a trail can actually be built in the Cascades, given the erosion from the rain and from regular foot traffic. Regular sections of exposed roots climb like stairs, and you may find yourself grabbing trees to pull yourself up. Patches of worn bark at hand level along the way show that you are not the first to employ this strategy.

Eventually the forest transitions to thinner undergrowth, with a lot of dead wood lining the floor. The decaying trees make for a soft and spongy surface that's easy on the feet and joints. Although you may feel you have come a long way, at 2,800 feet you are just about the halfway point in terms of the total elevation gain, which makes this a good place for a rest before continuing the second half of the uphill assault. There is no formal place to sit, so your best bet is to improvise and turn a fallen log into a bench.

At about 3,600 feet, the forest opens up and the trail slightly relents; it is still uphill the rest of the way, but the grade is not quite as extreme—a welcome relief. The first views begin to appear to either side as the trees give way to boulders and brush growth, including wild blackberries, ferns, and bear grass. Kinnikinnick covers the ground with stunted evergreens and Indian paintbrush poking through.

After another 700-foot gain, the trail reaches an alpine meadow perched on the crest of the final ridge. A spectacular rainbow of wildflowers populates the slope in spring and summer, with later blooms appearing the higher up you go. From the ridgeline, the world seems to drop steeply away to either side, especially to the right (south) where the buildings of the State Fire Training Center are virtually straight down. Although the climb is still demanding, the views near and far give your mind something else to focus on as you continue to ascend.

The trail abruptly reaches the summit at 4,841 feet, with its signature mailbox stuck in a pile of boulders. Inside, find the summit register and a collection of other random pieces of literature to keep you entertained as you relax among the bear grass.

However, your attention is best spent on the amazing view. To the north, the middle fork of the Snoqualmie River runs like a blue ribbon below the dominant crags and cliffs of Russian Butte. Mounts Si and Teneriffe are immediately to the west, with the radio towers of Rattlesnake Mountain visible across the Snoqualmie Valley. Mount Rainier and its huge Willis Wall rise to the south beyond Mount Washington and McClellan Butte. For the truly adventurous, a scrambler's trail heads along the summit ridge toward the southeast, first descending into a saddle and then climbing up the other side to a high point (4,926 feet) on the way to Mount Defiance.

Be careful on the descent. Despite the temptation, the steepness of the trail makes it difficult to go much faster on the way down than on the way up, and the roots and loose dirt make it easy to lose your footing. When you finally reach the bottom, you will be amazed at how far you actually managed to climb.

▶ NEARBY ACTIVITIES

Tucked into the back of the Union 76 gas station in Edgewick "Truck Town," the easily overlooked Rhodie's Smokin' BBQ and Pizza serves up some great posthike food. To reach Rhodie's, take Exit 34 off I-90 and head north for less than a quarter mile on 468th Avenue SE. Try a hefty Trailboss barbecue sandwich. After climbing Mailbox Peak, you deserve it.

MIDDLE FORK SNOQUALMIE RIVER TRAIL

KEY AT-A-GLANCE INFORMATION

LENGTH: 6 miles (round-trip) to river access point; 10 miles (round-trip) to Dingford Creek

CONFIGURATION: Out-and-back

DIFFICULTY: Moderate

SCENERY: Middle Fork Snoqualmie River, views of nearby peaks

EXPOSURE: Shaded

TRAFFIC: Medium; mountain bikers on odd-numbered days

TRAIL SURFACE: Dirt and gravel trails

HIKING TIME: 3–6 hours

ACCESS: Hikable year-round (may be snowy in winter); Northwest Forest Pass required for parking

MAPS: Green Trails—174 Mount Si, 175 Skykomish, 207 Snoqualmie Pass; USGS Lake Philippa, Snoqualmie Lake, and Snoqualmie Pass

FACILITIES: Restroom at trailhead; no drinking water available

Middle Fork Snoqualmie River Trail

Latitude: North 47d32.853m

Longitude: West 121d32.238m

▶ IN BRIEF

The Middle Fork Trail reaches deep into an area that is ripe for rediscovery. After years of neglect from the Forest Service, the low-elevation trail has suddenly had a rebirth, allowing hikers to explore along the banks of the scenic Middle Fork of the Snoqualmie River and access much of the mountain wilderness beyond.

▶ DESCRIPTION

If there is a dark side to the Alpine Lakes Wilderness, it can be found on the middle fork of the Snoqualmie River. The word wild describes equally well the natural environment of the mountain valley and its historical lawlessness: abandoned cars, dumped garbage, and even mobile methamphetamine labs are among the unwelcome artifacts that have appeared in the woods in the recent past, like a scene from *Deliverance*. Although these unsavory elements might have added a certain frontier authenticity to any visit to the region, not surprisingly many people decided to look elsewhere for their outdoor-recreation pursuits.

▶ DIRECTIONS

From I-5 south of downtown Seattle, go east on Interstate 90. Take Exit 34, 486th Avenue SE, and turn left (north) proceeding through the Edgewick "Truck Town" area. In less than 1 mile turn right on SE Middle Fork Road. Continue about 12 miles to the signed Middle Fork trailhead and parking area on the right. The alternate Dingford Creek trailhead is located just more than 6 miles farther up the Middle Fork Road (FR 56). The road is rough beyond the Middle Fork trailhead, so a high-clearance vehicle is recommended. The small parking area and trailhead is located on the right just before the bridge over Dingford Creek.

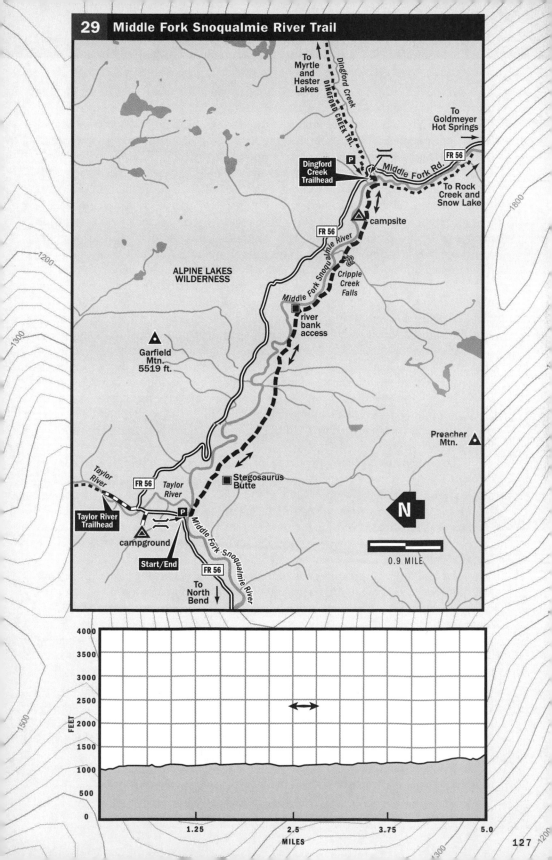

To Myrtle and Hester Lakes

Dingford Creek

DINGFORD CREEK TRL.

To Goldmeyer Hot Springs

P

Dingford Creek Trailhead

Middle Fork Rd.

FR 56

To Rock Creek and Snow Lake

campsite

FR 56

Middle Fork Snoqualmie River

Cripple Creek Falls

ALPINE LAKES WILDERNESS

Middle Fork Snoqualmie River

river bank access

Garfield Mtn. 5519 ft.

Preacher Mtn.

Stegosaurus Butte

N

Taylor River

FR 56 Taylor River

Taylor River Trailhead

P

campground

Start/End

Middle Fork Snoqualmie River

FR 56

To North Bend

0.9 MILE

FEET

4000
3500
3000
2500
2000
1500
1000
500
0

1.25   2.5   3.75   5.0

MILES

All that began to change a few years ago, when the Forest Service decided to take back the more than 100,000 acres of natural land accessible from along the river. Centerpiece of the reclamation project is the paving of the rough Middle Fork Road (FR 56). Depending on when you visit, the road could be a washboarded and rutted nightmare or, if the paving is complete, a smooth, newly sealed dream.

The linear Middle Fork Trail provides multiple hiking opportunities from several access points. The easiest place to begin is at the Middle Fork trailhead (also known as the Gateway Parking Area), elevation 1,000 feet, which has already seen some significant physical development as part of the region's overall rehabilitation. The wide parking lot seems prepared to deal with the increased traffic that the road improvements are sure to bring. Construction also began on a new drive-in campground on the northern side of the road near the Taylor River Confluence in fall of 2005.

There are two trailheads at the Gateway Parking Area but both lead to the same place, meeting 50 yards into the woods at the beautifully crafted Gateway Bridge over the Middle Fork River. The graceful bridge sports an unusual compression-arch, suspended-deck design with a single central span, and provides good views up and down the valley. On the far side, turn left and start heading upstream. The gravel single-track soon changes to dirt as the trail runs above some walls 20 feet above the clear water. On the right side, the slope climbs steeply away to some high cliffs overhead. This is the northern side of Stegosaurus Butte, a sharp, rocky fin rising about 1,000 feet that apparently bears some resemblance to the bony plates on the back of the dinosaur for which it is named, although you will be hard-pressed to discern that from here.

The trail gradually climbs away from the river on a series of short ups and downs through a forest of mixed second-growth deciduous and coniferous trees. Big leaf maples tower over ferns and devils club in the underbrush, and pretty orange chanterelle mushrooms grow on some of the fallen logs and giant stumps underneath. An area of downed trees and high, upturned root wads provides a great view across the valley to the seemingly impregnable walls of Garfield Mountain (5,519 feet) on the far side. The summit is frequently obscured by clouds billowing up the valley.

The trail flirts with the river bank for another mile, sometimes close to the edge and other times far above it. Although the trail seems to follow an excessively circuitous route, it actually takes a reasonably direct line; the deep bends and oxbows of the river cause the frequent separation. Views of Garfield come and go through the trees.

About 3 miles from the trailhead, you'll reach a clearing on the river's edge at an elevation of approximately 1,100 feet. The small open space makes a good place to stop, rest, and enjoy the view. A wide field of white rocks sits on the river bed on the opposite side, and some high cliffs are visible upstream, the abrupt terminus of the far northeastern ridge of Preacher Mountain (5,924 feet) to the south. The clearing is a little past the halfway point between the Middle Fork and Dingford Creek trailheads, and can potentially make a good turnaround point for a 6-mile out-and-back from Middle Fork or a slightly shorter trip from Dingford Creek.

Pass beneath the cliffs and continue for almost another mile to a bridge over a thundering falls on the right. Huge boulders and logs sit in the stream, known as Cripple Creek, fed by a cluster of alpine lakes far above in a bowl bounded by the eastern shoulder of Preacher Mountain and the northern side of Mount Roosevelt.

Another mile through the forest brings you to a spur trail on the left, heading sharply downhill to an undeveloped campsite. Soon after, look for a sign pointing to the left at a junction for Middle Fork Road and Dingford Creek Trail. The main Middle Fork Trail continues to follow the river upstream straight ahead, bound for Wildcat Creek about a mile away, Rock Creek and the Snow Lake Trail another half mile beyond that, and the privately owned Goldmeyer Hot Springs still another few miles distant. The hot springs mark the end of the Middle Fork Road, although the trail itself continues on to eventually reach Dutch Miller Gap below Summit Chief Mountain.

From the junction, turn left to reach a sturdy bridge over the river, then climb up the far bank to reach the end at Dingford Creek trailhead on FR 56. Note that if you are running a shuttle and need to leave a vehicle here or you have decided to start hiking from this point, this trailhead is not well-marked. Look for a turn-out on the right side of the road just before the bridge over Dingford Creek Falls.

For a point-to-point hike between the trailheads, there is a small elevation advantage to starting at Dingford Creek, which is 400 feet above Middle Fork. But the many short climbs and drops along the way are likely to eliminate any feeling of overall net elevation gain or loss in either direction.

Options abound for alternate ways to experience the Middle Fork Trail and the surrounding Alpine Lakes Wilderness. From Dingford Creek, hikers can continue up the Middle Fork Trail as mentioned earlier or tackle the tough climb on the northern side of the road on the Dingford Creek Trail, which rises 3,000 feet to Myrtle and Hester lakes, 5 miles distant.

It is also possible to return to the Taylor River trailhead on FR 56 via mountain bike, an option that is likely to remain viable even if the road becomes gated and closed to motor vehicle traffic somewhere along the way. In fact, the Forest Service decided in 2003 to allow mountain bikes on the Middle Fork Trail itself on odd-numbered calendar days, which makes a loop ride combining the trail and road a great option if you time your visit accordingly.

McCLELLAN BUTTE

KEY AT-A-GLANCE INFORMATION

LENGTH: 9 miles (round-trip)

CONFIGURATION: Out-and-back

DIFFICULTY: Difficult

SCENERY: Old-growth forest, subalpine meadows, historic rail-trail, summit scramble, views from summit

EXPOSURE: Mostly shaded; summit is exposed

TRAFFIC: Moderate

TRAIL SURFACE: Dirt with a short crushed-rock rail-trail segment

HIKING TIME: 5–8 hours

ACCESS: Hikable summer-fall (don't cross avalanche chutes when snow-filled); Northwest Forest Pass required for parking

MAPS: Green Trails—Bandera 206; USGS Bandera

FACILITIES: Restroom at trailhead, no drinking water available

McClellan Butte

Latitude: North 47d24.73m

Longitude: West 121d35.353m

IN BRIEF

Thanks to its rocky summit and central location, 5,162-foot McClellan Butte provides one of the best views of the high peaks lining I-90 between North Bend and Snoqualmie Pass. On the final ridge, an optional scramble presents an additional challenge, suitable for experienced hikers who are comfortable using handholds and facing considerable exposure.

DESCRIPTION

From the approach drive, the prominent peak of McClellan Butte does not seem to be far above the highway. Don't be deceived; the route to the top gains 3,700 feet over 4.5 miles, a demanding average gradient of 820 feet per mile, ranking this hike among the most difficult in the Snoqualmie River Valley.

Yet the trail is more than just an uphill slog passing through old-growth forest, subalpine meadows, and a series of avalanche chutes on its way to the top. The route also wraps around to the far side of the butte, crossing through a corner of the restricted Cedar River Watershed and presenting a unique southerly view away from the I-90 corridor.

Check the trailhead information board before beginning your hike. At an altitude of more than 4,000 feet, snow can linger in the avalanche chutes late into July and can be challenging to cross safely. Look for notes from the local rangers on this and other potential items of interest.

DIRECTIONS

From I-5 south of downtown Seattle, go east on I-90. Take Exit 42, Tinkham Road, and turn right (south). After about a quarter mile go right on a short road that ascends to the official McClellan Butte trailhead parking lot.

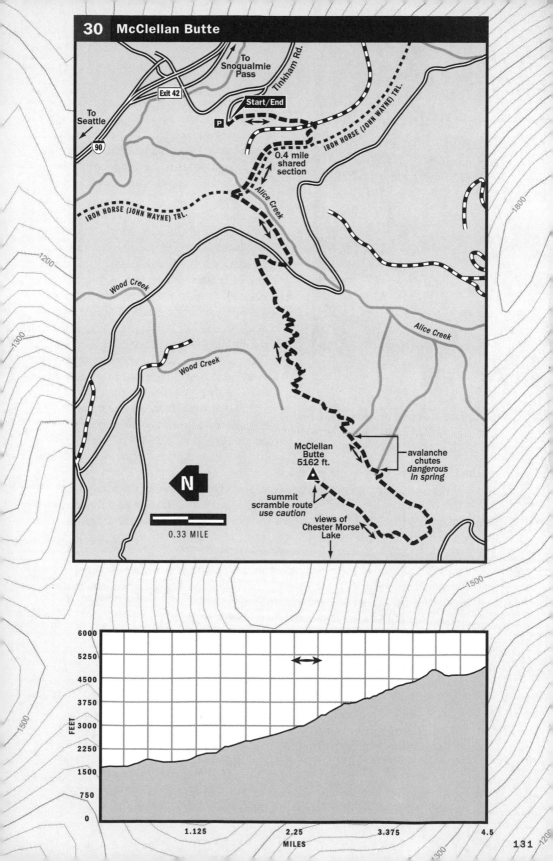

To Snoqualmie Pass

Tinkham Rd.

Exit 42

Start/End

To Seattle

90

P

IRON HORSE (JOHN WAYNE) TRL.

0.4 mile shared section

Alice Creek

IRON HORSE (JOHN WAYNE) TRL.

Wood Creek

Wood Creek

Alice Creek

N

0.33 MILE

McClellan Butte 5162 ft.

summit scramble route *use caution*

views of Chester Morse Lake

avalanche chutes *dangerous in spring*

6000
5250
4500
3750
3000
2250
1500
750
0

FEET

1.125   2.25   3.375   4.5
MILES

Summit scramble on McClellan Butte

The McClellan Butte Trail 1015 starts at an elevation of 1,600 feet from the western end of the parking lot. Almost immediately, pass underneath some power lines, the first of many traces of historical and modern development in this area. Within the first mile, expect to cross several sets of power lines and some gravel roads as you switchback uphill.

The second set of power lines you encounter runs through linear Iron Horse State Park. A reclaimed right-of-way from the old Chicago–Milwaukee–St. Paul–Pacific Railroad (commonly known as the Milwaukee Road), the Iron Horse stretches across most of Washington State. Snoqualmie Pass offers the easiest Cascade crossing between the Columbia River and the Canadian border, so the railway climbed the pass from the east and traveled down the Snoqualmie River Valley to Seattle just as I-90 does today.

The Milwaukee Road was converted to electricity through the Rockies in 1915 and then through the Cascades in 1917, making it the first electrified transcontinental railway in the United States. Although the tracks are long gone, the right-of-way still boasts forward-thinking technology in the form of optic fiber cables buried underground.

The McClellan Butte trail shares 0.4 miles with the John Wayne Pioneer Trail (also called the Iron Horse Trail), which travels more than 100 miles through Iron Horse State Park and was named a National Millennium Legacy Trail in fall of 1999. For many, John Wayne was the physical embodiment of the spirit of the west, and this rail-trail was named after him as a tribute. Although generally pictured riding into the sunset somewhere in the desert, The Duke was actually a frequent visitor to the Pacific Northwest and enjoyed exploring the waters around the Olympic Peninsula in his boat *Wild Goose;* he eventually donated 22 acres on Sequim Bay to what is now known as the John Wayne Marina. He has fictional ties to the region as well; in the 1960 film *North to Alaska* he portrayed Sam McCord, who visited Seattle during the gold rush era in search of his partner's girlfriend.

The shared section of the trail is well-signed at both ends. As you walk the wide gravel surface, look for a marker on the right showing 2,126 miles to Chicago. Also watch for the Alice Creek camp a quarter mile further along (with tent platforms, picnic tables, and a toilet), one of a series of public campsites available in Iron Horse State Park. Bypass an unmarked gravel spur off to the left which leads down to Alice Creek.

Reach the second trail junction and head uphill on the hikers-only trail. The first section of the route features notched logs, waterbars, bridges, and occasional steps, making the traveling easy despite the incline. Pass through some massive old-growth Douglas firs and enjoy the thick scent of cedar, which can permeate the lower forest.

Head straight across the final gravel road and begin the climb in earnest, as the trail becomes steeper and more rugged with less evidence of regular maintenance. For the next 2 miles, expect to grind up the mountain on a series of switchbacks, gradually working your way southwest. An occasional viewpoint to the left reveals I-90 below and shows how far you have come, although there is still a long way to go.

Just past the 3-mile mark, cross a series of creek beds that likely will be dry in the summer. A glance up to the right reveals the rocky crags of the summit, which the trail skirts with a backside approach. The creek beds grow successively larger and the last few are avalanche chutes, the final one characterized by pinkish rocks. Watch for snow here, which can be dangerous to cross as you navigate the boulders and brush.

Finally the trail bends to the right and then crests the ridge near 5,000 feet, presenting a view of Chester Morse Lake in the heart of the Cedar River Watershed. Descend for a quarter mile to reach a subalpine bowl with views out to the west, a small meadow, and a pond. Gradually head uphill once again, passing beneath some rocky cliffs, and then emerge on the summit ridge at the end of the hikers' trail. The opposite side of the ridge drops sharply into the avalanche chutes you crossed earlier, and the northern face of Mount Rainier appears through a notch on Mount Kent to the south. The glaciated giant looks close enough to touch but is actually more than 40 miles away.

A rocky fin leads northeast to the true summit, 100 feet higher and laced with mountain heather. The route is a short class-three scramble along the right side of the ridge. But despite plenty of good holds, it is exposed, and a fall from the scramble could result in serious injury or death. If you are unsure whether this is for you, then it probably isn't. Proceed with extreme caution and be aware of external factors, such as wet rocks or high winds, which could make the climb more dangerous.

Those continuing to the top will be rewarded with grand views to all sides and plenty of room to relax on the broad, flat boulders. Climbers or other hikers may be approaching up any of the faces, so be careful not to knock anything off; you never know who is below.

The view is particularly good of the peaks just across the valley, including Mailbox, Defiance, and Bandera. Look for Mount Stuart to the northeast, poking far above the intervening ridges at 9,415 feet. Below, the tiny cars crawl past on I-90, dwarfed by the mountains.

Return the way you came, and take extra care through the scramble; going down is typically more difficult than going up.

▶ NEARBY ACTIVITIES

Hiker, bikers, equestrians, cross-country skiers, and snowshoers can all take advantage of the John Wayne Pioneer Trail in Iron Horse State Park to trek for virtually any distance, short or long. Multiple access points and campsites along the way allow for easy overnight travel, and attractions like the 2.3-mile Snoqualmie Tunnel add special interest. For more information, visit the Iron Horse State Park Web site at **www.parks.wa.gov**.

IRA SPRING TRAIL TO MASON LAKE, MOUNT DEFIANCE, AND BANDERA MOUNTAIN

KEY AT-A-GLANCE INFORMATION

LENGTH: 6.5 miles (round-trip) to Mason Lake; 10 miles (round-trip) to Mount Defiance; 6.5 miles (round-trip) to Bandera Mountain false summit

CONFIGURATION: Out-and-back

DIFFICULTY: Moderate to Mason Lake, difficult to either summit

SCENERY: Mountain lake, a waterfall, two mountains to ascend, including a scramble route on a boulder ridge, and many great viewpoints along the way

EXPOSURE: Shaded on lower portions and around Mason Lake

TRAFFIC: High to Mason Lake, less on summit routes

TRAIL SURFACE: Dirt, with an abandoned gravel-road approach and boulder-hopping on Bandera

HIKING TIME: Half day to Mason Lake, all day for either summit

ACCESS: Hikable late spring–early fall; Northwest Forest Pass required for parking

MAPS: Green Trails–Bandera 206; USGS Bandera

FACILITIES: Restroom at trailhead; no drinking water available

---

Ira Spring Trail to Mason Lake, Mount Defiance, and Bandera Mountain

Latitude: North 47d25.477m

Longitude: West 121d35.003m

IN BRIEF

With multiple worthwhile destinations, this hike is really three trails in one—two difficult options climb the high peaks of either Mount Defiance or Bandera Mountain, while a moderate option leads to peaceful Mason Lake in between. No matter which one you choose, vibrant wildflowers, alpine wilderness, and great views will be your reward for the effort.

DESCRIPTION

The formerly sketchy Bandera Mountain–Mason Lake Trail saw major renovation in 2003 and was renamed the Ira Spring Trail a year later in memory of the famous outdoor advocate and photographer, who had just died from cancer at the age of 84. The tribute was especially fitting, both because the Spring Family Trust was established to support just this type of project and because the trail leads to a Pacific Northwest landscape with deep evergreen forests, grand mountain scenery, and sparkling alpine lakes that Spring would have loved to capture on film.

If there is any drawback to the new Ira Spring Trail, it's that despite the considerable improvements it still can't be described as easy. Mason Lake is the least-demanding destination, which nonetheless requires a tough climb of 2,000 feet over 3.3 miles. Add 1,200 feet and another 1.75 miles to reach the summit of Mount Defiance, or a little more than a mile to get to the

DIRECTIONS

From I-5 south of downtown Seattle, go east on I-90. Take Exit 45 and turn left under I-90 onto FR 9030, which bends left to parallel the Interstate. At a junction stay left (straight) on FR 9031 and continue 3 more miles to the road's end at the Mason Lake Trail–Ira Spring Trail parking lot and trailhead.

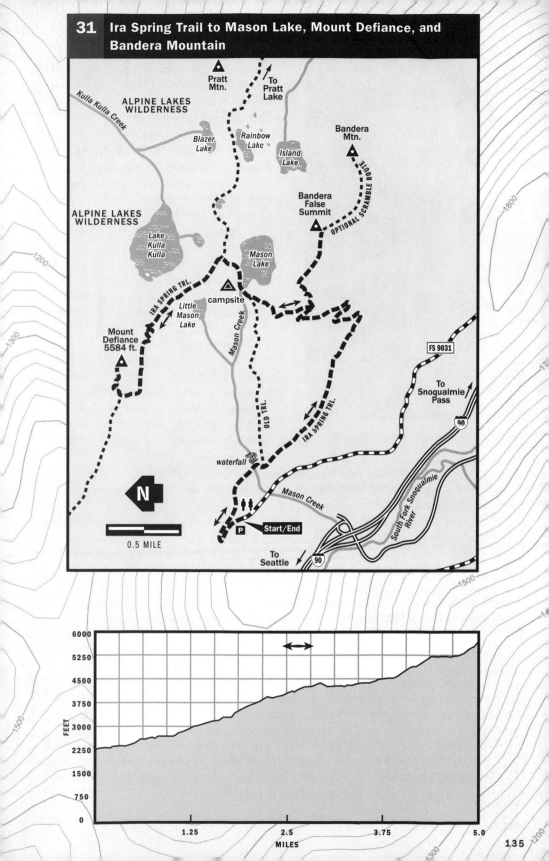

31 Ira Spring Trail to Mason Lake, Mount Defiance, and Bandera Mountain

Pratt Mtn.

To Pratt Lake

ALPINE LAKES WILDERNESS

Kulla Kulla Creek

Blazer Lake

Rainbow Lake

Island Lake

Bandera Mtn.

Bandera False Summit

OPTIONAL SCRAMBLE ROUTE

ALPINE LAKES WILDERNESS

Lake Kulla Kulla

Mason Lake

IRA SPRING TRL.

campsite

Little Mason Lake

Mount Defiance 5584 ft.

Mason Creek

FS 9031

To Snoqualmie Pass

90

OLD TRL.

IRA SPRING TRL.

waterfall

South Fork Snoqualmie River

N

Mason Creek

0.5 MILE

P Start/End

To Seattle 90

Interstate 90 from high ridge on Bandera Mountain

top of Bandera. Still, each destination is well worth the exertion. And the recent rehabilitation of the trail means there has never been a better time to visit.

Note that both Mason Lake and Mount Defiance are within the Alpine Lakes Wilderness and require self-issued permits from a box at the trailhead for access. No permit is required for the hike to Bandera, however, which does not enter the wilderness.

Whichever destination you choose, the first several miles of the route are identical for all three and involve climbing a high, south-facing ridge. The trail starts at near 2,300 feet on an abandoned gravel road, which quickly bends around to the east and enters a forest of alders. Several creeks—including Mason Creek with a particularly large and impressive waterfall worth stopping to photograph—flow down the slope from the left and pass under the roadbed. The water bounces down through a series of boulders and logs in a cascade of crashing foam and mist, with the top too far up to be seen through the trees.

The trail climbs steadily as it continues to head eastward, ascending on a long traverse. The trees gradually thin, providing views of the I-90 corridor and McClellan Butte directly across the valley, and are replaced by some lichen-encrusted boulders. Eventually the old road ends, but the trail branches off it uphill to the left and continues through several avalanche gaps before reaching its first switchback near 3,500 feet. Evidence of an old forest fire can be seen in some charred stumps scattered across the mountainside, sticking up out of the bear grass, huckleberry bushes, and wildflowers.

Several more switchbacks run back and forth across the fire-scarred slope and through some substantial piles of rock, where the trail displays some of the best handiwork of the tireless volunteers who labored to create it. The effort required to lay a flat dirt trail through a wide boulder field is nothing short of monumental, and the sandy surface provides great drainage, even in the rain and snow.

At 4,100 feet, you'll finally reach the signed split to Bandera Mountain on the right. The trail to Bandera above the junction is much rougher than the Ira Spring Trail, which is not far removed from a scramble through bear grass and exposed rocks. It is much steeper as well, running virtually straight uphill. However, it seems like the entire Snoqualmie Valley is at your feet and the wide-ranging views make it easy to forget the physical challenge. The south-facing slope gets plenty of sunlight, nurturing huckleberries, Indian paintbrush, purple lupine, and a host of other colorful wildflowers while keeping the ground generally dry.

Skirt some low trees and continue up the rocky ridge toward the crest. Occasional cairns show the way, but the boot-polished boulders are generally equally good indicators of the correct route, which is never hard to follow.

A small clearing marks the end of the hike at about 5,200 feet, just before it would be necessary to descend into a notch. The true summit is actually another half mile away, but it is only marginally higher at 5,241 feet and the crossing is little more than a bushwhack. Few hikers actually make the journey to the summit. And why should they? The view from the false summit is hard to beat, taking in a vast stretch of land that on a clear day includes everything from the peaks around Snoqualmie Pass to downtown Seattle and Mount Rainier. Mason Lake shimmers directly below to the north, along with Island Lake and several others. Lake Kulla Kulla sits below some exposed slabs on the northern buttress of Mount Defiance, whose distinctive pyramidal summit is the highest point anywhere to the west other than in the Olympic Range.

Mason Lake and Mount Defiance can be reached by continuing on the Ira Spring Trail from the junction at 4,100 feet. Follow the path until it reaches a saddle marking the official wilderness boundary, and then descend through an evergreen forest on the opposite side.

Cross the Mason Creek outflow to find the lake itself, sitting in an alpine bowl directly below the Bandera ridge. The trail wraps around through the trees on the northern shore, where a clearing among the boulders provides a good campsite and many places to sit and relax. There are plenty of opportunities to explore on your own as well, if this is your final destination.

To continue to Mount Defiance, follow the extension of the trail through the jumbled rocks and back into the forest. A sign reading Main Trail tacked high on a tree may help show the way, although it is easy to miss. The trail soon leads to a more obvious T-junction, with a sign for Mount Defiance Trail 1009 shown to the left, and a trail to Island Lake and distant Pratt Lake to the right. The dry and sandy tread hiked earlier will likely seem very far away, as mud puddles big enough to be called ponds can collect on the trail when it is wet.

Take the left fork and begin climbing once again on a shallow ridge, with glimpses of Lake Kulla Kulla visible through the stately trees to the right. As the trail continues to ascend it feels almost like an organic part of the forest, winding in and out of the moss-covered trunks until finally emerging into an avalanche gap at 5,100 feet, about 900 feet above Mason Lake.

Cross the chute and continue traversing west on an open, wildflower-studded slope with spectacular views similar to the summit ridge on Bandera (although the trail here is mercifully flat). After a long but glorious quarter mile, look for a narrow trail switchbacking straight up to the right just short of where you would re-enter the trees. This steep and rocky path provides the final push to the summit, where the ridge ends in a pile of boulders at 5,584 feet.

The view from the top of Defiance is just as panoramic as the one from nearby Bandera, with an even better vantage for observing the southwest corner of the Alpine Lakes Wilderness and the high summits of Kaleetan Peak, Mount Roosevelt, and Preacher Mountain across the Pratt River Valley to the northeast.

GRANITE MOUNTAIN LOOKOUT TOWER

KEY AT-A-GLANCE INFORMATION

LENGTH: 8 miles (round-trip)

CONFIGURATION: Out-and-back with summit loop option

DIFFICULTY: Difficult

SCENERY: Active lookout tower on summit with distant views, optional scramble route along a boulder-strewn ridge

EXPOSURE: Shaded on lower half, exposed on upper half

TRAFFIC: Moderate to high

TRAIL SURFACE: Dirt

HIKING TIME: 5–7 hours

ACCESS: Hikable late spring–fall (avalanche chutes can be dangerous in spring); Northwest Forest Pass required for parking

MAPS: Green Trails–Snoqualmie Pass 207; USGS Snoqualmie Pass

FACILITIES: Restroom at trailhead, no drinking water available

Granite Mountain Lookout Tower

Latitude: North 47d23.863m

Longitude: West 121d29.221m

IN BRIEF

This tough but rewarding hike leads to one of the highest peaks west of Snoqualmie Pass and includes some 2,000 feet of climbing in the alpine zone; the trek is capped by a long boulder-hop up the final ridge. From the summit lookout tower, Granite Mountain enjoys a commanding view of the surrounding area and much of the central Washington Cascades. Four high volcanoes frame the unforgettable scene.

DESCRIPTION

Most of the summits along I-90 can provide excellent views, and Granite Mountain is no exception. However, there is a reason Granite was selected as a fire lookout site when so many others were not. Even among the exemplary collection of peaks between North Bend and Snoqualmie Pass, Granite stands out, reaching just a little bit higher with a grander view to match. The price of admission is the demanding haul up the mountain's long south slope, a trip that's guaranteed to exact its toll in sweat and lactic acid.

Granite Mountain shares a trailhead with several other destinations, listed with specific mileages and trail numbers on a prominent sign at the northern side of the parking lot, where trail reports and other useful information are also displayed. All the hikes start on the Pratt Lake Trail 1007 before branching off to their separate endpoints. Note that the hike to the Granite Mountain Lookout is listed as 4 miles one-way, but it certainly feels farther given the tough character of the climb.

DIRECTIONS

From I-5 south of downtown Seattle, go east on I-90. Take Exit 47, Denny Creek–Asahel Curtis. Turn left over I-90, then turn left again and drive less than a half mile to the parking lot and trailhead.

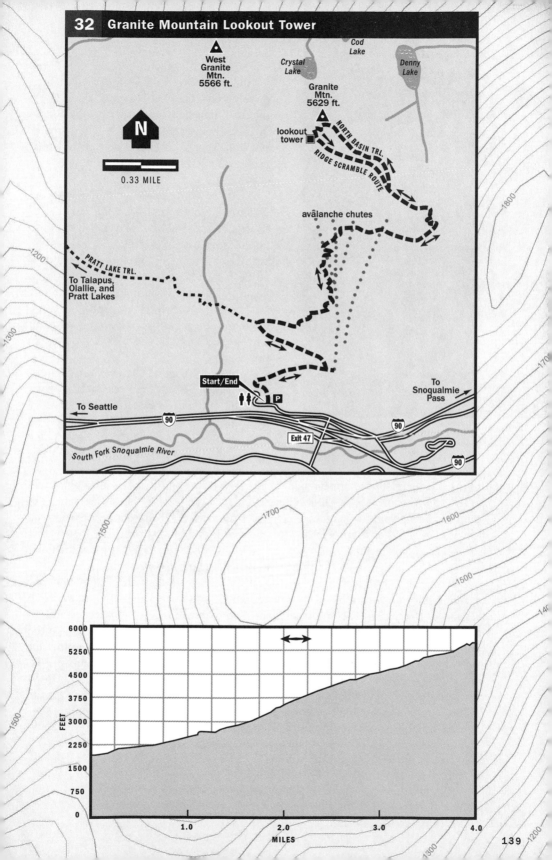

West Granite Mtn. 5566 ft.

Cod Lake

Crystal Lake

Denny Lake

Granite Mtn. 5629 ft.

lookout tower

NORTH BASIN TRL.

RIDGE SCRAMBLE ROUTE

N

0.33 MILE

avalanche chutes

PRATT LAKE TRL.

To Talapus, Olallie, and Pratt Lakes

Start/End

P

To Snoqualmie Pass

To Seattle

90

90

Exit 47

South Fork Snoqualmie River

90

1200

1300

1800

1700

1500

1700

1600

1500

1500

1400

1300

1200

FEET

6000

5250

4500

3750

3000

2250

1500

750

0

1.0

2.0

3.0

4.0

MILES

Granite Mountain lookout

The trail begins on a rocky uphill, rising quickly above the trailhead at 1,880 feet. A series of seasonal streams flow down the mountainside and cross underfoot as the route contours eastward, reaches a major switchback at 2,200 feet, and then bends back to the left beneath a forest of tall Douglas firs.

After about a mile, a sign marks the Granite Mountain Trail, where it branches to the right from the Pratt Lake Trail. The climb becomes noticeably steeper and reaches the bottom of a series of avalanche chutes near 3,000 feet, not far below the official Alpine Lakes Wilderness boundary. These chutes are hazardous in winter and spring and are often a problem early in the hiking season if a heavy snowpack lingers on the mountain's upper slopes.

Skirt the edge of the avalanche chutes on a series of tight switchbacks before finally crossing over to the eastern side at the top near the 2.5-mile mark. The open gullies provide good views of the Snoqualmie Valley below, and are often full of colorful wildflowers and puffy bear grass in the spring and summer.

Large rocks start to appear along the trail, evidence of the mountain's namesake underlying granite. As you climb above 4,000 feet and enter the alpine zone, the steepness relents and the landscape continues to open up. This section can be cruelly deceptive—even though it seems the top must be just above the next rise, there is still a long way to go. The area is also exposed to the weather, which could mean anything from cold wind and rain to a burning sun, depending on seasonal conditions.

At around 5,000 feet, some social trails branch to the left and lead to the foot of a long ridge of granite boulders that reaches all the way to the summit, still 600 feet above. The main trail continues into an open alpine bowl and crosses toward the mountain's scenic, quiet northern side before climbing through stunted trees to the lookout tower. Many hikers take the most direct route to the top, enjoying the fun and easy scramble through the massive rocks. In some years, snow remains on the official trail well into July, making the boulders an even more attractive option. However, both routes lead to the same destination. And, of course, it is possible to make a short loop by climbing one and descending the other, getting a feel for both.

At 5,629 feet, Granite Mountain is high enough that it is possible to feel some minor effects of the altitude over the last few hundred feet of climbing. The thin air will be most apparent to anyone coming up from sea level, which means essentially all hikers from the Puget Sound lowlands.

The sturdy wooden lookout is perched on the southern end of the summit crest, capping a jumble of lichen-encrusted rocks. The lichen adds a mix of green and black to the gray and white slabs, and even throws in a splash of pink. Unfortunately, the lookout is kept locked and is not available for public rental, as it is still in use by the National Forest Service. Fire-spotting is mostly done by helicopters these days, but rangers and volunteers are sometimes stationed in the tower for a variety of reasons.

If someone is on duty and it is possible to get inside, the interesting fire-finder compass in the center of the structure is worth investigating. Surrounding peaks up to a radius of about 9 miles are labeled and can be lined up with a set of crosshairs to provide bearing and elevation data, traditionally used to report the locations of potential wildfires. The compass is also useful for identifying many geographic landmarks visible from the lookout.

On a clear day no one will have any trouble picking out Mount Rainier and Mount Adams to the south and Mount Baker and Glacier Peak to the north; all are unmistakable. Although not quite as scenic as the mountain peaks, I-90 also requires no guide for identification, as it winds through the valley far below. All around, a sea of peaks, valleys, lakes, and rivers invites quiet contemplation.

ANNETTE LAKE AND ASAHEL CURTIS NATURE TRAIL

 KEY AT-A-GLANCE INFORMATION

LENGTH: 6 miles (round-trip) for Annette Lake; about 1 mile for Asahel Curtis Nature Trail

CONFIGURATION: Out-and-back to lake; loop on nature trail

DIFFICULTY: Easy on nature trail, moderate to Annette Lake, difficult scramble to Silver Peak

SCENERY: Scenic Annette Lake, old-growth forest, educational nature trail loop, an optional bushwhack and boulder route to Silver Peak for experienced scramblers

EXPOSURE: Shaded

TRAFFIC: High

TRAIL SURFACE: Dirt with rocks and roots to lake, dirt and boardwalk on nature trail

HIKING TIME: 4–6 hours for Annette Lake; add 30–45 minutes for the Nature Trail, and 3–4 hours for Silver Peak

ACCESS: Hikable late spring–fall, depending on snowpack; Northwest Forest Pass required for parking

MAPS: Green Trails–Snoqualmie Pass 207; USGS Lost Lake and Snoqualmie Pass

FACILITIES: Restroom at trailhead; no drinking water available

Annette Lake and Asahel Curtis Nature Trail

Latitude: North 47d23.572m

Longitude: West 121d28.48m

IN BRIEF

Annette, the only significant lake on the southern side of the Snoqualmie Valley, is an easier destination than many similar lakes in the well-known Alpine Lakes Wilderness to the north. Filling a subalpine bowl beneath several 5,000-foot peaks, Annette is accessed via a pleasant trail through some old-growth forest. The nearby Asahel Curtis Nature Trail and a wilderness scramble up Silver Peak expand the available hiking options.

DESCRIPTION

The Annette Lake trailhead shares a parking lot with the Asahel Curtis Nature Trail, worth exploring as a quick side trip or even a short and easy destination by itself. The nature trail forms a loop of about a mile through some of the best old-growth forest anywhere around Snoqualmie Pass, in a representative forest typical of western Washington and Oregon. The trail stays above some swampy ground on a boardwalk while interpretive signs help identify various features of the ecosystem, from root wad to canopy and everything in between. The most impressive trees here are western hemlock, Douglas fir, and western red cedar; other species like Pacific silver fir, noble fir, and western white pine are present as well.

Asahel Curtis, for whom the nature trail is named, was a founding member of The Mountaineers and an accomplished climber who served as chief guide at Mount Rainier National Park in 1917. His achievements include summiting Rainier many times and completing the first

DIRECTIONS

From I-5 south of downtown Seattle, go east on I-90. Take Exit 47, Denny Creek–Asahel Curtis, and turn right. At the T-shaped intersection, turn left onto FR 55 and drive nearly a half mile to the parking lot entrance on the right.

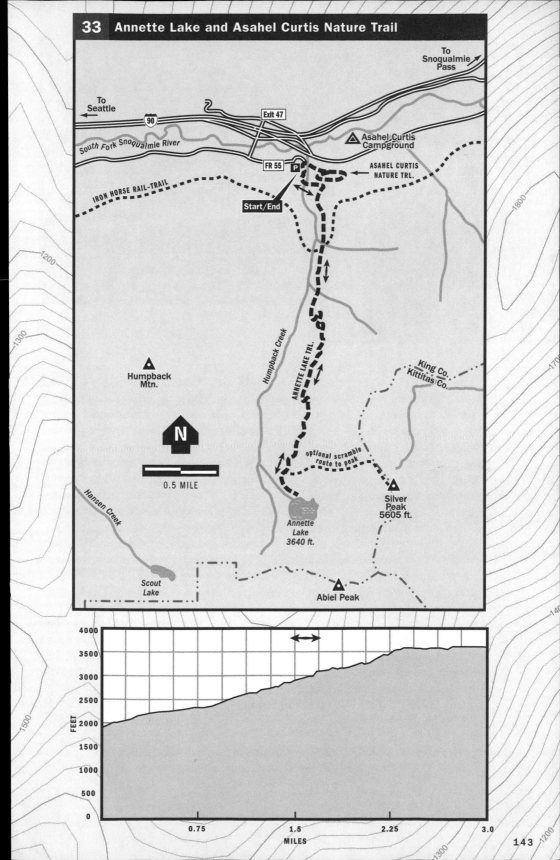

To Snoqualmie Pass

To Seattle

90

Exit 47

South Fork Snoqualmie River

FR 55

P

Start/End

IRON HORSE RAIL-TRAIL

Asahel Curtis Campground

ASAHEL CURTIS NATURE TRL.

Humpback Creek

ANNETTE LAKE TRL.

King Co.
Kittitas Co.

Humpback Mtn.

N

0.5 MILE

optional scramble route to peak

Silver Peak 5605 ft.

Annette Lake 3640 ft.

Hansen Creek

Scout Lake

Abiel Peak

FEET

4000
3500
3000
2500
2000
1500
1000
500
0

0.75   1.5   2.25   3.0

MILES

Annette Lake

documented ascent of Mount Shuksan in 1906 with W. Montelius Price. But Curtis is probably best known for his photographs documenting the natural landscape of the Pacific Northwest, including the early years of Mount Rainier National Park just as it was first reached by road. His work was often overshadowed, however, by that of his more famous brother Edward, who ran a photography studio out of Seattle and whose controversial images of the fading cultures of Native Americans are now preserved in the Library of Congress as one of the most important historical records of the era. Edward Curtis' portrait of Chief Joseph of the Nez Perce is now famous, and the renowned photographer once filmed the Snake Dance of the Arizona Hopi in a rare, early motion picture.

The Annette Lake Trail leaves the parking lot headed nearly due south, climbing steadily from the starting elevation of 1,900 feet. Enter a dense forest of alders and cross Humpback Creek on a bridge, with a pretty waterfall flowing down through some boulders on the right. The trail remains on the eastern side of the creek for the rest of its run up the valley.

Reach an old, unmaintained forest road within a half mile, cross to the right, and follow a sign for Annette Lake. Soon thereafter, pass underneath some power lines in a clearing and then emerge on the gravel Iron Horse State Park rail-trail near 2,400 feet. Look for another sign to Annette Lake Trail about 20 yards to the right and re-enter the trees; you'll be heading uphill.

Some of the old-growth starts to become apparent after another quarter mile. Although this patch of forest is less impressive than the area showcased along the Asahel Curtis Nature Trail, there are still plenty of significantly large and ancient trees. An inventively designed section of the trail actually runs along the top of a giant downed log, complete with flat steps laboriously carved and leveled out of the rounded surface.

Running through a mix of switchbacks and flatter sections, the trail climbs steadily while angling up the valley's eastern wall. Near 3,500 feet, you'll cross some steep brush fields with open views to the right. Humpback Creek runs far below, and rocky, exposed Humpback Peak is visible above at 5,174 feet. With another 100 feet of climbing, the trail reaches a high point, crosses some talus slopes, then begins a gradual descent with a few muddy ups and downs to enter the bowl that holds the lake, which is less than another half mile away.

Annette Lake, sitting at 3,640 feet, is surrounded by trees on all sides and bounded by Silver Peak (5,605 feet) to the east, the long ridge of Humpback Peak to the west, and the high basalt walls of Abiel Peak (5,365 feet) to the south. A small seasonal waterfall pours into the lake on the far eastern shore, collecting runoff from the western slopes of Silver. On the near side, the lake outflow empties into the Humpback Creek Valley; this is not the source of the creek itself, which originates in a drainage gap a quarter mile away. Expect to share the tranquil and picturesque lake with other users, and possibly even fly-fisherman who cast their lines out of boats and float-tubes on the water.

Camping is not allowed on the day-use-only northern shore, but good campsites are available on the western shore across the outflow creek. It is possible to continue farther around the lake by bushwhacking along the water's edge, but the thick brush and steep walls soon make this endeavor prohibitively difficult, and there are certainly no good campsites to be found.

Dedicated scramblers will invariably be drawn to the upper slopes of Silver Peak, which is usually climbed from the Pacific Crest Trail on the opposite side but can also be reached from here. Backtrack slightly along the trail from the lake and then pick a way uphill through the woods due east, aiming for the nearest visible clearing. With a little effort you can reach the start of the long boulder field that climbs to the northern ridge and then the summit. Should you choose this adventurous side trip, you'll be rewarded with commanding views of the Snoqualmie Pass region.

FRANKLIN FALLS AND OLD SNOQUALMIE PASS WAGON ROAD TRAIL

 KEY AT-A-GLANCE INFORMATION

LENGTH: 2 miles (round-trip)

CONFIGURATION: Loop

DIFFICULTY: Easy

SCENERY: Franklin Falls and the picturesque South Fork Snoqualmie River Gorge, old-growth forest, a walk along a historic wagon route

EXPOSURE: Shaded

TRAFFIC: Get an early start to beat crowds and get parking.

TRAIL SURFACE: Dirt (well-maintained with steps and bridges)

HIKING TIME: 1–2 hours

ACCESS: Hikable late spring–fall; Northwest Forest Pass required for parking

MAPS: Green Trails–Snoqualmie Pass 207; USGS Snoqualmie Pass

FACILITIES: No facilities at trailhead; Denny Creek Campground has restrooms and water

Franklin Falls and Old Snoqualmie Pass Wagon Road Trail

Latitude: North 47d24.79m

Longitude: West 121d26.535m

▶ IN BRIEF

The trail to Franklin Falls combines history and natural beauty along a compact and easily accessible loop. A visit to the falls makes for a particularly enjoyable half-day's outing for anyone who wants to explore the Snoqualmie Pass Region but isn't looking for a demanding mountain hike.

▶ DESCRIPTION

It sounds like a joke or the effects of some terrible flood: a scenic waterfall in the middle of I-90—not off to the side somewhere or even visible from the pavement but right in the center—with traffic driving by on either side. Yet this improbable juxtaposition of natural and man-made elements exists just west of Snoqualmie Pass, where the two directions of I-90 are split. More than 25,000 people pass within a quarter mile of Franklin Falls every day, and most would never guess that it exists. Amazingly, an old-growth forest still hangs on in the area, as well, seemingly oblivious to the cars and trucks humming by overhead.

Long before there was an I-90, however, human traffic passed much closer to the falls on the Old Snoqualmie Wagon Road, developed by pioneers heading west toward Seattle. Without

▶ DIRECTIONS

From I-5 south of downtown Seattle, go east on I-90. Take Exit 47, Denny Creek–Asahel Curtis, and turn left, going under both I-90 overpasses. At the T-shaped intersection, turn right. Then in a short distance turn left onto FR 58 toward Denny Creek. In about 2 miles pass FR Road 5830 toward the Denny Creek and Melakwa Lake Trail. Just before the bridge over the river, you'll find the trailhead for the Franklin Falls Trail on the right. Park anywhere along FR 5830 near the trailhead, or drive to the end of FR 5830 for additional parking spots.

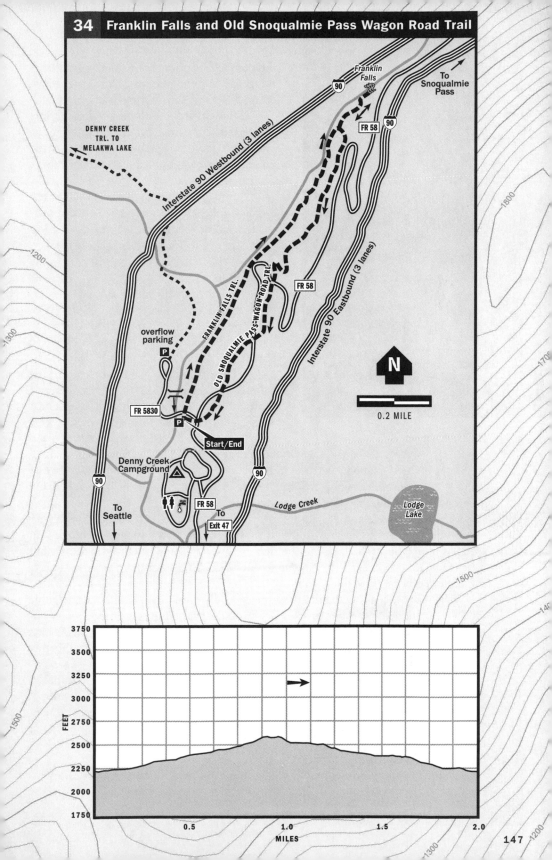

Franklin Falls

To
Snoqualmie
Pass

90

FR 58

90

DENNY CREEK
TRL. TO
MELAKWA LAKE

Interstate 90 Westbound (3 lanes)

FR 58

FRANKLIN FALLS TRL.

OLD SNOQUALMIE PASS-WAGON-ROAD-TRL.

Interstate 90 Eastbound (3 lanes)

overflow
parking

P

N

0.2 MILE

FR 5830

P

Start/End

Denny Creek
Campground

90

To
Seattle

FR 58

To
Exit 47

Lodge Creek

Lodge
Lake

90

FEET

3750

3500

3250

3000

2750

2500

2250

2000

1750

0.5   1.0   1.5   2.0

MILES

Franklin Falls

the miracles of modern engineering that elevate the current roadway, the horse-drawn wagons had to stay at the bottom of the valley on their arduous journey through the mountains. The road often amounted to little more than two wheel-worn ruts in the mud. Nonetheless, it was the primary route across the central Washington Cascades.

Unlike the cars on the interstate, today's hikers tend to travel at a pace similar to that of the pioneers, which makes the former site of the Wagon Road a great place to explore the natural beauty and history of the area on foot.

At the Franklin Falls trailhead, the correct trail is signed as Franklin Falls 1036. The return for the 2-mile loop is on the other side of the junction where FR 5830 branches off FR 58.

The hike starts out heading northeast along the south fork of the Snoqualmie River. The water is clear with a greenish tinge, and runs fast through a mix of gray and reddish rocks. There are plenty of good places to stop and dip your toes in the rushing water, including a polished rock chute in an exposed slab that could double as a water slide a short distance upstream. There is even a small sandy beach on the bank and a pool at the bottom when the river is low.

The trail is wide and easy to follow, with some private rustic cabins visible on either side of the river. Old-growth stands of western red cedar, western hemlock, and Douglas fir appear in the forest to the right, displaying some truly outstanding giant specimens. An epic cedar with a circumference easily 20 feet or more stands watch at the bottom of a set of wooden stairs.

The stairs ascend the bank as the river quickly drops away into a narrow gorge on the left, guarded by a wooden safety fence on the rim. More seemingly good swimming holes appear below, but they are unreachable at the bottom of the sheer rock walls. Various tributary streams flow into the Snoqualmie River, including Denny Creek on the far side (although it is difficult to spot through the trees).

In just less than a mile, a trail joins from the right at a junction, the start of the Old Snoqualmie Wagon Road and the return route on the second half of the loop. Stay straight ahead along the fence for another 0.1 mile to reach the splendor of Franklin Falls, where the river pours over a 70-foot cliff into a natural amphitheater of black and reddish rocks, misting everything nearby. The westbound lanes of I-90 cross overhead on a bridge to the left, clearly visible above.

Return to the previous junction and turn onto the Old Wagon Road. Surprisingly, although the falls tend to attract considerable crowds, many hikers return the way they came, ignoring the simple loop option. The 1-mile descent back to the trail-head is pleasant and comfortable, with a spongy and forgiving surface of decaying wood underfoot that is easy on the joints. The perspective on the forest is different as well, with the river mostly out of sight.

Hard evidence of the old road is well-hidden, and only the most diligent or lucky observer is likely to find anything specific to mark the pioneers' passing. It is difficult enough to even imagine covered wagons making it through the mud and trees of the forest. Not so well-hidden, however, is modern paved FR 58, which must be crossed several times along the way. At each intersection, look for an inconspicu-ous wooden post on the opposite side to show the continuation of the trail, usually within 10 yards to the left or right.

The end of the Old Wagon Road returns you to the junction of FR 58 and FR 5830, as mentioned earlier, where it is a short walk across the parking lot back to your vehicle.

▶ NEARBY ACTIVITIES

From the parking area, you can hike to two good waterfalls on the Denny Creek Trail, which starts from the end of FR 5830: Keekwulee Falls is about 2 miles up the trail, and Snowshoe Falls is another quarter mile beyond.

KITSAP PENINSULA AND WHIDBEY ISLANDS

GREEN MOUNTAIN STATE FOREST:
GOLD CREEK, BEAVER POND, AND WILDCAT TRAIL LOOP

 KEY AT-A-GLANCE INFORMATION

LENGTH: 7.7 miles for entire loop, 4 miles (round-trip) to summit

CONFIGURATION: Loop or out-and-back

DIFFICULTY: Moderate to difficult

SCENERY: Summit views west to the Olympic Mountains and east to Seattle over Puget Sound ponds and marshes, and wildflowers

EXPOSURE: Mostly shaded (a few exposed sections)

TRAFFIC: Moderate (note that trail is open to bikes, horses, and motorcycles, though seldom seen)

TRAIL SURFACE: Dirt

HIKING TIME: 4–7 hours

ACCESS: Hikable year-round; no fees for parking or park access

MAPS: USGS Wildcat Lake

FACILITIES: Restroom at trailhead; no drinking water available

Green Mountain State Forest:
Gold Creek, Beaver Pond and
Wildcat Trail Loop

Latitude: North 47d33.078m

Longitude: West 122d49.642m

IN BRIEF

The Kitsap Peninsula has numerous hiking options. But there is only one Green Mountain, a prominent high point in the middle of a mostly flat and low-lying landscape. Luckily, the second-highest peak in the region provides plenty of good reasons to visit other than just its exclusivity, including an extensive network of trails and great summit views.

DESCRIPTION

The Kitsap Peninsula is full of recreation opportunities, with a host of campgrounds, boat launches, and parks available for use. Many Seattle residents keep waterfront cottages on the shores of the Hood Canal or on any of a number of popular lakes and flock across Puget Sound each weekend in the summer for the chance to get away. Yet, despite the primarily undeveloped landscape everywhere outside Bremerton, public trails that climb to significant peaks on Kitsap are few and far between.

DIRECTIONS

From downtown Seattle: Take the ferry across Puget Sound to Bremerton. After exiting the ferry, drive west on WA 304 and follow signs to WA 3. Turn right (north) on WA 3 and take the Chico Way exit. Turn left onto Chico Way, then turn right onto N Lake Way. In a quick quarter mile, turn right again onto Seabeck Highway and continue just more than 3 miles to Holly Road on the left. Follow Holly Road for more than 4 miles, then turn left onto Tahuya Lake Road (signed Tahuyeh), which eventually becomes Gold Creek Road. After passing Tahuya Lake look for the Gold Creek trailhead parking lot on the left. From Tacoma: Travel on WA 16 (west) across the Tacoma Narrows bridge and continue all the way to WA 3 (north); then follow the directions from Chico Way above.

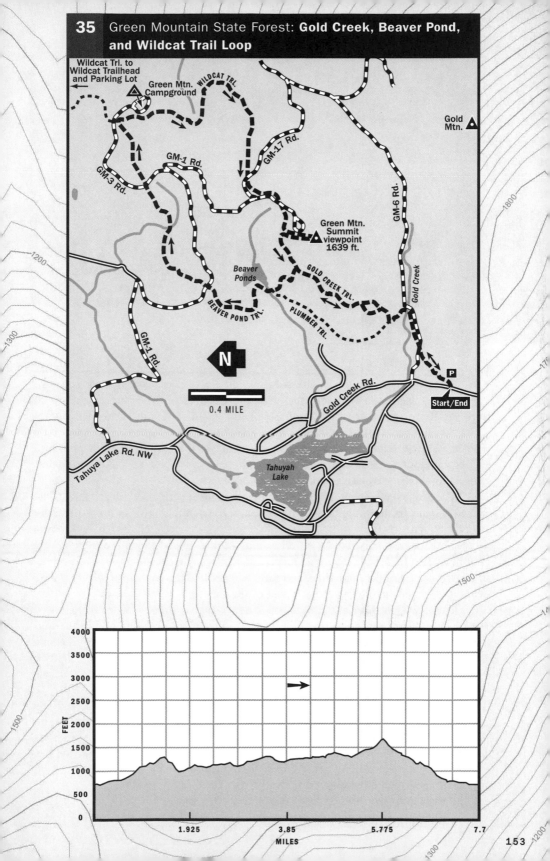

Wildcat Trl. to
Wildcat Trailhead
and Parking Lot

Green Mtn.
Campground

WILDCAT TRL.

Gold
Mtn.

GM-1 Rd.

GM-17 Rd.

GM-3 Rd.

GM-6 Rd.

Green Mtn.
Summit
viewpoint
1639 ft.

Beaver
Ponds

GOLD CREEK TRL.

Gold Creek

BEAVER POND TRL.

PLUMMER TRL.

GM-1 Rd.

N

0.4 MILE

P

Gold Creek Rd.

Start/End

Tahuya Lake Rd. NW

Tahuyah
Lake

1200

1300

1800

1500

1500

FEET

4000

3500

3000

2500

2000

1500

1000

500

0

1.925

3.85

5.775

7.7

MILES

Summer sky from Green Mountain
summit

The obvious exception is Green Mountain State Forest, a managed woodland run by the Washington Department of Natural Resources. At the heart of the 6,000-acre forest are the twin summits of Green and Gold mountains, the two highest points on the peninsula. Gold might hold a slight edge in altitude, but Green is the one to visit, the latter featuring an extensive network of multiuse trails, a central campground, and wide-ranging views from the summit. If you're looking for a hike on Kitsap, this is the place to go.

The slopes of Green Mountain are still considered a "working forest," so selected stands of trees are periodically harvested for timber. This is not a protected wilderness area; its trails serve a range of recreational users, including hikers, equestrians, mountain bikers, and even all-terrain vehicle riders and motorcyclists. The mountain is sufficiently large and spread out, though, that conflicts between groups are rare, and natural geographic segregation helps to keep human-powered visitors separate from engine-powered ones most of the time.

The new Gold Creek trailhead sits about a quarter mile away from the site of the old one; it was reborn as part of a grand improvement plan initiated in the mid-1990s to combat the vandalism, abuse, and neglect that were then plaguing the state forest. The spacious parking lot is now well-maintained, providing room for plenty of vehicles and a latrine. A radio tower visible on the ridge to the northeast marks the destination of the hike on the mountain's summit.

The dusty trail begins at the northern end of the parking lot through the stumps of a former clear-cut, elevation 650 feet. Foxgloves, daisies, and many other wildflowers fill the field with color in the summer as the path runs through several forks in the low brush. Follow a series of blue and white Trail signs to find the best way. Turn right on abandoned gravel road, signed GM-6 (which leads up from the old trailhead), and then cross chattering Gold Creek on a sturdy footbridge.

Immediately over the bridge, make a sharp left onto the Gold Creek Trail and climb a short rise. The trail is marked with a low vertical post in the ground, typical for the area. As part of the recent rehabilitation, many unofficial trails have been blocked off and closed; they're visible as you continue ascending on the dry, sandy tread. Stay right to remain on the Gold Creek Trail past a junction with the Plummer Trail, turn left at a small clearing, and then choose either path at a strange fork whose two branches converge again another quarter mile up the hill.

The surrounding ecosystem—with madrones, rhododendrons, salal, and low, scrubby trees as the norm—is quite different from a typical Cascade lowland environment. Much of the difference can be attributed to the Olympic Mountains only 20 miles to the west, which cast a substantial rain shadow over the region and keep it quite a bit drier than its latitude would generally indicate.

Near 1,300 feet, cross beneath some old power lines with a west-facing view down to Tahuya Lake and the Olympics beyond. Descend slightly to a major intersection, about 1.5 miles from the trailhead. To the right, the Gold Creek Trail continues uphill and joins the Vista Trail to the summit, providing a short out-and-back option. This is also the return route for the extended loop to the top, which is described below.

Turn left down the hill on the Beaver Pond Trail and then bend back around to the right, heading north. Ferns appear in the understory and small creeks flow down the mountainside, shaded by tall trees that slow evaporation. Stay straight to remain on the Beaver Pond Trail past the Plummer Trail and then cross a creek and turn right, heading upstream. The first beaver pond (one of two swampy, stagnant pools full of reeds, lilies, and downed logs) appears soon after.

Cross foxglove-lined road GM-1 at an elevation of just more than 1,000 feet. Despite the presence of motorcycles and all-terrain vehicles elsewhere on the mountain, the only sounds you are likely to hear in the forest are natural: birds singing, frogs croaking, insects buzzing. Follow the Beaver Pond Trail for another half mile through a pleasant forest to cross road GM-3 and start climbing again on the far side.

Reach the GM-3 road a second time at a junction with the Wildcat Trail from the north. Stay right on the near side of the road to join the Wildcat and pass by the Green Mountain Campground in the trees. Noticeably wider and smoother than the single-track Beaver Pond Trail, the Wildcat Trail climbs for a mile on the eastern side of the mountain with views out to Seattle and Mount Rainier through some gaps on the left. The radio installation on the top of Gold Mountain appears around a bend, and then the summit of Green Mountain swings into view as well.

Cross road GM-17 near 1,250 feet and then meet GM-1 just above. The trail crosses the road, then runs parallel to it on the left side for 100 yards in a clear-cut before crossing back again. After a quarter mile through a thick, dark forest of low trees, turn left at a junction with the Vista Trail. Pass along the parking lot at the end of GM-1 (it is possible to drive here) and climb another 200 feet to emerge at the 1,639-foot summit. Although this is just about 1,000 feet above the trailhead, the total vertical gain via the long loop is closer to twice that amount.

The main, rocky overlook provides views over Gold Mountain to the cranes of Bremerton to the east, with Bainbridge Island, the high rises of Seattle, and the distant Cascades behind. On a clear day, it is possible to make out the white cone of Mount Baker far off to the north. Past some picnic tables on the western side of the summit, another viewpoint looks out through trees to the Hood Canal and some of the high peaks of the Olympic Range, often veiled by clouds.

Start down on the Vista Trail and turn left at the junction with the Gold Creek Trail to complete the loop in another quarter mile. Return to the trailhead the way you came.

▶ NEARBY ACTIVITIES

Wildcat Lake County Park provides conventional recreation opportunities like swimming, volleyball, picnicking, and fishing in a scenic lakefront setting. To reach the lake, turn right on Gold Creek Road W from the trailhead and then turn right again on Northwest Holly Road after about 3 miles. The park is another 3 miles on the right, at 9025 Holly Road. For more information, visit the Wildcat Lake County Park Web site at **www.kitsapgov.com/parks/regionalparks/wildcat_lake_cp.htm**.

HOOD CANAL AND THELER WETLANDS

▶ IN BRIEF

Biology, botany, and ecology are just a few of the subjects taught in the living classroom of the Theler Wetlands. With an educational community center and more than 3 miles of trails that explore the saltwater and freshwater marshes at the head of the Hood Canal, even seasoned naturalists are sure to come away from a hike at Theler with new knowledge, understanding, and appreciation of the natural world.

▶ DESCRIPTION

When Samuel Theler deeded his 72-acre wetland property to the local community, it's doubtful he really knew the value of what he was giving away; at that time in the late 1960s there was little popular demand for wetlands preservation. The modern environmental movement was only in its earliest stages, far from the considerable political force it would later become. These days, the Hood Canal Wetlands Project, which includes the Theler Wetlands, has grown to 135 acres and has become a local favorite.

However, in the decades since Theler's generous donation, the Belfair community has frequently

▶ DIRECTIONS

From downtown Seattle: Take the ferry across Puget Sound to Bremerton. After exiting the ferry, drive west on WA 304 following signs to WA 3. Turn left (south) on WA 3 and continue through Gorst to the town of Belfair. The trailhead is located in the parking lot of the Mary E. Theler Community Center, 1 mile past the main intersection in Belfair, on the right (west) side of WA 3 across from the Belfair Elementary School. From Tacoma: Travel on WA 16 (west) across the Tacoma Narrows bridge and continue all the way to WA 3 in Gorst. Then follow WA 3 (west) to Belfair and find the trailhead as described above.

ⓘ KEY AT-A-GLANCE INFORMATION

LENGTH: 2.5 miles (round-trip) on River Estuary Trail; nearly 4 miles to explore all trails

CONFIGURATION: Out-and-back with side trails

DIFFICULTY: Easy

SCENERY: Education center with interpretive garden, abundant wildlife, bird-watching, and views of scenic marshlands and Hood Canal

EXPOSURE: Exposed on Marsh and River trails, shaded on Swamp Trail

TRAFFIC: High

TRAIL SURFACE: Mostly gravel (barrier-free) with boardwalk over marshlands and swamps

HIKING TIME: 1–3 hours

ACCESS: Hikable year-round; no fees for parking or park access

MAPS: USGS Belfair

FACILITIES: Restroom at trailhead; no drinking water available

Hood Canal and Theler Wetlands

Latitude: North 47d26.293m

Longitude: West 122d50.163m

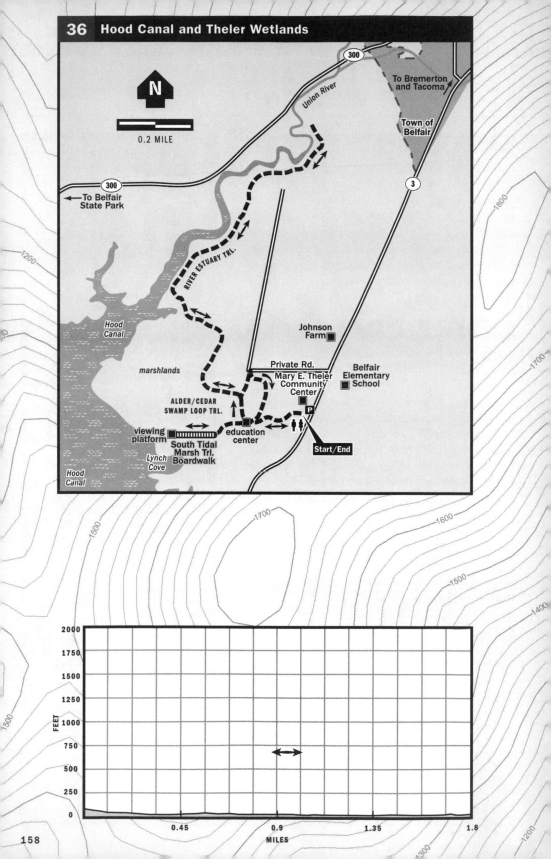

N

0.2 MILE

300

Union River

To Bremerton
and Tacoma

Town of
Belfair

300

← To Belfair
State Park

3

RIVER ESTUARY TRL.

Hood Canal

Johnson
Farm

marshlands

Private Rd.

Mary E. Theler
Community
Center

Belfair
Elementary
School

ALDER/CEDAR
SWAMP LOOP TRL.

P

viewing
platform

education
center

South Tidal
Marsh Trl.
Boardwalk

Start/End

Lynch
Cove

Hood
Canal

2000

1750

1500

1250

1000

FEET

750

500

250

0

0.45

0.9

1.35

1.8

MILES

Hood Canal from South Tidal
Marsh Trail boardwalk

squabbled over just how the property should be used and whether or not a related financial trust has been appropriately managed, arguments that unfortunately continue today around a proposed Pacific Northwest Salmon Center. At the heart of the debate is the regrettably vague directive given by Theler himself about the fate of his land, words that are now interpreted and analyzed with some of the same passion and scrutiny that the Supreme Court might apply to determine the Founding Fathers' "original intent" in writing the Constitution.

For better or worse, the task of administering the gift fell to the North Mason School District, which chose to devote the land to educational purposes. Whether Sam Theler intended it or not, this forward-thinking decision provides many benefits, both for Belfair residents and for anyone else who visits the wetlands and discovers the natural treasures within.

Park in front of the Mary E. Theler Community Center, named for Sam's wife. Start on the gravel road that runs downhill and enters the preserve through a big gate, barrier-free and wheelchair-accessible like the entire network of trails on the site. Descend through two rock walls to reach a boardwalk through the forest, with many plants common to the area identified along the way, like skunk cabbage, Pacific bleeding heart, bear grass, twinberry, and serviceberry.

These plants are only a warm-up for what follows—a comprehensive interpretive garden with enough different species that even a serious botanist might be hard-pressed to name them all. At the heart of the garden stands several structures: the Mary E. Theler Exhibit Building, the Hood Canal Watershed Center, and the North Mason School District Classroom, all designed to educate and inform the public about the local environment; particular emphasis is placed on programs for children. There is even an outdoor "lecture hall" and a huge gray-whale skeleton hanging overhead.

Three different trails head out from the educational center, each worth exploring. The South Tidal Marsh Trail runs on an elevated boardwalk over the rim of the canal to the edge of Lynch Cove. Despite dead-ending at a viewing platform after only a quarter mile, the marsh trail offers plenty to see along the way. Visiting this location during high and low tides can provide vastly different experiences; a huge mudflat hidden beneath the water is only exposed when the tide is out.

This is a great place to watch for ospreys and bald eagles, just a few of the multitude of bird species that visit the area or call it home. A rudimentary list might also include loons, grebes, plovers, sandpipers, gulls, terns, doves, owls, chickadees, hummingbirds, wrens, thrushes, sparrows, warblers, not to mention more-common herons, ducks, and geese. The dizzying number of bird species potentially present is a direct testimony to the diversity of life supported in the estuary environment at the heart of the wetlands, where the freshwater of the Union River intermingles with the saltwater of the Hood Canal.

The Alder–Cedar Swamp Trail offers an alternate look into wetland diversity by showcasing a forested bog, characterized by an abundance of red alders and western red cedars. Along the third-of-a-mile walk, interpretive signs provide nuggets of interesting information, such as the true definition of a swamp: a wetland with a tree canopy. Sword ferns are common in the damp understory, also favored by frogs and other small amphibians.

The River Estuary Trail is the longest option available and offers the best hiking opportunity, heading 1.25 miles upstream along the Union River to create a 2.5-mile, out-and-back trip. The trail starts out toward the river on a raised berm with wetlands on both sides that are perfect habitat for a variety of ducks. A sea of cattails, grasses, and reeds grow out of the shallow water, along with some nasty-looking thistles and blackberry bushes at the edge. The privately owned Johnson Farm lies off to the right, bordering the Theler property.

The trail continues on gravel to the edge of the broad and shallow river, then follows the bank to the northeast. During the fall run, salmon can be observed swimming upstream to spawn, and several other species of fish populate the river year-round. A good set of polarized lenses can help make them easier to spot through the surface glare. But the fish do not make themselves too obvious, lest they end up as food for raptors who watch carefully overhead.

Proceed up the river to the end of the trail and then retrace your steps to the beginning, as the only exit from the trail system is at the trailhead where you began.

▶ NEARBY ACTIVITIES

Belfair State Park provides many recreational opportunities along the Hood Canal shoreline, including a freshwater lagoon for swimming. The park is located 3 miles west of the town of Belfair on N Shore Road (also known as SR 300), which runs right along the canal. A public boat launch is available another 2 miles father along. For more information, visit the Belfair State Park Web site at **www.parks.wa.gov**.

EBEY'S LANDING STATE PARK AND NATIONAL HISTORIC RESERVE

▶ IN BRIEF

Ebey's Landing is one of the most spectacular and historically significant locations anywhere on Puget Sound. Reminiscent of the golden hills above San Francisco Bay, the high bluffs provide sweeping views of the water from the Olympic Peninsula to Vancouver Island. Bald eagles perch in the trees overhead. And the long stretch of driftwood-strewn shoreline around Perego's Lagoon is any beachcomber's dream.

▶ DESCRIPTION

Isaac Ebey landed on the western side of Whidbey Island in 1850, drawn by a geographically unusual grassland he found just north of Admiralty Head. (Unfortunately, he was beheaded some years later by members of the Haida tribe as a result of an ongoing dispute.) The open prairie did not have to be cleared of trees for development, a particularly valuable commodity among the dense virgin forests of the Pacific Northwest,

▶ DIRECTIONS

From Interstate 5 north of Seattle, take Exit 182, WA 525, toward the Mukilteo Ferry. Continue on WA 525, also signed as Mukilteo Speedway, for nearly 9 miles to the town of Mukilteo and drive onto the ferry to Clinton on Whidbey Island. In Clinton, continue on WA 525, which eventually becomes WA 20, for approximately 28 miles to Coupeville. On the outskirts of Coupeville turn left off WA 20 onto Ebey Road. In a short distance, continue straight where another road bends left and follow Ebey Road all the way to the shoreline. The parking area for Ebey's Landing is on the right where Ebey Road turns left to follow the shoreline. Ebey's Landing can also be reached from the northern end of Whidbey Island by following WA 20 from Burlington on I-5.

ⓘ KEY AT-A-GLANCE INFORMATION

LENGTH: 3.5 miles (plus 1.7-mile optional out-and-backside trip)

CONFIGURATION: Loop

DIFFICULTY: Moderate

SCENERY: Bird-watching, beach walking, colorful Perego Lagoon, spectacular ocean views from the Bluff Trail

EXPOSURE: Exposed the entire way

TRAFFIC: Medium

TRAIL SURFACE: Half dirt, half sandy beach walking

HIKING TIME: 2–4 hours

ACCESS: Hikable year-round; no fees for parking or park access

MAPS: USGS Coupeville

FACILITIES: Restroom at trailhead; no drinking water available

Ebey's Landing State Park and National Historic Reserve

Latitude: North 48d11.545m

Longitude: West 122d42.514m

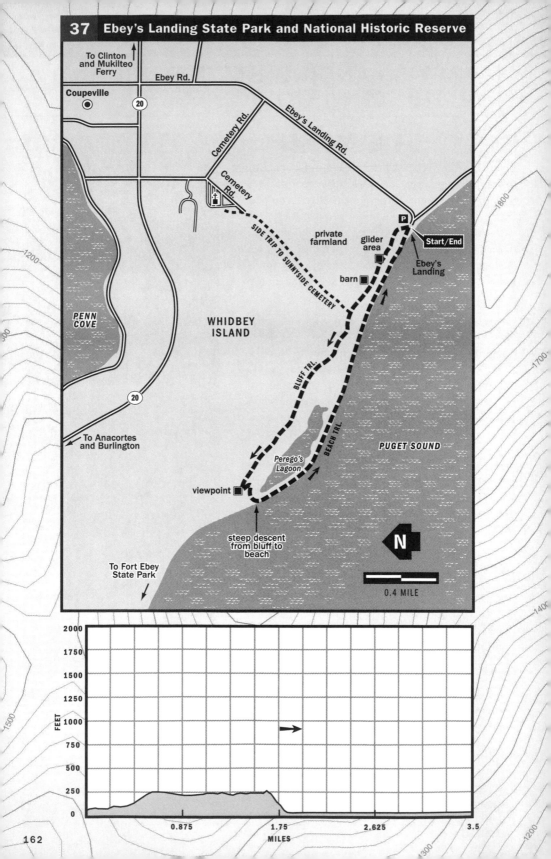

To Clinton
and Mukilteo
Ferry

Ebey Rd.

Coupeville

20

Cemetery Rd.

Ebey's Landing Rd.

Cemetery Rd.

SIDE TRIP TO SUNNYSIDE CEMETERY

P

Start/End

private
farmland

glider
area

Ebey's
Landing

barn

WHIDBEY
ISLAND

PENN
COVE

BLUFF TRL.

BEACH TRL.

PUGET SOUND

20

To Anacortes
and Burlington

Perego's
Lagoon

viewpoint

steep descent
from bluff to
beach

N

To Fort Ebey
State Park

0.4 MILE

1800

1200

1700

900

1400

1500

1300

1200

FEET

2000
1750
1500
1250
1000
750
500
250
0

0.875   1.75   2.625   3.5
MILES

making it the perfect place for a farm. A century and a half later, the property is mostly unchanged, with the open fields still in use for agriculture and the beaches below retaining much of their original wild and untouched state. And visitors can expect to leave with great memories and photographs.

Ebey's Landing was established in 1978 as the first U.S. National Historic Reserve, and even from the access road it's easy to see why the government thought the area was worth preserving. Apart from its considerable historic value as one of the oldest settlements in Washington State, the beauty of the natural surroundings is obvious in the steep headlands that stretch up and down the coast.

Start hiking from the northern end of the parking lot through the dry grass above the sandy beach and then climb some wooden stairs to the right. The entire hike forms an elongated loop, which is easier to travel in the counterclockwise direction by starting up the bluff and then returning along the shoreline.

The stairs lead up to the working farmland of Ebey's Prairie, where the trail skirts the western end of the alfalfa fields and begins to ascend the bluff. A designated area is set aside for model-glider hobbyists, who fly their graceful aircraft over the beach and the fields thanks to updrafts and ocean breezes.

A wooden fence marks the end of the privately owned farmland. From this point, the Ebey's Prairie Trail heads inland along the fence to reach Sunnyside Cemetery, a worthwhile side trip that adds 1.7 miles to the total distance. The cemetery houses the graves of Isaac Ebey and many other early pioneers and is guarded by the historic Crockett Blockhouse, a square-timbered structure built for defending the area.

The Bluff Trail continues uphill through a mix of wildflowers, Oregon grape, and reedy grasses, leveling off about 200 feet above the beach. From the top, the views are unparalleled across Admiralty Inlet to Port Townsend, the high peaks of the Olympic Range, Dungeness Spit, and the noticeably barren Protection Island. Victoria and Vancouver Island lie across the Strait of Juan de Fuca to the north. In between, all manner of oceangoing vessels sail by, including freighters, ferries, pleasure craft, and even the occasional aircraft carrier or submarine.

You can look straight down on kelp fronds growing in the greenish water just offshore and the vibrant mix of earth tones that surround the shallows of Perego's Lagoon, which becomes visible as the trail pushes on to the north. The lagoon usually looks like a lake, fully separated from Puget Sound by a thin strip of beach, but the outer barrier is occasionally breached by high waters from the sea.

Many species of birds reside on the bluff, including gulls, sparrows, robins, and thrushes. Watch for bald eagles that sit in the stunted and twisted trees on the top of the headlands and survey the water below for fish and other prey. Coyotes make rare appearances on the exposed slope as well, quickly disappearing into the woods.

The Bluff Trail dead-ends at a high lookout with a good view to the south, back the way you came. Descend on a sandy trail dropping straight down to the beach just before the viewpoint. The main advantage of completing the loop in the counterclockwise direction is taking this steep slope downhill, instead of up.

On the shore, it is possible to continue north along the bottom of the cliffs as far as Fort Ebey State Park, a little more than 2 miles away. This portion of the seashore is generally deserted, an undisturbed beachcomber's paradise that's passable during just about any tide. Arranging a car shuttle at the end allows for a great one-way hike.

Perego's Lagoon from the
Bluff Trail

However, the standard return along the beach has plenty to offer, as well. The sun-bleached driftwood is stacked so deep it looks like a mammoth boneyard, sure to keep children occupied for hours. Treasures of all kinds can be found in the sand along the way, especially when the tide pools are exposed between the barnacle and algae-covered rocks.

▶ NEARBY ACTIVITIES

Ebey's Landing is bracketed by two fascinating former military installations—Fort Ebey State Park to the north and Fort Casey State Park to the south. Underutilized Fort Ebey features an extensive concrete bunker system above an unspoiled beach. The more popular Fort Casey also has a concrete bunker, impressively capped by two massive guns still aimed out over Admiralty Inlet, as well as a historic lighthouse, open playing fields, and the famous Fort Casey Inn, converted from the original World War I officers' quarters. Both parks are right off of WA 20. For more information, visit the Fort Casey and Fort Ebey Web sites at **www.parks.wa.gov**.

USELESS BAY TIDELANDS

▶ IN BRIEF

Useless Bay is a true oddity; the only hike in this book without any semblance of a trail. Instead, the bay provides a few miles of wild saltwater shoreline on Puget Sound for free wandering and discovery. An out-and-back trip on the beach to Double Bluff makes a good 4-mile round-trip hike, but many visitors will find the plentiful and welcome distractions along the way to be worthwhile destinations in and of themselves.

▶ DESCRIPTION

Useless Bay joins Point No Point, Deception Pass, and Cape Disappointment in a long list of colorful geographic place names given to locations on the rugged coast of the Pacific Northwest; the terms were typically assigned by early seafaring explorers who had trouble navigating the region's notoriously hazardous currents and stormy seas. For land-based visitors to these spectacular settings, however, there is little connection to the sailors' troubles–and Useless Bay is no exception. The tidal mudflats that likely make the bay useless for anchoring purposes make it anything but useless for beachbound adventurers, who can find all manner of marine riches along the shoreline.

Although the beach at Useless Bay can be hiked at any time, it is best to plan your trip on an

ℹ KEY AT-A-GLANCE INFORMATION

LENGTH: 4 miles (can be extended beyond Double Bluff)

CONFIGURATION: Out-and-back

DIFFICULTY: Easy

SCENERY: Abundant marine life at lower tides, beach walking; views across Puget Sound all the way to Seattle

EXPOSURE: Exposed the entire way

TRAFFIC: Low after leaving the crowds near the parking area.

TRAIL SURFACE: Sandy beach

HIKING TIME: 3–4 hours

ACCESS: Hikable year-round; no fees for parking or park access

MAPS: USGS Hansville

FACILITIES: Restrooms and water at trailhead

▶ DIRECTIONS

From I-5 north of Seattle, take Exit 182, WA 525, toward the Mukilteo Ferry. Continue on WA 525, also signed as Mukilteo Speedway, for nearly 9 miles to the town of Mukilteo and drive onto the ferry to Clinton on Whidbey Island. In Clinton, continue on WA 525 for more than 8 miles to Double Bluff Road on the left just before the town of Freeland. Drive to the end of Double Bluff Road, where Shore Avenue bends left, and find the Useless Bay beach access parking area.

Useless Bay Tidelands

Latitude: North 47d58.935m

Longitude: West 122d30.856m

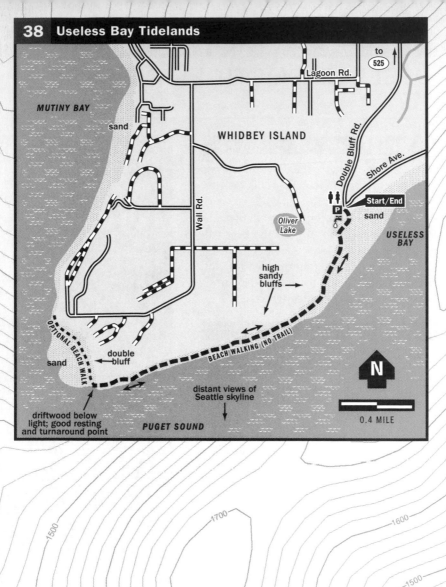

MUTINY BAY

sand

WHIDBEY ISLAND

Lagoon Rd.

to 525

Double Bluff Rd.

Shore Ave.

Start/End

sand

USELESS BAY

Wall Rd.

Oliver Lake

1800

high sandy bluffs

P

OPTIONAL BEACH WALK

double bluff

sand

BEACH WALKING (NO TRAIL)

1700

N

0.4 MILE

driftwood below light; good resting and turnaround point

distant views of Seattle skyline

PUGET SOUND

1200

1300

1500

1700

1600

1500

1400

1300

1200

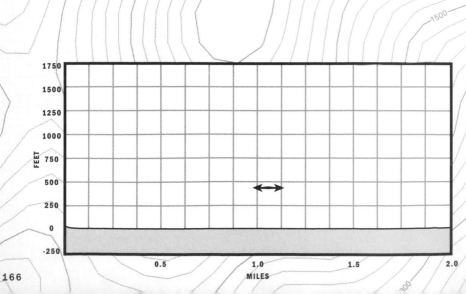

ebb tide, when the beach is effectively twice its normal size and the flourishing life below the high-water line is exposed. Check local tide charts for more information.

The Useless Bay Tidelands are technically part of the Washington State Park system. But the land is not shown as a park on most maps and the area remains undeveloped, except for a few facilities adjacent to the parking lot. Private beachfront houses run along the shore to the east toward Deer Lagoon and Sunlight Beach, with small pleasure-craft moored out on the water. If you arrive at low tide these boats might be resting on the mud, which stretches almost a quarter mile away from the shore without any significant drop-off.

The extensive shallows are formed by the prominent point at Double Bluff, which intercepts northbound tidal currents in Puget Sound and forces the flow into Useless Bay to deposit sand and dirt while sheltering the bay from southbound currents that might otherwise carry the sediment away. These same two forces also result in the high quantities of flotsam and jetsam that collect on the shore, noticeably more than on the typically west-facing beaches up and down the coast of Whidbey Island.

From the parking lot, head west along the sand toward the high bluffs. Although dogs must be leashed for the first quarter mile, beyond a prominent windsock four-footed explorers are as free to wander as their two-legged companions, who swim, wade, dig for clams, poke around in the logs and grasses above the high-water line, and participate in a host of other recreational activities on the water's edge.

The sandy cliffs rise almost 300 feet above the beach at the nearest headlands, forming a natural psychological barrier for most visitors. Once you are around the point and the parking lot has disappeared from view, the shoreline receives very little traffic. Surprisingly, the Seattle skyline is visible straight out to the south, poking above the intervening landmass of the Magnolia neighborhood about 25 miles away. Nonetheless, the city seems very distant and far removed from this piece of remote and wild coast.

A staggering variety of marine life can be found on the beach. And bird-watchers will enjoy spotting such diverse species as bald eagles, belted kingfishers, grebes, terns, goldeneyes, and great blue herons. Harbor seals occasionally swim by or even come up on the land.

But it is the smaller life forms that tend to be the most interesting, particularly in the intertidal zone. At first glance it might seem there is not much to see, yet patient inspection reveals entire worlds of activity, suggesting the emergence of primordial life from the ocean millions of years ago. All manner of cockles, mussels, and barnacles cling to the rocks, fighting for space with anemones and other mollusks. Green seaweed and algae provide shelter for scampering crabs. And multiple tide pools hide minnows, snails, and starfish. Buried clams spray water in mini-fountains from beneath the sand, giving away their hidden positions, while insects swarm overhead.

Fascinating shells, cast-offs from bottom-dwelling organisms in deeper water, are everywhere as well. Most are bleached as white as the ubiquitous driftwood and come in standard clam-like shapes and sizes. But less-common fans, spirals, and cones appear in exotic colors like red, brown, and even purple. Plenty of evidence of human marine activity also ends up at Useless Bay—some welcome and some not—

but it is always interesting to speculate how these items might have come to be tossed up here by the waves.

The hike to Double Bluff at the western end of the bay is only 2 miles one way, but covering the distance can be deceptively difficult and time-consuming. Walking through the sand and rocks is much slower than on a firmer and smoother surface, there is virtually no shade or protection from the sun, and almost everything along the way invites lengthy contemplation. It will be particularly hard to get children all the way to the end since they will find so much of interest en route. However, if the 4-mile round-trip journey to Double Bluff is not enough, it is possible to continue around the point and hike northwards along the next beach, below some nice waterfront houses.

EVERETT, EDMONDS, AND US 2 STEVENS PASS AREA

SPENCER ISLAND NATURAL WILDLIFE RESERVE

 KEY AT-A-GLANCE INFORMATION

LENGTH: 4.5 miles (round-trip) plus optional northern-island trails

CONFIGURATION: Out-and-back

DIFFICULTY: Easy and flat

SCENERY: Wildlife watching and bird-watching, wetlands, interpretive boardwalk trails, river and mountain views

EXPOSURE: Mostly exposed

TRAFFIC: Medium

TRAIL SURFACE: Mixture of dirt, gravel, paved, and boardwalk

HIKING TIME: 2–4 hours

ACCESS: Hikable year-round during daylight hours; no fees for parking or park access

MAPS: USGS Everett

FACILITIES: Restroom at nearby Langus Riverfront Park; no drinking water available

Spencer Island Natural Wildlife Reserve

Latitude: North 47d59.634m

Longitude: West 122d10.757m

▶ IN BRIEF

Spencer Island sits at the center of the biologically flourishing Snohomish River Estuary, home to countless animals and plants, including more than 350 known species of birds. A series of trails explores the rich life of the wetlands, great for naturalists, bird-watchers, and hikers.

▶ DESCRIPTION

Just north of downtown Everett, freshwater from the mouth of the Snohomish River mingles with the saltwater of Possession Sound, creating a highly dynamic environment and forming critical habitat for hundreds of species. However, these same dynamic forces are frequently not so kind to the land itself. Rising and sinking saltwater tides coupled with seasonal flooding cause the ground to endlessly shift and erode, only to be built up somewhere else. Sitting at the center of the estuary, Spencer Island often gets the brunt of the relentless waters, and in many ways it continues to exist thanks only to an extensive series of dikes and levees designed to keep the river and the ocean at bay.

The system is certainly not failsafe, though, and the largely wood-chip dikes are in constant need of repair. The fragility of the system was graphically displayed in 2003, when catastrophic

▶ DIRECTIONS

From Interstate 5 in Everett, take the Marine View Drive exit (Exit 195) and turn left onto East Marine View Drive. Continue north then turn right onto WA 529 over the Snohomish River Bridge toward Marysville. Take the first right, then immediately turn right again following signs to Langus Riverfront Park. Turn left at the stop sign at Ross Avenue and continue past the marinas to another intersection and veer right onto Smith Island Road. At the southern end of Langus Riverfront Park is a parking lot and trailhead under I-5.

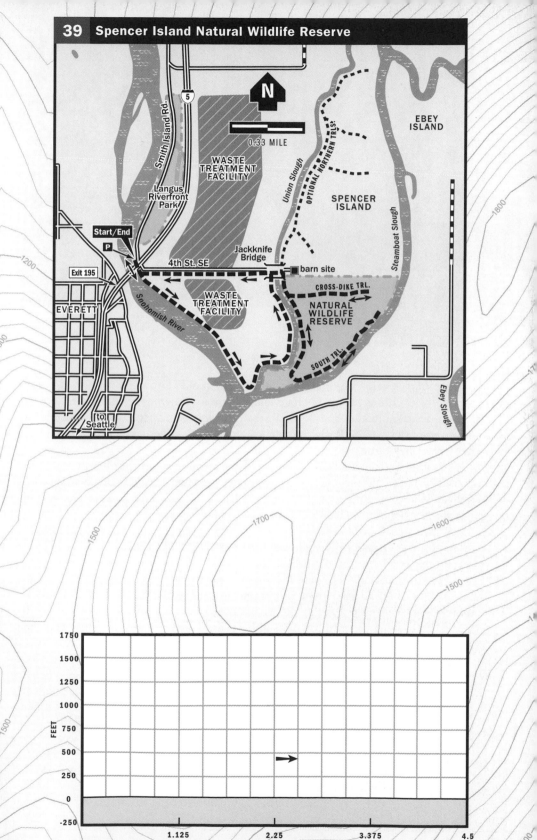

N

0.33 MILE

I-5

Smith Island Rd.

WASTE TREATMENT FACILITY

Langus Riverfront Park

Union Slough

OPTIONAL NORTHERN TRLS.

EBEY ISLAND

SPENCER ISLAND

Steamboat Slough

Start/End

P

Exit 195

4th St. SE

Jackknife Bridge

barn site

CROSS-DIKE TRL.

EVERETT

Snohomish River

WASTE TREATMENT FACILITY

NATURAL WILDLIFE RESERVE

SOUTH TRL.

Ebey Slough

[to] Seattle

1800

1700

1200

1300

1200

1500

1700

1600

1500

1500

1500

FEET

1750

1500

1250

1000

750

500

250

0

-250

1.125

2.25

3.375

4.5

MILES

Cattails at Spencer Island

damage from several large breaches and a fire smoldering within one of the dikes caused the closure of several key trails and significantly altered the landscape. Recovery and construction work—both to repair the considerable damage and also for ongoing maintenance to prevent further problems—still continue and should be expected for the foreseeable future.

Just as the island sits at the center of the swirling waters of the estuary, so too does it lie in the middle of a mix of government jurisdictions, creating a strange juxtaposition of conflicting uses. The southern half is administered as a Natural Wildlife Reserve by Snohomish County Parks and Recreation, while the northern half, run by the Washington Department of Fish and Wildlife, is open for hunting in season. Yet even with this apparently paradoxical division, the island remains a great place to explore the fascinating Snohomish Estuary.

From the parking lot, there are two different ways to reach the island. The most direct route is on Fourth Street SE heading straight to the Jackknife Bridge, a little more than a half mile away to the east. However, a more interesting route to the bridge leads along the river to the south on the Langus Waterfront Trail and then back up the shoreline of the Union Slough, about 1.5 miles altogether.

The Langus Waterfront Trail promises little in the way of a natural experience at the start, as it is fully paved and almost directly under I-5. The first half mile is only marginally better, with significant industrial development on the far shore and the path bordering the Everett wastewater facility on the left. The exposed treatment pools can occasionally be glimpsed through the trees, and unfortunately the odor tends to waft over the trail unless merciful winds blow it back the other way.

However, things start to improve a little farther along, where tangled blackberry bushes and some benches appear on either side. By the time you reach Union Slough after 0.8 miles, the setting becomes much more pleasant. Follow the slough northward through grasses, reeds, and trees, looking out over the southern end of Spencer Island just across the water to the right.

Jackknife Bridge spans Union Slough where the trail rejoins Fourth Street SE from the parking lot. Cross the bridge to reach the island at a well-signed junction on the far side. The ruins of a barn sit straight ahead among a sea of cattails, all that remains of the now-closed cattle-ranching operation that spawned the original set of dikes to hold back the water. A boardwalk near the old barn site leads to an interpretive sign.

It was once possible to complete a 3.5-mile grand loop all the way around the perimeter of the island, but the damage to the dikes in 2003 unfortunately eliminated that popular route. The best remaining routes are on the South Trail and the Cross-Dike Trail, which total about 2 miles. These trails are in the natural reserve and away from bicyclists, dogs, boats, and hunters, so they are sure to provide the most attractive option for the majority of hikers.

Start south on the dirt trail, a right turn as you step off the bridge. Another short interpretive boardwalk leads to an overlook on the left, with excellent views over the reeds; helpful information about the marsh ecosystem is provided by easily noticeable displays. On a clear day, a chain of prominent peaks is visible in the Cascades, including Whitehorse Mountain, Three Fingers, and Mount Pilchuck, with Mount Baker rising far to the north. If the wind is calm, look for reflections of the snow-clad peaks in the still waters below.

Just past the boardwalk, the Cross-Dike Trail leads off to the left on a raised berm through the center of the island. For now, continue along Union Slough on the South Trail. Soon you will reach a bridge (likely seen earlier from the Langus Waterfront Trail on the opposite bank) that may host bird-watching photographers. The bridge provides a flat and stable tripod platform, necessary for the giant zoom lenses they use.

Bend around to the left at the bottom end of the island, now following Steamboat Slough on the uneven levee surface. Some dilapidated houseboats and barges float on the opposite bank and other occasional watercraft go by. A collection of snags stands along the trail here, formed when the trees were inundated by water over the breached levees and subsequently died. The trees' loss is the bird-watchers' gain; all manner of avian species like to perch in the bare treetops, especially hawks, eagles, and other raptors that use the high vantages to look for food. Part-way up the trunks, man-made bat boxes provide shelter for winged hunters of an altogether different kind.

Soon you'll reach the site of a washed-out bridge where the trail once continued northward to meet the far end of the Cross-Dike Trail. Snohomish County plans to replace this bridge and another that is missing at the east end of the Cross-Dike Trail. Until then, return the way you came. On the way back, you should turn right to explore the heart of the island on the raised embankment of the Cross-Dike Trail. With no vegetation other than the low reeds, panoramic views of the area are available on all sides, providing some of the best opportunities for wildlife observation anywhere at Spencer. Ducks and a host of other waterfowl are impossible to miss any time of year. Also, deer, beavers, and even seals and otters can occasionally be spotted.

After the Cross-Dike Trail, a short walk north returns you to the Jackknife Bridge. From here, it is possible to head straight back to the parking area by following Fourth Street SE and completing a loop, or you may retrace your steps around the longer Langus Waterfront Trail to the left. You also can head along the near side of Union Slough to explore the northern portion of Spencer Island. The main trail stays along the bank of the slough, with numerous out-and-back options available on side trails into the interior.

MEADOWDALE COUNTY PARK AND BEACH

KEY AT-A-GLANCE INFORMATION

LENGTH: 2.5 miles (round-trip)

CONFIGURATION: Out-and-back

DIFFICULTY: Easy to moderate

SCENERY: Lunds creek and gulch, Meadowdale Beach, playfields, and a variety of trees with identification plaques

EXPOSURE: Shaded along the trail, exposed at the beach

TRAFFIC: High

TRAIL SURFACE: Mixture of dirt and gravel

HIKING TIME: 1–2 hours

ACCESS: Hikable year-round; no fees for parking or park access

MAPS: USGS Edmonds East

FACILITIES: Restroom at trailhead; no drinking water available

Meadowdale County Park and Beach

Latitude: North 47d51.432m

Longitude: West 122d18.998m

▶ IN BRIEF

Meadowdale is a valuable rarity among the many good Puget Sound beachfront parks, thanks to restricted road access to the shore. This makes it a great choice for hikers who will enjoy the descent on an easy trail along Lunds Creek, which runs through a beautiful forest on the way to the beach.

▶ DESCRIPTION

Not surprisingly for a waterfront parcel of land in the heavily developed Edmonds region, Meadowdale Park passed through many private hands before being acquired by the Snohomish County Parks and Recreation Department in 1968. Of the private owners, the most significant was surely the Meadowdale Country Club, which built and maintained a clubhouse, swimming pool, and other facilities on site. Most of the evidence of the club is long gone. The memory of John Lund, an early homesteader in the late 1800s, is most obvious today—the hike runs through Lunds Gulch, carved out over the ages by the waters of Lunds Creek.

The trail, which starts on the opposite side of the parking lot from a good-sized madrone tree, curves around a broad bend through the field to the east. Start down the wide surface, circling through the grass, and then enter the forest. The gradual descent and smooth trail make this hike a good option for families with small children, who will find the route interesting but not too difficult.

▶ DIRECTIONS

From I-5 north of Seattle, take Exit 183, 164th Street SW, and turn left (west). After 164th Street SW curves south onto 44th Avenue W, turn right onto 168th Street SW, which immediately crosses over WA 99. Turn right onto 52nd Avenue W, then turn left onto 160th Street SW. Turn right onto 56th Avenue W, then turn left onto 156th Street SW and proceed straight into the Meadowdale Park parking lot.

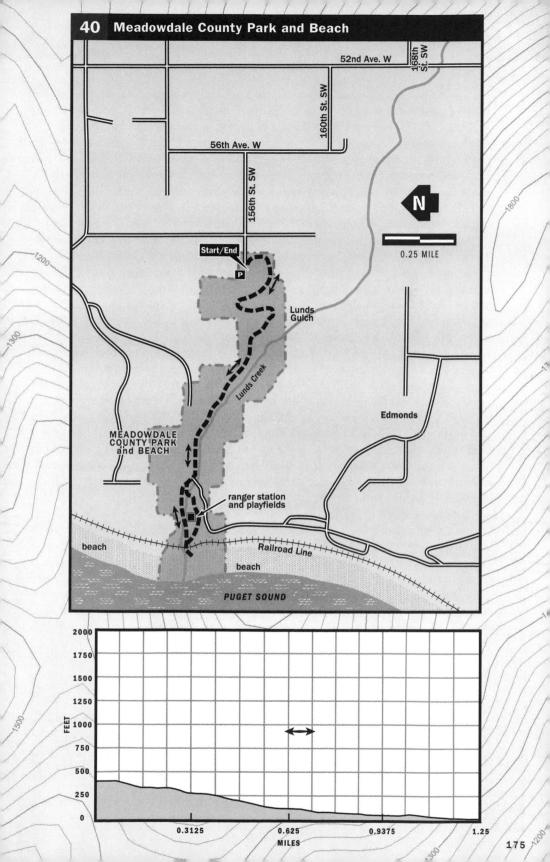

Some wooden stairs and a split-rail fence mark the beginning of a steeper descent into the narrow valley of Lunds Gulch. The fern-covered walls rise 200 feet to the rim, and Lunds Creek soon appears in a gully to the left as the trail runs beneath a mix of maples, Douglas firs, cottonwoods, and alders. Despite its very limited length, the creek carries a number of species of fish, including some salmon that make the run upstream from the ocean to spawn. The mix of freshwater and saltwater at the creek's mouth acts as a tiny estuary, where the young smolts go through the substantial physical changes that allow them to make the transition from life in the freshwater of their birth to the saltwater of their adult lives, the unique adaptation of anadromous fish.

Moss-covered big leaf maples now seem to be the dominant tree species in the forest, but a series of enormous western hemlock stumps near the half-mile mark give some idea of what the original ecosystem here might have been like. Look for the old springboard notches in the wood, used to support the working platforms the loggers used to fell the ancient giants. A few low-to-the-ground interpretive signs help identify some of the major plant species and point out their distinguishing characteristics, such as the heart-shaped leaves of the black cottonwood.

As you near the beach, high alders lean out over the trail from either side, creating an effect similar to a towering arbor trellis. The setting is magical when the sunlight filters through the majestic living archway to the ground below. The trail emerges from the trees and then crosses the creek on a bridge next to a park ranger station on the left. A road connects the ranger's facility to surface streets on the southern side of the gulch, but access is currently restricted, keeping the crowds away. Only disabled individuals who would otherwise be unable to descend the longer trail from the top are permitted to use this approach. Pass through a grassy clearing with a picnic shelter and a volleyball pit and then duck into a short concrete tunnel under railroad tracks to finally reach the beach.

Lunds Creek empties into Possession Sound through the sand, depositing the sediment and runoff it has collected along its course. At low tide, a tiny barrier island serves as a breakwater just offshore. And numerous small tide pools are exposed, ripe for examination. Pieces of sun-bleached driftwood are scattered around the gravelly beach, cast up by the whims of the tide.

Much like the more-popular beaches at Golden Gardens and Carkeek Parks to the south, Meadowdale is a great place to watch the sun set over the Olympic Mountains. Just to the northwest, Possession Point marks the extreme southeastern end of Whidbey Island, and the northern tip of the Kitsap Peninsula sits straight out to the west.

Spend any length of time along the water, and there is a good chance that a freight train will come thundering up the tracks. The sight and sound of the locomotives hauling a mile-or-more-long chain of cars certainly does not enhance the wilderness aspect of the hike, but the spectacle is thrilling nonetheless.

The beach serves as a frequent haul-out site for harbor seals that come up on shore from the water to help regulate their body temperatures, interact with other individuals, and rest or sleep. Young pups that have not yet learned to fear people are particularly vulnerable while on land and should not be disturbed, especially if they are nursing. Seals may potentially be found here at almost any time of year.

After exploring the beach, retrace your steps up Lunds Creek to the trailhead. You will need to climb back up the 400 feet lost on the descent to complete the round-trip journey of approximately 2.5 miles.

WALLACE FALLS STATE PARK

▶ IN BRIEF

This deservedly popular hike leads to an impressive series of waterfalls in the Skykomish River Valley, nine of which drop more than 50 feet and whose centerpiece is the 265-foot Middle Falls. The falls aren't the only attraction, however, as old-growth forest, a wide network of trails, and local history all converge at this year-round park.

▶ DESCRIPTION

From the trailhead, the two most striking features of the landscape are the power lines which stretch along the northern end of the parking lot and the sunset-clock display, the latter reminding day-use visitors to leave before the gates are locked for the night. Needless to say, neither of these items fit into most people's vision of an outdoors experience. The situation doesn't improve much over the hike's first quarter mile, where the trail runs eastward beneath the crackling and humming wires on a gravel access road. However, all of that is soon left behind as soon as the trail turns into the trees, revealing the true nature of Wallace Falls State Park.

Right away, the trail reaches the first fork. The left branch is the Old Railroad Grade, open to foot traffic, bikers, and equestrians. Head through the gate on the right to access the hikers-only Woody Trail. The path is not named for its obvious

ⓘ KEY AT-A-GLANCE INFORMATION

LENGTH: 4 miles (round-trip) to Middle Falls and 5.4 miles (round-trip) to Upper Falls

CONFIGURATION: Out-and-back and loop options

DIFFICULTY: Moderate

SCENERY: Four waterfalls with great vantage points, mossy tree-lined trails, interpretive trail, old railroad grade, and campgrounds

EXPOSURE: Shaded

TRAFFIC: Hike midweek or start early (parking lot fills up on weekends)

TRAIL SURFACE: Dirt (Woody Trail) and gravel (old railroad grade)

HIKING TIME: 2–4 hours

ACCESS: Hikable year round, gates are open 8 a.m.–dusk; Washington State Park Pass required for parking (daily passes available at trailhead)

MAPS: Green Trails–Index 142; USGS Gold Bar

FACILITIES: Restroom at trailhead, water at campground

▶ DIRECTIONS

From I-5 at the northern end of Everett, take Exit 194, US 2 (east). Travel US 2 through the towns of Monroe, Sultan, and Startup. Once you reach the town of Gold Bar, look for the Wallace Falls State Park sign and take a left onto First Street. Then turn right onto May Creek Road and in a short distance stay left at the Y-shaped junction onto Ley Road. Stay left again at the end of Ley Road to enter the state park parking lot.

Wallace Falls State Park

Latitude: North 47d52.031m

Longitude: West 121d40.706m

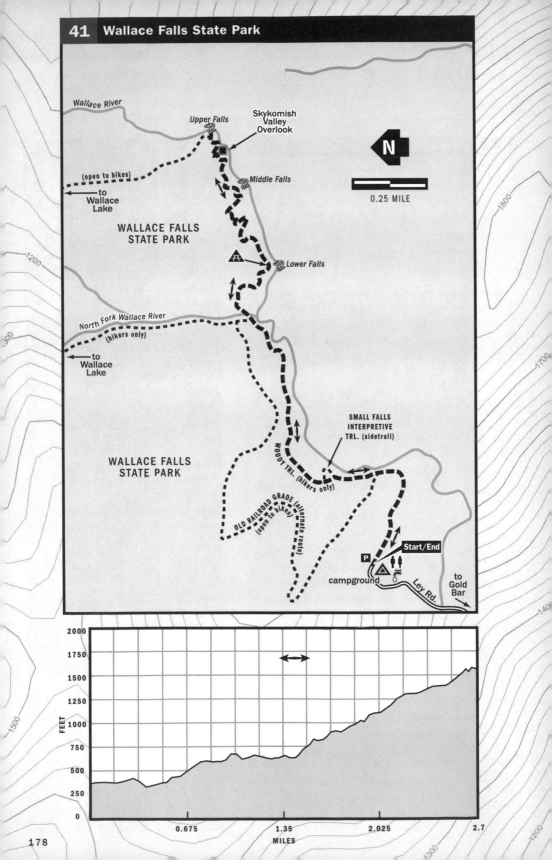

cartoon forest character but instead as a tribute to State Senator Frank Woody, a long-time advocate of youth programs at parks like this one.

Beyond the fence, the Woody Trail narrows to single-track and begins a steady ascent along the northern bank of the Wallace River. Moss hangs in thick coats over the trees, heavy enough to be reminiscent of the Hoh Rain Forest on the Olympic Peninsula. The growth of the moss is aided by mist rising from the fast-moving river, keeping the forest here particularly damp.

The Small Falls Interpretive Trail branches to the left on a boardwalk. Laid out by an Eagle Scout in 1995, the short detour explores a cascading tributary of the Wallace River and explains the methods and history of logging in the area on a series of informative signs.

At the 1-mile mark, the Railroad Grade Cut-Off Trail climbs over a small rise and leads to the Old Railroad Grade Trail. On the way back, this trail provides a good option for creating a small loop, although the route is a mile longer than the Woody Trail.

The Old Railroad Grade was once used to haul logs and timber from the forest to the town of Gold Bar, where they could be sent down the Skykomish River or loaded onto the Great Northern Railroad. It was the arrival of James J. Hill's transcontinental Great Northern line in the late 1800s that allowed the town to flourish, firmly connecting it to growing urban centers on both sides of the mountains.

The value that the growing nation placed on the first cross-country rail connections is hard to imagine today, but the story of the Great Northern gives some idea. In order to establish a railroad linking Lake Superior to the Pacific, Hill was granted some 44 million acres of land, slightly more territory than currently makes up the entire state of Washington. The rail line, established in a checkerboard pattern of public and private ownership, would travel through a wide band approximately 120 miles wide and more than 2,000 miles long.

James Hill instantly became one of the wealthiest and most powerful men in the United States, controlling with his corporation about 25,000 acres of land for every single mile of track he eventually built—and that was before his crucial railroad had ever made a single transcontinental run. Like so many of the vastly influential men of his time, Hill was a strange mix of monopolist, entrepreneur, and robber baron, depending on how his legacy is viewed. The checkerboard patchwork of land ownership that marks most current timber concessions and continues to shape the landscape of the West is also part of Hill's legacy, dating back to the original system of land grants first set down by the government in 1864.

Continue on the Woody Trail and cross the North Fork of the Wallace River at 1.5 miles on a sturdy wooden bridge, and then start a steady climb up the other side through a series of switchbacks. After another 0.3 miles, the picnic shelter provides a good resting point with a view of the Lower Falls, the first of the three main plunges.

Above the picnic shelter the trail becomes more rugged, with exposed roots and rocks. The 2-mile mark is signed with a wooden post in the middle of an uphill section, just short of the fenced overlook for the Middle Falls. At 265 feet, the Middle Falls is one of the highest waterfalls in the state and the most striking anywhere in the park. The river tumbles down through two separate drops, with a series of small pools in between. For some hikers, this makes an excellent turnaround point for a 4-mile out-and-back trip.

Above Middle Falls, the trail becomes steeper and darker, sheltered by the high trees. Even at the height of the summer it tends to be cool here in the perpetual dusk, among the shadows of the thick growth. Just past the 2.5-mile mark the Skykomish Valley Overlook opens out to the right, providing views of the valley below if the weather is good.

The Upper Falls mark the traditional turnaround point for most hikers, 2.7 miles from and 1,200 feet above the trailhead. The falls themselves are another double-tiered-pool drop like the Middle Falls, although not as high.

With close to 4,800 acres of land, Wallace Falls State Park provides plenty of options for longer and more demanding trips. Above the Upper Falls, the trail climbs another 200 feet to Wallace Lake, 2.5 miles away, with Jay and Shaw lakes even farther along. Most of this route follows a logging road favored by mountain bikers; it loops back to both the Old Railroad Grade Trail and a network of Department of Natural Resources roads leading all the way to the town of Startup. A hikers-only trail opened in summer of 2005, roughly following the North Fork of the Wallace River from the end of the railroad grade to Wallace Lake and allowing foot traffic to stay clear of the bikers.

▶ NEARBY ACTIVITIES

Get an intimate look at local history at the Gold Bar Museum and Historical Society on the northern side of US 2 between First and Second Streets in Gold Bar. The exhibits focus on the logging industry and the Great Northern Railway, which together put the city on the map. It is best to call ahead before visiting since hours are limited: (360) 793-2138.

LAKE SERENE AND BRIDAL VEIL FALLS

▶ IN BRIEF

Lake Serene might be the perfect swimming hole. With a fantastic location below the northern wall of Mount Index, crystal-clear water, and a collection of sun-soaked boulders along the shore for diving, it's hard to imagine any better place to spend a summer's day. The tough hike in only adds to the experience, keeping away the worst of the crowds and making the swim seem that much more inviting.

▶ DESCRIPTION

The Washington Cascades are blessed with countless lakes, tarns, and ponds, but there are precious few that can rival Lake Serene. The location is unforgettable, in a bowl at the bottom of the sheer 3,000-foot northern face of Mount Index. Although the peak's signature crags can be easily identified from almost anywhere in the Skykomish Valley, it's the view straight up from the lake that truly shows the mountain's massive vertical relief. If that's not enough, the lake is directly fed by melting snow and ice, leaving the water clean, pure, and cold—and unbelievably refreshing on a hot, sunny day.

If Lake Serene were just off the road, it surely would be overrun every summer weekend and a good portion of the rest of the time as well. Thankfully, access to this alpine treasure needs to be earned, and not everyone is prepared to pay the price. All potential visitors must first complete a strenuous 3.7-mile hike with a 2,000-foot

▶ DIRECTIONS

From I-5 at the northern end of Everett, take Exit 194 US 2 (east). Follow US 2 through the towns of Monroe, Sultan, Startup and Gold Bar. Around milepost 35 (before the road to Index) turn right onto Mount Index Road. In a short distance, turn right into the parking lot for Lake Serene Trail.

ℹ KEY AT-A-GLANCE INFORMATION

LENGTH: 7.4 miles (round-trip) to lake, 3.4 miles (round-trip) to the falls

CONFIGURATION: Out-and-back

DIFFICULTY: Difficult

SCENERY: Bridal Veil Falls, Lake Serene under the high walls of Mount Index, old-growth forest; views across the Skykomish Valley.

EXPOSURE: Mostly shaded

TRAFFIC: High

TRAIL SURFACE: Dirt with slippery rocks and roots in places

HIKING TIME: 4–6 hours

ACCESS: Hikable late spring–fall; Northwest Forest Pass required for parking

MAPS: Green Trails—Index 142; USGS Index

FACILITIES: Restroom at trailhead, no drinking water available

Lake Serene and Bridal Veil Falls

Latitude: North 47d48.544m

Longitude: West 121d34.427m

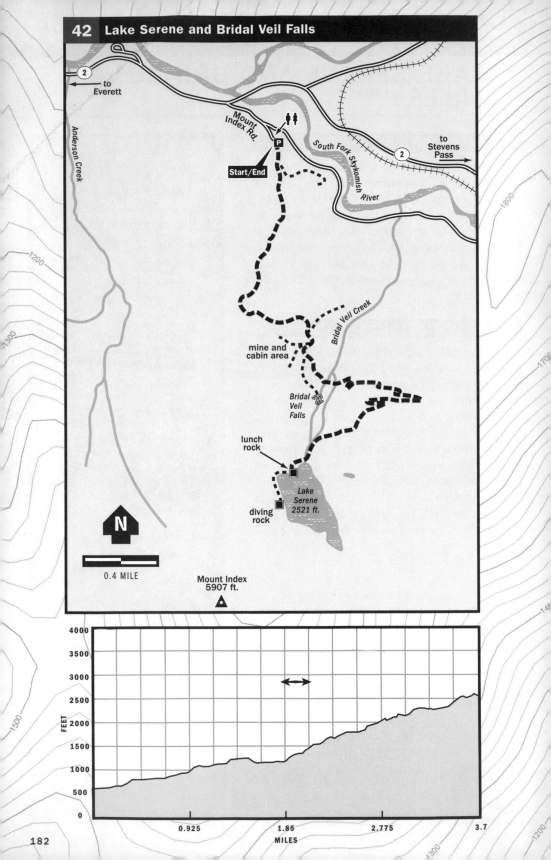

to Everett

Mount Index Rd.

P

Start/End

South Fork Skykomish River

to Stevens Pass

Anderson Creek

Bridal Veil Creek

mine and cabin area

Bridal Veil Falls

lunch rock

diving rock

Lake Serene 2521 ft.

N

0.4 MILE

Mount Index 5907 ft.

1200

1300

1500

1800

1700

FEET

4000
3500
3000
2500
2000
1500
1000
500
0

0.925   1.85   2.775   3.7

MILES

elevation gain. Yet for anyone seeking a shorter journey, thundering Bridal Veil Falls makes a great alternate destination for less than half the effort, an amazing added bonus among an embarrassment of riches.

The trail begins at an altitude of just less than 600 feet on an old road with a very rocky surface. The road forks within the first quarter mile, connecting to a larger network of reclaimed vehicle access points all along the southern side of the Skykomish Valley. Stay right, following a sign with a hiker symbol.

The forest here is in shade most of the time, shielded from the sun by the high walls of Mount Index to the south and the thick canopy of alders and big leaf maples overhead. Expect the trail to be wet and muddy all year and for the trail to cross several small creeks and streams as it climbs through the trees on a shallow incline.

At about 1.5 miles from the trailhead the road branches a second time. Once more stay right, following a hiker sign, and then reach another intersection soon after. The right branch enters a small maze of

Bridal Veil Falls

gravel roads exploring an old copper-mining claim. A ruined prospector's cabin is shown on some maps, but it is not easy to find. The main route, to the left, starts a gradual descent toward Bridal Veil Creek.

The signed trail to Middle Bridal Veil Falls comes up a few hundred yards farther along. Although the side trip adds over a half mile and 300 feet of vertical gain to the total hiking distance, it should be considered an absolute must for everyone.

The rugged single-track to the falls climbs steeply through rocks and roots, staging a direct assault on the mountainside. A set of wooden stairs leads to the spectacular cascade, where Bridal Veil Creek plunges down a giant slab of exposed rock, tossing up curtains of mist out over the Skykomish Valley. Unless the water is very high, it is possible to walk out onto the rocks below the falls or cross to the far side to get a better view. Use caution and stay well back from the edge, however, as the rocks are wet and slippery.

The falls make a great place to rest, with plenty of space to sit down and enjoy the thundering water and the great view across the valley from the 1,500-foot vantage. Look for the cliffs on the opposite side, known as the Index Town Wall and popular with rock climbers.

For some hikers, Bridal Veil Falls makes a worthwhile destination all on its own, and this is their turnaround point. Yet beautiful Lake Serene, another scenic jewel some 1,000 feet above, still awaits.

Descend from the falls to return to the main trail, and then follow the sign to Lake Serene, 2 miles away. Cross Bridal Veil Creek on a sturdy footbridge with a view of the impressive lower falls through the trees to the right; a slide falls similar in form to the middle falls farther up. The trail runs below yet another waterfall in the next quarter mile, close enough that anyone passing underneath is sure to feel the spray.

Beyond this point, the trail gives up any pretense of moderation and starts on a demanding and relentless climb. The mountainside is so steep as to allow only seven major switchbacks before the top, resulting in many sections with wooden stairs and other aids to ease the ascent. The sheer slope also makes logging very difficult, with old-growth western hemlock still standing here that would have been cut long ago in the flats closer to the bottom of the valley.

At 2,400 feet, emerge from the trees to meet a view of Mount Index straight ahead and the Skykomish River far below to the right. Another mucky quarter mile of climbing leads to the crest of the trail and then, at last, the shoreline of the lake.

Cross the outflow stream to the right on a wooden bridge and proceed to the Lunch Rock, a broad slab of unmistakable granite overlooking the eastern shore where most hikers congregate. It is also possible to scramble farther around the edge of the lake to some substantial boulders at the bottom of the talus field below the rock walls of Mount Index. The tricky crossing is worth it for the improved solitude and excellent diving platforms on the far side.

The massive face of Index tends to keep much of Lake Serene in shadow later in the day, but when the morning sun shines down unabated the setting is glorious. The emerald waters of the lake can almost look like the Caribbean, in contrast with the forbidding walls of Cascade rock just behind. Amazingly, there are some climbing routes up Mount Index that start from the lake, but they are extremely difficult and hazardous and are rarely attempted. For most hikers, reaching the lake will be reward enough.

HEYBROOK RIDGE AND LOOKOUT TOWER

▶ IN BRIEF

This short-and-sweet hike can easily be completed in a single morning or afternoon, including plenty of time spent both lingering on the trail along the way and enjoying the sweeping views of the lower Skykomish River Valley and its stunning surrounding peaks from the fire lookout at the top.

▶ DESCRIPTION

It's not hard to see why Heybrook Ridge was chosen for a fire lookout. Like all such sites, the ridge has a near-perfect location for observing a wide swath of the surrounding countryside—the impressive lower Skykomish River Valley. But unlike most lookouts, which typically extract a heavy toll in sweat and labor for access, Heybrook (at 1,824 feet) is one of the of the lowest-elevation towers anywhere in the Washington Cascades. Instead of the grueling climbs most Forest Service staffers would have to endure to reach their posts, often while hauling water and supplies, reaching Heybrook requires walking little more than a mile of trail from busy US 2. For the generally unencumbered day-hiker, the 1,000-foot climb right outside of Index is a wonderful gift, a true big-mountain view that is almost too easy to attain.

The Heybrook Ridge Trail could not be simpler to follow, as it is completely devoid of junctions, side trips, and alternate routes all the way to the top. Start out from the trailhead heading east, parallel to the highway, and then turn left up the hill. Despite being a long way inland, the

▶ KEY AT-A-GLANCE INFORMATION

LENGTH: 2.8 miles (round-trip)

CONFIGURATION: Out-and-back

DIFFICULTY: Moderate

SCENERY: Eight-story fire-lookout tower with observation deck below the cabin, stunning views of Mount Index and other nearby mountains

EXPOSURE: Mostly shaded

TRAFFIC: Low to moderate

TRAIL SURFACE: Dirt

HIKING TIME: 2 hours

ACCESS: Hikable year-round (may be snow-covered at the top in winter); Northwest Forest Pass required for parking

MAPS: Green Trails–Index 142; USGS Index

FACILITIES: None at trailhead

▶ DIRECTIONS

From I-5 at the northern end of Everett, take Exit 194, US 2 (east). Travel on US 2 through the towns of Monroe, Sultan, Startup and Gold Bar. After passing the turnoff to Index, continue nearly 2 miles to the parking lot and trailhead on the northern side of US 2.

Heybrook Ridge and Lookout Tower

Latitude: North 47d48.501m

Longitude: West 121d32.101m

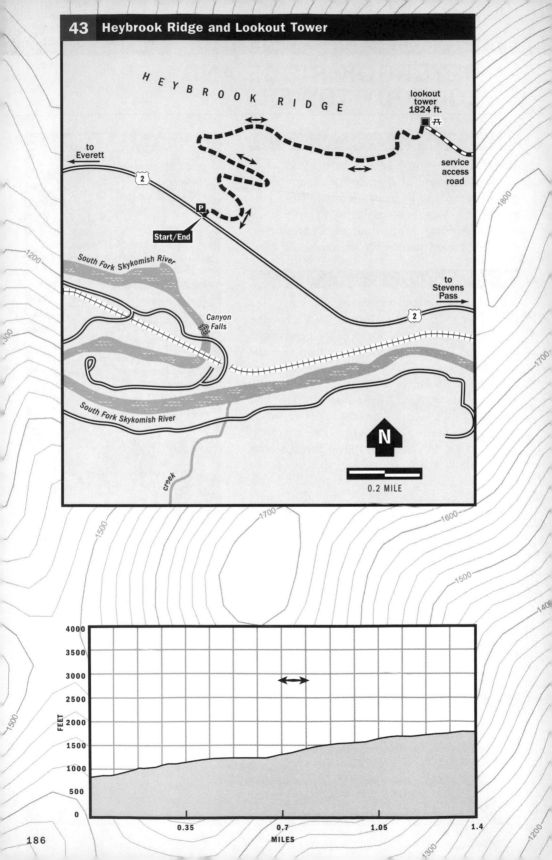

forest here is only 800 feet above sea level and is typical of the lowlands on the western slope of the Cascades. Moss grows like thick velvet, draped over every exposed inch of the host trees. Passing underneath the branches while the sunlight filters through is like hiking in a living cathedral of green.

The footing soon becomes rough and rocky as the trail gets steeper and generally trends toward the north. Giant erratic boulders and a few exposed slabs of polished rock hint at the area's ancient glacial history, while some stumps between the tall trees recount the more recent effects of man upon the landscape.

After about a half mile, follow a broad bend around to the right. Amazingly, at just more than 1,200 feet this is already the halfway point in terms of both horizontal distance and vertical gain. Once through the turn, the trail continues to climb through stately Douglas firs until it reaches the crest of a broad ridge. Although the forest prevents any views, the ground drops gently away on the left toward the North Fork of the Skykomish River.

Follow the southern side of the ridge for another quarter mile to abruptly emerge at the top of a brush-laden chute. The summit is only a few steps farther, just up the hill to the left where the high fire lookout rises above the trees.

The commanding wooden tower has been through various permutations and renovations since its original construction in 1925. Most recently refurbished in the 1990s, Heybrook Lookout now stands about 70 feet high. The tower is usually open for public access as far as the outdoor observation level, just below the cabin; a staircase zigzags up the eight stories to reach it.

The deck provides a grand view. Directly across the valley to the south, Mount Index's three jagged peaks (north, middle, and main) dominate the skyline. The steep rock walls below the long summit ridge rise more than 2,500 feet straight up from the forest below. Lake Serene rests at the bottom of the huge wall, although it is several hundred feet higher than the Heybrook Lookout and therefore not visible from this vantage. The whitewater of Bridal Veil Falls, the lake's outflow, can be made out, tumbling down through the trees. And Mount Persis stands behind Mount Index to the right, with a similar rocky summit ridge.

A section of US 2 is visible to the east, below the distinctive twin spires of Mount Baring, two sharp points thrust into the sky. At 6,125 feet, Baring is about 200 feet higher than Index and 5,000 feet above the South Fork of the Skykomish, which runs along the highway. On the northern side of Baring, Gunn Peak and Merchant Peak stand across the Barclay Creek Valley.

The view to the north is largely obscured by trees and nearby ridges, although there are many prominent peaks in that direction. To the west, it is possible to see out the end of the valley and onto the flatlands around Monroe and on toward Puget Sound.

Below the lookout, a pair of picnic tables near the trees to the east offers a good place to sit down and have something to eat, although the only view they provide is of the tower itself. The gravel surface underneath connects to a network of Forest Service roads continuing eastward along the ridge, which some hikers may find worth exploring, although there is no better vista to be found than the one here.

BARCLAY LAKE, STONE LAKE, AND EAGLE LAKE

KEY AT-A-GLANCE INFORMATION

LENGTH: 4.5 miles (round-trip) to Barclay Lake and 7.5 miles (round-trip) to Eagle Lake

CONFIGURATION: Out-and-back

DIFFICULTY: Easy (Barclay Lake) or difficult (Eagle Lake)

SCENERY: Plant life, subalpine meadows, wildflowers (in Paradise Meadow), old cabin; mountain views

EXPOSURE: Mostly shaded, some exposure in Paradise Meadow

TRAFFIC: Heavy to Barclay Lake, low to Eagle Lake

TRAIL SURFACE: Dirt with some rocky sections past Barclay Lake

HIKING TIME: 3–8 hours

ACCESS: Hikable spring–fall (Eagle Lake, summer–fall); Northwest Forest Pass required for parking

MAPS: Green Trails—Monte Cristo 143; USGS Baring

FACILITIES: None at trailhead

Barclay Lake, Stone Lake, and Eagle Lake

Latitude: North 47d47.741m

Longitude: West 121d28.003m

IN BRIEF

This is the best of hikes, this is the worst of hikes. Well, not really. But it is a tale of two trails. The first offers a relaxing walk through beautiful forest to reach Barclay Lake, and the second continues on a rough and steep climb to remote Eagle Lake, less than 2 miles farther away but much harder to reach. In between, unheralded but scenic Stone Lake rests in a high mountain saddle.

DESCRIPTION

The Barclay Lake trailhead sits in the middle of several impressive high peaks, most notably the rocky spires of Baring Mountain and Mount Index and the crags of Gunn and Merchant peaks, which give some indication of the character of the surrounding terrain. However, the trail to Barclay Lake is much less demanding than the environment would make it seem and is accessible to almost anyone. Reaching Eagle Lake, on the other hand, requires tough physical exertion and the use of route-finding skills.

Maintained by the Skykomish Ranger District of the Mount Baker–Snoqualmie National Forest, the trail is open solely to hikers and begins from the eastern end of the parking lot next to the information board. Right away the path plunges into the dark woods. Despite being largely second-growth, the trees here look like a primeval forest

DIRECTIONS

On I-5 at the northern end of Everett, take Exit 194 US 2 (east). Travel on US 2 through the towns of Monroe, Sultan, Startup, and Gold Bar. After passing the turnoff to Index, continue just more than 5 miles to the tiny town of Baring and take a left, immediately crossing railroad tracks. This road becomes Forest Road 6024 and dead-ends 4.5 miles from US 2 at the Barclay Lake trailhead and parking area.

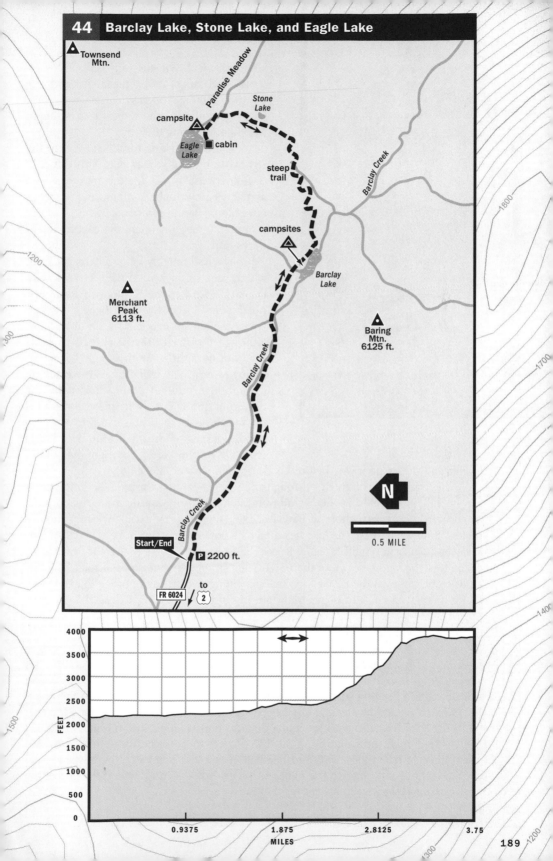

Townsend
Mtn.

Paradise Meadow

Stone
Lake

campsite

cabin

Eagle
Lake

steep
trail

Barclay Creek

campsites

Barclay
Lake

Merchant
Peak
6113 ft.

Baring
Mtn.
6125 ft.

Barclay Creek

N

0.5 MILE

Barclay Creek

Start/End

P 2200 ft.

to
2

FR 6024

1800

1700

1400

1200

1300

1200

1500

1300

Elevation profile:

FEET

4000
3500
3000
2500
2000
1500
1000
500
0

0.9375   1.875   2.8125   3.75

MILES

Merchant Peak above Eagle Lake

straight out of *Grimm's Fairy Tales*. Mosses, ferns, and fungi cover the trees and the ground, making it is easy to imagine trolls, elves, and other mythical creatures hiding in the shadows along the way.

A bushwhacking route leads off to the right within the first half mile. This difficult-to-follow path is not for the inexperienced and is used by climbers attempting the western side of Baring Mountain, where a steep scramble up a gully offers the easiest access to the top.

The trail roughly follows Barclay Creek, which runs through the valley on its way to the south fork of the Skykomish River just northwest of the town of Baring. In dry spells the stream may have little or no flow, although the size of the creek bed suggests that during spring runoff it can become a raging torrent. The trail crosses the creek on a footbridge built in 2003, funded by the nonprofit Spring Family Trust for Trails. This organization seeks to preserve the Washington wilderness that Ira Spring loved and revealed to the world through his photographs and tireless lobbying before his death from cancer at age 84.

The trail gently undulates through the woods, gaining elevation so gradually it can be difficult to tell that the overall trend is uphill. After a little more than a mile, it reaches the northern shore of Barclay Lake, where several excellent campsites are tucked among the trees. The lake lies directly below the massive northern face of Baring Mountain, whose cliff faces look like the walls and towers of a giant fortress. At 6,125 feet, the summit is more than 3,700 feet straight up, all exposed rock. There is a noticeable echo off the far wall for anyone willing to disturb the peace to test it out. Unfortunately, the lake has generally muddy beaches, making it less than a great place to swim.

For many hikers, this friendly destination makes an excellent turnaround point. If you are seeking additional challenge and solitude, continue around the shore to find the route to Eagle Lake up the ridge to the north. The Eagle Lake trail is not shown on most topographic maps and can be tricky to locate and follow. Look for an unmarked trail heading straight up the hill to the left just past the path to the toilet. If you reach the inflow creek to the lake at the last campsite, you have gone too far.

The boot-beaten track starts immediately uphill, marked intermittently by some ribbons, although these can be unreliable. Expect to do some route-finding as you climb through fallen logs, dirt, and needles. If you lose your way, the best bet is to continue uphill and angle to the right. As long as you stay on the western side of the creek, eventually you should recover the trail.

Enter a boulder field a half mile up, near 3,200 feet. These boulders continue in sections most of the way to Stone Lake, still some 700 feet higher. The trail is easier to follow here than below thanks to a series of cairns, although the general trend is the same as before: straight uphill. Near 3,400 feet, the trail crosses the creek and continues ascending on its eastern side. Look behind you for a great view of Baring Mountain across the Barclay Lake basin.

The trail finally relents at the southern end of Stone Lake, really just a pond; its name is probably derived from a rockslide that reaches into the clear water on the eastern shore. The route reaches a relatively high point here and then descends on the far side into Paradise Meadow and the Eagle Creek valley.

Paradise Meadow sits in a vast subalpine bowl, surrounded by Townsend Mountain (5,936 feet) to the north, Merchant Peak (6,113 feet) to the west, and Eagle Rock (5,615 feet) at the far eastern end of the valley. Indian paintbrush and wild blueberry bushes stretch along Eagle Creek, among grasses, flowers, and stunted pines. The trail crosses the creek several times through some muddy sections as it winds towards the northwest.

At 3,888 feet, Eagle Lake is slightly higher than Stone Lake and almost twice as big as Barclay. A good tent campsite is located where the trail first reaches the lake on its eastern side, and an old cabin is also available for public use about 200 yards around the shoreline to the southwest. The cabin has collected a host of equipment and junk over the years, but the front porch is a great place to rest and gaze out over the lake. Fish jump out of the clear water, chasing nymphs and bugs on the surface; bleached dead wood lines the shore. The rocky face of Merchant Peak rises directly above the western end, although the true summit is not visible from here. The return trip is the way you came.

▶ NEARBY ACTIVITIES

The Washington State Department of Fish and Wildlife operates a salmon hatchery on the Wallace River in Gold Bar. The public is allowed to tour the working facility and see various types of smolts in their tanks before being released into the wild. Look for a big brown sign for the State Salmon Hatchery on US 2, across from the West Gold Bar rail station at milepost 27.

SILVER CREEK AND MINERAL CITY TOWN SITE

KEY AT-A-GLANCE INFORMATION

LENGTH: 6 miles (round-trip); 9 miles if parking at the lower lot and walking the rough four-wheel-drive-only road

CONFIGURATION: Out-and-back

DIFFICULTY: Moderate with some difficult creek ravine crossings

SCENERY: Numerous mineshafts to peer into, historic mining town site; views of a scenic creek, deep gorge, many waterfalls, and nearby peaks

EXPOSURE: Mostly shaded

TRAFFIC: Low

TRAIL SURFACE: Dirt

HIKING TIME: 4–5 hours

ACCESS: Hikable year-round (avoid high-water runoff and deep snow, which could make the trail treacherous); no fees for parking or park access

MAPS: Green Trails—Monte Cristo 143; USGS Monte Cristo

FACILITIES: None at trailhead

Silver Creek and Mineral City Townsite

Latitude: North 47d54.629m

Longitude: West 121d26.314m

▶ IN BRIEF

Plenty of hikes explore Washington's pioneer history in the wilderness, but none can match the immediacy, rawness, or dramatic setting of this one. Several abandoned mine shafts line the trail, a deteriorating one-time road to the remnants of Mineral City. Along the way, the route climbs through a beautiful gorge deep in the Mount Baker–Snoqualmie National Forest, carved out by the crystal waters of Silver Creek and fed by multiple waterfalls on both sides.

▶ DESCRIPTION

The history on the Silver Creek Trail begins even before the hike does. The abandoned community of Galena once stood at the turnoff from the North Fork Skykomish River Road, a sister settlement to Mineral City farther up the valley. The region's mining heritage is obvious—Galena was named

▶ DIRECTIONS

From I-5 at the northern end of Everett, take Exit 194, US 2 (east) through the towns of Monroe, Sultan, Startup, and Gold Bar. Turn off US 2 toward the town of Index on the paved North Fork Skykomish River Road (FR 63; may be signed as Index-Galena Road). Pass by the road to Index and continue about 8.5 miles from US 2 to a left turn that crosses the river (unsigned). After crossing the bridge, take the first right on an unsigned dirt road. At this point, if you don't have a high-clearance four-wheel-drive vehicle, look for a parking spot and hike up the road. If you are comfortable driving up a narrow four-wheel-drive-only road, you will reach the actual trailhead and save about 1.5 miles of hiking each way. There is only room for 4 or 5 vehicles at this trailhead. Note that FR 63 may be closed in winter, but it should be open as far as the Galena turnoff.

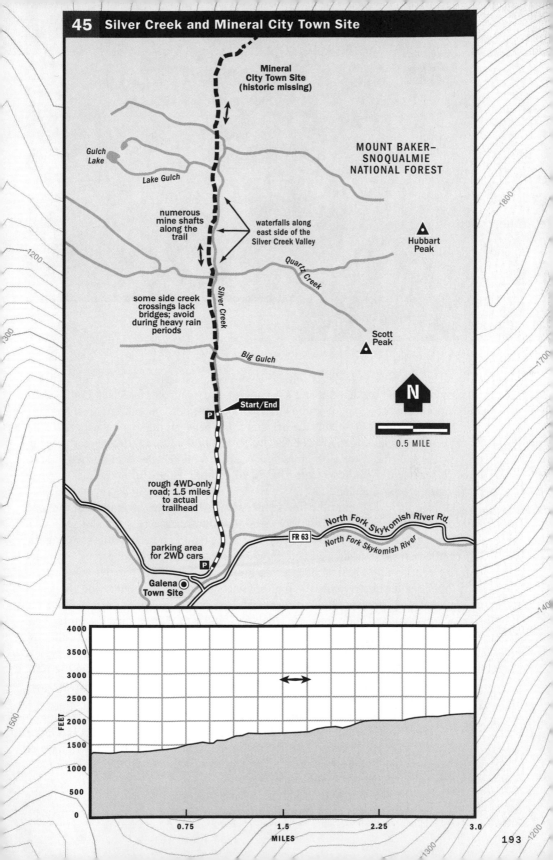

Mineral
City Town Site
(historic missing)

Gulch
Lake

Lake Gulch

MOUNT BAKER–
SNOQUALMIE
NATIONAL FOREST

numerous
mine shafts
along the
trail

waterfalls along
east side of the
Silver Creek Valley

Hubbart
Peak

Silver Creek

Quartz Creek

some side creek
crossings lack
bridges; avoid
during heavy rain
periods

Scott
Peak

Big Gulch

N

Start/End

P

0.5 MILE

rough 4WD-only
road; 1.5 miles
to actual
trailhead

North Fork Skykomish River Rd.

FR 63

North Fork Skykomish River

parking area
for 2WD cars

P

Galena
Town Site

4000
3500
3000
2500
2000
1500
1000
500
0

FEET

0.75   1.5   2.25   3.0

MILES

Abandoned mine entrance along
Silver Creek Trail

after the standard term for lead sulfide, a common, naturally occurring ore that is a primary source of metallic lead and a frequent geologic marker for silver. Both Galena and Mineral City were once boomtowns in the 1800s, but later fell into decline.

The final approach road is the original route between the two towns, graded for an expected railroad line that was never built. The trail follows the same path, beginning where the rutted road becomes impassable to all vehicles at a barrier of scattered blocks and boulders. Expect a steady uphill climb, although it is never particularly steep or demanding.

A huge rockfall around the first corner shows that the heavy erosion of the road will only continue the rest of the way. A boot-beaten track across the slide has usually been established by previous hikers, but care should be taken while crossing the loose surface, especially after rain or snow. The tricky conditions are a good reminder that this is not an appropriate hike for children.

After a short quarter mile the first obvious mine entrance appears on the left, a dark tunnel deep into a wall of reddish-orange rock. Two wooden rails run into the shaft along the floor, undoubtedly a track for hauling ore more than a century ago. This is an excellent example of an adit mine, a horizontal passage designed to follow an individual seam through the bedrock. Now largely archaic, the adit style is typical for the historic mining activity in the area, including the other shafts along the trail. These mines may be filled with standing water and are particularly prone to collapse, so enter at your own risk.

Just beyond the mine, a tributary creek drops through its own narrow slot into the main gorge from the left. At one time a wooden bridge crossed the gap, but it has disappeared, most likely swept away by debris and flood waters. Hikers will have to negotiate the way on their own, which may require a scramble through the mud and rock down one side and back up the other.

The loss of this bridge foreshadows what is to come for most of the rest of the way. Nature seems intent on reclaiming the trail to Mineral City by any means necessary, including flood, landslide, and rot. Several more wooden bridges in various stages of decay and collapse cross feeder streams tumbling into Silver Creek from the west. Although these bridges were solidly built and have stood for more than a century, each year they grow slightly more questionable, so proceed with caution; slippery and crumbling timbers are the rule, even on the good ones.

But the occasionally treacherous passage is well worth the effort. Every failing bridge spans a creek with a beautiful waterfall, often multistage drops down the valley wall with several pools and plunges. Below, the turquoise waters of Silver Creek churn through rapids and falls of their own, carving an ever-deeper channel into the slippery rocks. When the flow is right, whitewater kayakers run the river and provide a thrilling spectacle for hikers watching from above.

Pass several more mine entrances and enter a wide grove of birch trees. The valley opens up slightly through the birches, and views of some of the higher peaks in the surrounding area become available. With about 0.75 miles to go, follow a path branching off to the left, ignoring the main road that soon dead-ends at the river's edge.

The last section of trail reaches an open area at the confluence of Silver Creek and another creek flowing in from the left. This is the old Mineral City town site, so obliterated by mud and debris that it has become barely recognizable. Multiple landslides and floods have swept through, leaving very little evidence of human habitation other than a stack of giant logs. It takes a vivid imagination to picture the 15 blocks of stores, saloons, and hotels that used to stand here. This once-bustling outpost in the mountains can no longer even qualify as a ghost town, since the buildings themselves have disappeared.

Particularly determined and adventurous hikers may be able to continue beyond the town to Silver Lake and Poodle Dog Pass several miles farther up the valley. The route once linked Mineral City to the community of Monte Cristo on the other side of Silvertip Peak, but it is now a fading way trail, and may be little better than a bushwhack.

▶ NEARBY ACTIVITIES

On your way home, try the Mountain View Diner at the eastern end of Gold Bar for a filling posthike meal. The diner serves up a variety of hearty plates and attracts an interesting mix of customers, both locals and tourists. Look for the Mountain View along the southern side of US 2, or call (360) 793-3345 for more information.

IRON GOAT TRAIL

KEY AT-A-GLANCE INFORMATION

LENGTH: 6 miles (round-trip)

CONFIGURATION: Out-and-back

DIFFICULTY: Moderate

SCENERY: Historic railroad (including tunnels, snowshed walls, and artifacts), interpretive signs, wildflowers, well-maintained hiking trail; numerous viewpoints

EXPOSURE: Mostly shaded

TRAFFIC: Low to medium

TRAIL SURFACE: Mostly dirt with short sections of boardwalk and gravel

HIKING TIME: 3–6 hours

ACCESS: Hikable late spring–fall; Northwest Forest Pass required for parking

MAPS: Green Trails—Stevens Pass 176; USGS Scenic

FACILITIES: Restroom at trailhead; no drinking water available

SPECIAL COMMENTS: The Iron Goat Trail is still a work in progress, requiring volunteer labor and donations for completion. For more information or to become involved in the project, visit the official Iron Goat Trail Web site at **www.irongoat.org.**

Iron Goat Trail

Latitude: North 47d43.76m

Longitude: West 121d12.403m

IN BRIEF

History and nature converge on the Iron Goat Trail unlike anywhere else, a tribute to both the beauty of the environment in its pristine condition and man's amazing ability to transform it. Hiking the Iron Goat is like exploring a living museum in the wilderness, showcasing some great engineering achievements and the men who changed the world forever by building them. Throw in wildflowers, high mountain views, and a virtually flat, single-track trail, and the Iron Goat is an absolute must for any Washington State hiker.

DESCRIPTION

Many people believe Stevens Pass was named for Isaac Stevens, the first governor of the Washington Territory from 1853 to 1857. But it is actually a tribute to railroad engineer John F. Stevens, who managed the construction of more than 1,000 miles of James J. Hill's Great Northern Railway at the end of the 19th century. Hill, sometimes called "The Empire Builder of the Northwest," hoped to lay track from St. Paul, Minnesota, all the way to Seattle to link the rich natural resources around Puget Sound to the markets of the east. But to realize this dream, a difficult Cascade crossing had to be built, and Stevens was the answer.

DIRECTIONS

From I-5 at the northern end of Everett, take Exit 194, US 2 (east). Travel on US 2 through several small towns toward Stevens Pass. At milepost 55 turn left onto the Old Cascade Highway (FR 67). Continue just more than 2 miles from US 2 then turn left onto FR 6710. Travel on FR 6710 for about 1.5 miles to the Martin Creek trailhead and parking area. The alternate Wellington trailhead is located on FR 050 off the Old Stevens Pass Highway, which begins on the northern side of US 2 between mileposts 64 and 65.

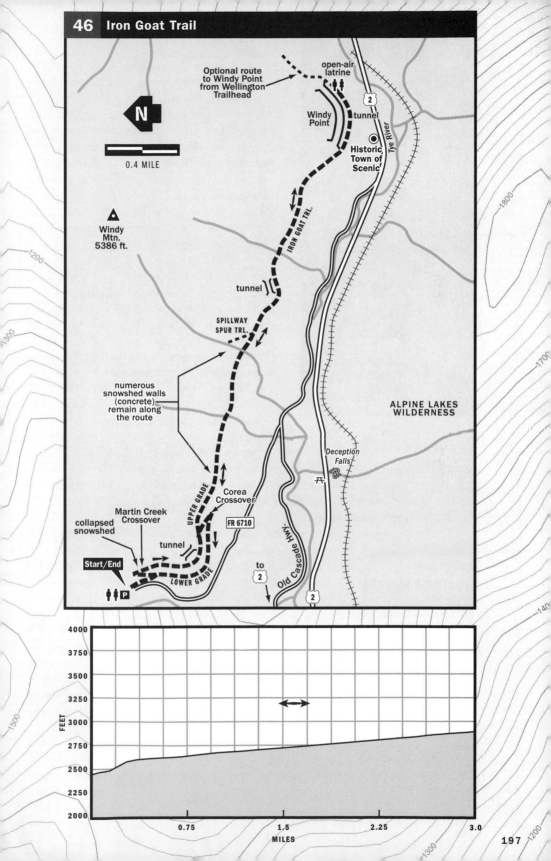

N

0.4 MILE

Optional route
to Windy Point
from Wellington
Trailhead

open-air
latrine

2

tunnel

Windy
Point

Tye River

Historic
Town of
Scenic

IRON GOAT TRL.

Windy
Mtn.
5386 ft.

tunnel

SPILLWAY
SPUR TRL.

numerous
snowshed walls
(concrete)
remain along
the route

ALPINE LAKES
WILDERNESS

Deception
Falls

UPPER GRADE

Corea
Crossover

FR 6710

Martin Creek
Crossover

collapsed
snowshed

tunnel

Old Cascade HWY.

Start/End

P

LOWER GRADE

to
2

2

Stevens had made his name by discovering Marias Pass through the Rocky Mountains with the help of a Native American guide in late 1889. At only 5,300 feet, Marias was the lowest-elevation crossing of the Rockies, located on the southern edge of what is now Glacier National Park. Managing to find the pass in frigid winter weather, Stevens saved the Great Northern millions of dollars and the need to travel hundreds of extra miles on a circuitous route through the notoriously rugged Bitterroot Range.

Hill counted on Stevens to duplicate his success in the Cascades, but it was actually Stevens' assistant C. F. B. Haskell who located a suitable pass in 1890 and named it in honor of his boss. In a rush to get the trains running as fast as possible, a tricky route was chosen across the mountain gap using eight separate switchbacks; this later proved to be extremely hazardous. Heavy snowfall and frequent avalanches often closed the tracks in winter, prompting Stevens to oversee construction of what is now known as the First Cascade Tunnel, a 2.6-mile passage under the Wenatchee Mountains and a remarkable engineering achievement. A series of showsheds were built over long sections of the track, and additional tunnels were later added for further protection, all constructed under difficult and dangerous conditions.

Yet Stevens's greatest success came not in the mountains of the Pacific Northwest, but thousands of miles away in the jungles of Central America. On the recommendation of Hill, President Theodore Roosevelt appointed Stevens as chief engineer of the Panama Canal in 1905. Apparently, Hill had looked beyond any personal animosity he might have felt toward the president—whose antimonopolist, trust-busting legislation was not exactly favorable to the Great Northern Corporation—and decided to support a project he believed vital to American strategic interests by sending one of his most valuable employees. Although Stevens resigned his post and left the isthmus of Panama only two years later (long before the "big ditch" was completed in 1913), his innovative use of the railroad to remove the excavated earth, commitment to fair treatment of the laborers, and successful campaign to eradicate tropical diseases are together credited by most historians for the final success of the massive project that changed the face of global trade forever.

All of this history is close enough to touch on the Iron Goat Trail, which follows the old right-of-way used by the Great Northern and gets its name both from the Great Northern logo, a mountain goat on a precipice, and from the idea of trains as iron horses.

There are two main trailheads on the Iron Goat, one at Martin Creek and the other about 6 miles east at Wellington; each is at a pivotal point on the former railway. Martin Creek was once the site of an exceptional switchback tunnel, where trains crossed between a lower and an upper grade just west of the current trailhead. This tunnel was known as the Horseshoe Tunnel due to its U shape, but unfortunately the switchback is not currently part of the Iron Goat restoration. At the other end, Wellington sits next to the western entrance to the First Cascade Tunnel on the site of one of the worst rail accidents in U.S. history. On March 1, 1910, a massive avalanche swept two trains down the mountain and took half the town with it, killing 96 people. Afterward, the settlement was renamed Tye to try to erase the connection between the name Wellington and the disaster, but the name Wellington is now in use once again. Although it is possible to complete a point-to-point traverse of the entire trail with a shuttle vehicle, this hike starts from the Martin Creek trailhead and turns around at Windy Point Tunnel, just about halfway.

The trail starts east from Martin Creek on a boardwalk and then quickly changes to the gravel and dirt of the lower grade. Amazingly, the footing feels almost perfectly flat, although trains once struggled to climb this stretch. The trail runs at an average 2.2 percent grade, meaning it gains 2.2 vertical feet for every 100 horizontal feet—steep for rail travel but imperceptible to hikers.

Reach a junction in less than a quarter mile, signed as Martin Creek Crossover (to Upper Grade). Head up the slope to the left through a lush forest of maples, alders, and ferns and then turn right on the upper grade, about 120 feet farther up the side of the mountain. Note that it would have required a train to travel a little over a mile through the Horseshoe Tunnel to gain the same altitude.

The upper grade is narrower than the lower grade and starts next to the rotting timbers of a collapsed snowshed, the first of many along the way. Today, it is hard to imagine the serious avalanche danger that would have prompted construction of the shed, as a forest of Douglas firs and western hemlocks now covers the mountainside. However, the steep slopes were once stripped bare, cleared by logging and forest fires, which were frequently started by sparks from passing locomotives. The denuded land had a hard time holding the wet and heavy snowpack.

The first tunnel, a gaping hole blasted through the side of the mountain, comes up on the left. It is worth walking up to the mouth to get a true sense of the size of the opening and imagine the trains chugging through, although entry into the hazardous tunnel is not recommended. Just past the tunnel, a beautifully restored black-and-white post marks this as mile 1,716, measured from the eastern terminus of the line in St. Paul. These highly visible posts can be found at each mile interval, and are useful for gauging distance.

Another quarter mile leads to a second junction heading downhill to the right, signed as Corea Crossover (to Lower Grade), allowing for completion of a short loop on the return. For now, stay on the upper grade.

For the next 2 miles, the Iron Goat offers a host of historical, archeological, and natural delights too numerous to name and best left to each individual to discover. Rotting timbers, towering concrete snowshed walls, metal debris, old work camps, stone supports, and another gaping tunnel are all part of the treasures to be found along the way, scattered between the trees and wildflowers. Perhaps inspired by the engineering feats of the original laborers, the restoration work on the trail itself shows a great level of inventiveness and creativity, often taking advantage of buried railroad supports, concrete pilings, and other existing relics.

Frequent viewpoints look south over the Tye River Valley to the right and the Alpine Lakes Wilderness beyond. Watch and listen for the trains of the Burlington Northern Santa Fe line that still run in the valley below, what's left of the Great Northern after several mergers with other railroads. The trains are headed for the Second Cascade Tunnel, whose inauguration in 1929 caused the abandonment of the entire upper line that has now been reclaimed as the Iron Goat Trail. The second tunnel runs underneath Big Chief Mountain and the Stevens Pass ski area for 7.8 miles, the longest in the Western Hemisphere at the time of its building and still the longest anywhere in the United States—yet another engineering marvel of the railway through Stevens Pass.

Windy Point makes a good place to turn back for a 6-mile round-trip. A quarter-mile tunnel was built here in 1913 to ease the passage around a dangerous, exposed curve on the edge of 5,386-foot Windy Mountain. A great viewpoint looks straight down on US 2, the old town site at Scenic, and the western mouth of the Second Cascade Tunnel. And if nature should happen to call, an open-air latrine down the slope to the right provides a spectacular view from "the throne."

On the return trip, remember to follow the Corea Crossover to complete the loop along the lower grade. Corea was the name of a telegraph station for monitoring train movements along the tracks, and the ruins of the site are marked along the way with one of many thoughtful interpretive signs.

GRANITE FALLS AND THE MOUNTAIN LOOP HIGHWAY

LIME KILN TRAIL AT ROBE CANYON HISTORIC PARK

KEY AT-A-GLANCE INFORMATION

LENGTH: 6.4 miles (round-trip) to river; 4.8 miles (round-trip) to lime kiln

CONFIGURATION: Out-and-back with a short loop at trail's end

DIFFICULTY: Easy to moderate

SCENERY: Historic lime kiln and old artifacts along a little-used rail-trail; views down to South Fork Stillaguamish River; access to river bank

EXPOSURE: Mostly shaded, exposed along a portion of dirt road

TRAFFIC: Low to medium

TRAIL SURFACE: Mostly dirt with a couple of sections of gravel

HIKING TIME: 4–5 hours

ACCESS: Hikable year-round; no fees for parking or park access

MAPS: Green Trails—Granite Falls 109; USGS Granite Falls

FACILITIES: Restroom at trailhead; no drinking water available

Lime Kiln Trail

Latitude: North 48d04.641m

Longitude: West 121d55.964m

▶ IN BRIEF

Despite its laid-back demeanor, the quiet town of Granite Falls was once a thriving economic hub. The local railway disappeared long ago with the logging and mining firms it used to serve, but many archeological remnants of the industrial-era operation still remain, waiting to be discovered by those who know where to look. This hike runs along the southern side of the Stillaguamish River, exploring the region's colorful past and culminating at the unique ruins of an old lime kiln, standing in the beautifully regenerated forest.

▶ DESCRIPTION

Access to the south fork of the Stillaguamish between Granite Falls and Verlot has generally been restricted to the river's northern bank. The rich history of the southern side was largely hidden, refusing to give up its secrets to the casual visitor.

All that changed in the fall of 2004 with the inauguration of the Lime Kiln Trail, centerpiece of the Robe Canyon Historic Park. The new trail

▶ DIRECTIONS

From Interstate 5 at the northern end of Everett, take Exit 194, US 2 (east). At the eastern end of the long bridge over the marshlands, take the left-lane exit onto WA 204, which climbs up to the town of Lake Stevens. At the intersection with WA 9, turn left (north) and proceed to a right turn onto WA 92 toward Granite Falls. At the far end of Granite Falls, turn right on S Alder Avenue and continue to a T-shaped intersection. Turn left on E Pioneer Street, which becomes Menzel Lake Road signed for Lake Rossiger. After about 1 mile, turn left onto Waite Mill Road. After the school bus turnaround, stay left on a gravel road that climbs uphill. Look for the entrance to the parking area on the left signed for Robe Canyon Historic Park and Lime Kiln Trail.

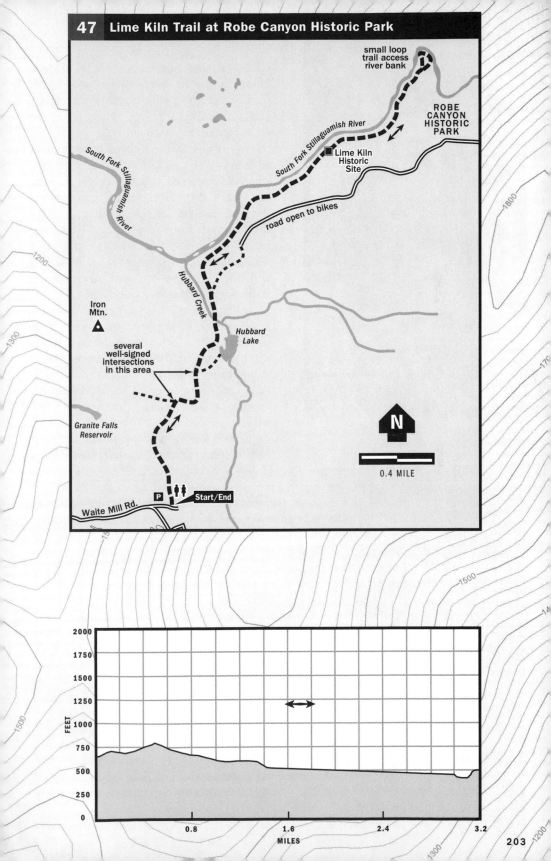

small loop
trail access
river bank

ROBE
CANYON
HISTORIC
PARK

South Fork Stillaguamish River

Lime Kiln
Historic
Site

road open to bikes

South Fork Stillaguamish River

Hubbard Creek

Iron
Mtn.

Hubbard
Lake

several
well-signed
intersections
in this area

Granite Falls
Reservoir

N

0.4 MILE

P

Start/End

Waite Mill Rd.

1200

1300

1800

1700

1500

1400

1300

1200

FEET

2000
1750
1500
1250
1000
750
500
250
0

0.8   1.6   2.4   3.2
MILES

Front view of the lime kiln

circles around the eastern side of Iron Mountain on an easement through private land to join the former route of the Everett and Monte Cristo Railway. From there, the route penetrates deep into the canyon on the river's high southern bank before ending at the location of a former bridge, now long since disappeared. Although this is the end of the trail, the park continues linearly along the river canyon for several more miles to the original Robe town site. Hopefully, future development will extend the Lime Kiln Trail to the east where it can be linked with the Old Robe Trail and other existing trails originating from around Verlot.

Until then, the Lime Kiln Trail still makes a great hiking destination on its own, combining the beautiful natural environment with a window into the region's fascinating history. The trail's builders also took extra care in construction and development, crafting a well-designed journey into the wilderness.

Look for the trailhead on the northern end of the parking lot, and start hiking through a dark forest of ferns and low maples. About a quarter mile in, a sign marks the beginning of some private property. It is particularly important to stay on the trail through this section, although a tangled and virtually impenetrable mess of salmonberry bushes on either side effectively prevents passage anywhere but along the footpath.

Stay right at a junction, signed Robe Canyon Park and Lime Kiln, and emerge onto a wide gravel road. Shade is limited here, as an old clear-cut is still in the early stages of regeneration and few trees of any size remain. In early summer, purple and white foxgloves add shafts of color on either side, where the flowering plants thrive in the ample sunlight.

Follow the old logging roads downhill to the right at the next intersection and then bend around to the left to reach a Y-junction. Both of these turns are once again clearly marked. Stay left for another quarter mile to reach the signed entrance to Robe Canyon Historic Park, the end of the passage through the private property. The trail re-enters the trees and shrinks back to single-track on a rough surface of gray and reddish rocks, now about a mile from the trailhead.

Cross a wide wooden bridge over Hubbard Creek. The creek flows out of Hubbard Lake, just through the trees to the right although not visible from here. On the far side of the bridge, the trail surface returns to gravel road for another quarter mile, where a single-track heads left into the trees, signed for Lime Kiln Trail. This turn is the start of the hikers-only section, although bicyclists and equestrians can continue along the road until it ends.

Descend along Hubbard Creek toward the Stillaguamish River and find the start of the old Everett and Monte Cristo Railway, built in the early 1890s and abandoned in 1934. Turn right to join the old railroad grade, hardly distinguishable from the previous trail except for its particular flatness.

The river runs at the bottom of the canyon, about 100 feet below to the left. Large cedars and big leaf maples grow from the steep slope, spreading their ample branches at eye-level along the trail, providing an unusual vantage point for inspecting the forest canopy. Ferns gather in sheltered glades where side creeks flow down on their way to meet the Stillaguamish.

At first, evidence of any former human activity is hard to find, with only the occasional piece of rusted debris or cable poking up through the dirt. Soon after entering the Cutoff Junction Historic Site, however, all manner of cast-off items can be found scattered beneath the trees. Look for pieces of ceramic plates, bowls, and glass jars along with bricks, leather boots, and even old iron-stove components. Particularly striking are a large number of rusted circular-saw blades, whose jagged teeth stand in high contrast with the softer textures and smooth edges of the natural forest. These fascinating relics are testaments to the strange transformation that takes place when worthless junk is left anywhere for a sufficiently long period of time—it turns into something of great interest and value.

The history lesson reaches its apex at the old lime kiln, standing about 20 feet high. Lime kilns date back at least as far the ancient Egyptians, who used lime mortar for their stone buildings; this kiln, however, is a textbook example of the design for such structures used during the Industrial Revolution. The tower is built on a slope to facilitate the addition of limestone to the top, with wood and other burning materials fed into a fire through an opening on the side. Powdered lime would be removed from the main access arch at the bottom, which now faces the trail. The final product would be used for a host of applications, including construction, agriculture, and cleaning.

The kiln's gray rock walls are now covered in green mosses, lichens, and ferns, giving it an appearance like something out of the ruined civilizations of the Mayas, Incas, or Aztecs. It's easy to forget that it has only been standing for about a century.

The trail continues past the lime kiln for another 0.7 miles through some former logging sites to reach a Y-junction, the beginning of a short loop. Stay right for a few hundred yards to a viewpoint over the river, where the Everett and Monte Cristo Railroad once crossed to the far side of the canyon on a bridge. Almost all evidence of the span has disappeared, inviting speculation as to where the two ends might have been anchored in the rocks and on what angle the structure crossed the water.

This is the end of the trail and the turnaround point for the hike, at least pending further development of the Robe Canyon Historic Park. The hoped-for future linking of the Lime Kiln Trail with the Old Robe Trail would require construction of another bridge over the river.

On the way back, be sure to explore the short loop from the previous junction that leads down through salal and low brush to the river bank. With a little effort it is possible to scramble down to the rocks on the river bed, a great place to enjoy some rest and relaxation.

MOUNT PILCHUCK STATE PARK: MOUNT PILCHUCK LOOKOUT

KEY AT-A-GLANCE INFORMATION

LENGTH: 5 miles (round-trip)

CONFIGURATION: Out-and-back

DIFFICULTY: Moderate

SCENERY: Scenic trail, historic lookout cabin open to public; summit views

EXPOSURE: Shaded on about half the route; lookout cabin provides shelter at the summit

TRAFFIC: Heavy (hike midweek, if possible)

TRAIL SURFACE: Dirt and rock, large boulders

HIKING TIME: 3–5 hours

ACCESS: Hikable summer–fall (road remains snowed-in during spring); Northwest Forest Pass required for parking

MAPS: Green Trails–Granite Falls 109; USGS Verlot

FACILITIES: Restroom at trailhead; no drinking water available

Mount Pilchuck State Park: Mount Pilchuck Trail

Latitude: North 48d04.244m

Longitude: West 121d48.847m

IN BRIEF

Although the only man-made structure here is the summit lookout, Mount Pilchuck could not be any better designed even if it had been specifically planned and constructed by hand. When it comes to getting the most bang for your buck, no other peak offers such great rewards for so little effort. This landmark hike should not be missed by anyone.

DESCRIPTION

Most 5,000-foot peaks near Seattle rise so steeply and abruptly they require some 4,000 feet of climbing to reach the summit. Thanks to an approach road that winds high above the Stillaguamish River Valley, 5,324-foot Mount Pilchuck can be crested via a relatively short trail with only 2,200 feet of vertical gain. Once you attain the lookout, the view is so grand it seems all of western Washington is spread out below you.

At an altitude of more than 3,100 feet, the parking lot alone offers impressive views, and some people drive up the road just to take a look. To the northeast, Three Fingers Mountain rises high above the Stillaguamish (which locals call

DIRECTIONS

From I-5 at the northern end of Everett, take Exit 194, US 2 (east). At the eastern end of the long bridge over the marshlands, take the left-lane exit onto WA 204, which climbs up to the town of Lake Stevens. At the intersection with WA 9 go left (north). Proceed to a right turn onto WA 92 toward Granite Falls. Continue through Granite Falls and go left on S Alder Avenue, which becomes the Mountain Loop Highway. After passing Verlot and immediately after crossing the Stillaguamish River, go right on an unmarked road. This paved and gravel road (FR 42) ascends up to the Mount Pilchuck parking area.

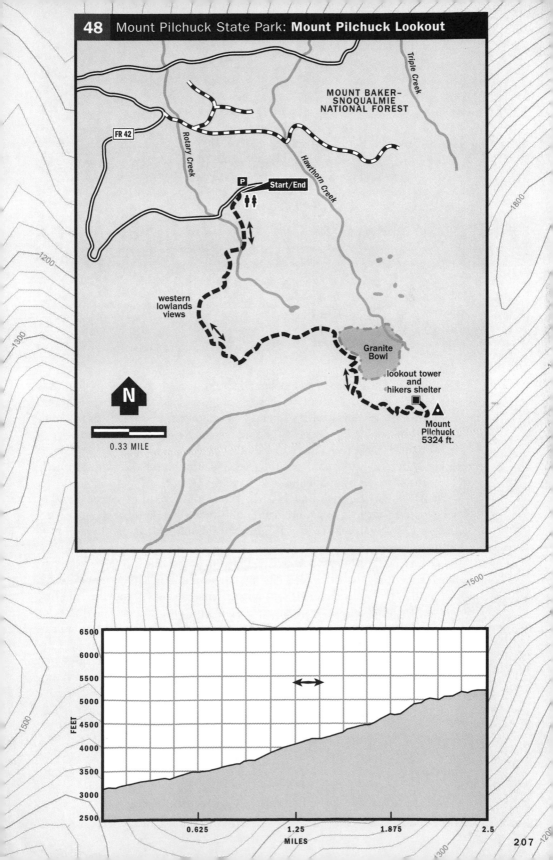

Triple Creek

MOUNT BAKER–
SNOQUALMIE
NATIONAL FOREST

FR 42

Rotary Creek

Hawthorn Creek

P

Start/End

western
lowlands
views

Granite
Bowl

lookout tower
and
hikers shelter

Mount
Pilchuck
5324 ft.

N

0.33 MILE

1200

1300

1500

1500

1800

1500

1300

1200

FEET

6500
6000
5500
5000
4500
4000
3500
3000
2500

0.625   1.25   1.875   2.5

MILES

Mount Pilchuck lookout

The Stilly), and several vantage points look straight up through the trees at Pilchuck's rocky pinnacle. The lot has plenty of space, so even on the busiest days there is bound to be room. Expect those busy days to come quite frequently, especially in the summer, as the trail is suitable for hikers of all kinds, including many children and pets.

Unfortunately, the sheer number of people passing through the area causes some problems beyond heavy traffic on the trail. This trailhead has had some break-ins, so be sure not to leave any valuables in the car.

Marked as Mount Pilchuck Trail 700, the route originates at the western end of the parking lot next to the information board and is posted at 3 miles in length, one-way, although it is actually closer to 2.5 miles. For the first 100 yards, the trail is as wide and rocky as a gravel road, but it soon narrows as it climbs to the south.

The area is jointly administered by Washington State Parks and Recreation and the National Forest Service. Watch for a sign marking the entrance to Mount Pilchuck State Park nestled next to some reeds and huge skunk cabbage plants after the first quarter mile. The trail is well-maintained and worn, with regular waterbars for drainage and a raised surface lined by logs on either side. Steps have been built in several areas where needed, and the uphill grade is moderate and relatively easy-going for about the first mile. Occasional viewpoints open out to the west through a mixed forest of young conifers interspersed with some far older trees and sun-bleached snags.

Near 3,600 feet the path picks its way through a large boulder field, the beginning of a rocky surface that continues most of the way to the top. Fortunately, steady views appear as well. Each one is better than the last, especially in the last mile, which is by far the steepest and most demanding.

The trail exits the forest for good at 4,000 feet, emerging into a vast granite bowl beneath the northern side of the summit. The lookout is visible far above, silhouetted against the sky on the highest crag. The setting here is spectacular and geologically unusual for the area, like a piece of the High Sierras was lifted from California and dropped at the edge of the western Cascades. Pikas whistle their alarm from the white rocks, while several small tarns shimmer below.

The route skirts the western side of the exposed granite, passing by the ruins of a tramline that once served the summit. Weathered timbers, giant bolts, and rusted pulleys are all visible along the way, evidence of the hardships of building high in the mountains before the advent of the helicopter.

Wrap around to the southern side of the mountain before reaching the final ridge. Traverse the ridge, scramble through the last few boulders, and then clamber up the ladder to the lookout. The climb can be a little tricky, but there is no real exposure and everyone should be able to complete it.

The handsome lookout has a long history, intimately tied to the development of the area. The first access trail up Mount Pilchuck was constructed along Black Creek and Pinnacle Lake in 1909, ascending the peak's eastern flank. A more direct 7-mile route was established within a year from near the town of Robe, crossing the Stillaguamish River on a hand-driven cable car. Much of that route is not too far from the trail still in use today.

In 1921, the first lookout was completed on the summit. Subsequent redesigns and renovations occurred in 1941, 1971, and 1989, bringing it to its current form as a year-round hiker's shelter. Heavy snow shutters can be lowered over the windows in winter to shield the building and its occupants from storms and the brunt of the wind. The Everett chapter of The Mountaineers is responsible for the most recent remodeling of the structure as well as its current upkeep, a great service to the public.

Inside the cozy shelter, benches line the walls beneath the 360-degree-angle windows, a perfect place for lunch. Informational panels recount the history of the lookout with text and photographs, and panoramic displays indicate the countless landmarks on all sides.

The view offers a virtual who's who of the high peaks of the central Washington Cascades, including Baker, Shuksan, Three Fingers, Whitehorse, El Dorado, Glacier, Sloan, Big Four, Dickerman, Pugh, and Rainier. To the west, the town of Granite Falls lies directly below, with Everett, Lake Stevens, Camano Island, and Puget Sound out to the Olympic Peninsula beyond. Enjoy your rest on top of the world before starting the descent.

▶ NEARBY ACTIVITIES

There are multiple amenities and services available in Granite Falls, where the Mountain Loop Highway meets WA 92. As you enjoy a posthike meal or drink, look for Mount Pilchuck, clearly visible towering over the eastern end of town. For more information, visit the Town of Granite Falls Visitor Web site at **www.granitefalls wa.com**.

HEATHER LAKE

KEY AT-A-GLANCE INFORMATION

LENGTH: 5.25 miles (round-trip), including a 0.75-mile loop around the lake

CONFIGURATION: Out-and-back with loop around the lake

DIFFICULTY: Moderate

SCENERY: Old-growth trees and massive stumps, lake bowl

EXPOSURE: Shaded in forest, exposed around lake

TRAFFIC: Heavy (hike midweek, if possible)

TRAIL SURFACE: Dirt, short scenic boardwalk at lake

HIKING TIME: 3–5 hours

ACCESS: Hikable spring–fall; Northwest Forest Pass required for parking

MAPS: Green Trails—Granite Falls 109; USGS Verlot

FACILITIES: Restroom at trailhead

Heather Lake

Latitude: North 48d04.962m

Longitude: West 121d46.497m

▶ IN BRIEF

The trail to Heather Lake offers an interesting and rewarding hike with just enough challenge to make the swim at the end all the more inviting—at least during high summer. If you prefer solitude, the lake also makes for a worthwhile destination during some of the colder months, thanks to its low elevation and dramatic setting beneath 1,500-foot cliffs.

▶ DESCRIPTION

Heather Lake is the westernmost of a chain of lakes spread out on the northeastern side of Mount Pilchuck, including Bear Lake, Hemple Lake, and Lake Twenty-Two, all formed by natural bowls that collect runoff above the South Fork of the Stillaguamish River. Nestled in an impressive cirque, the lake lies less than 1 mile from the top of Pilchuck but almost 3,000 feet beneath it. The summit, however, cannot be seen from the lake, thanks to the high ridges that rise sharply from the southern shore. These ridges funnel the water down into the basin and often keep the snowpack here late into summer, shading it from the sun.

▶ DIRECTIONS

From I-5 at the northern end of Everett, take Exit 194, US 2 (east). At the eastern end of the long bridge over the marshlands, take the left-lane exit onto WA 204, which climbs up to the town of Lake Stevens. At the intersection with WA 9, turn left (north). Proceed to a right turn onto WA 92 toward Granite Falls. Continue through Granite Falls and turn left on S Alder Avenue, which becomes the Mountain Loop Highway. After passing Verlot and immediately after crossing the Stillaguamish River go right on an unmarked road. Travel on this paved and gravel road (FR 42) about 1.4 miles to a parking area on the right across the road from the Heather Lake trailhead.

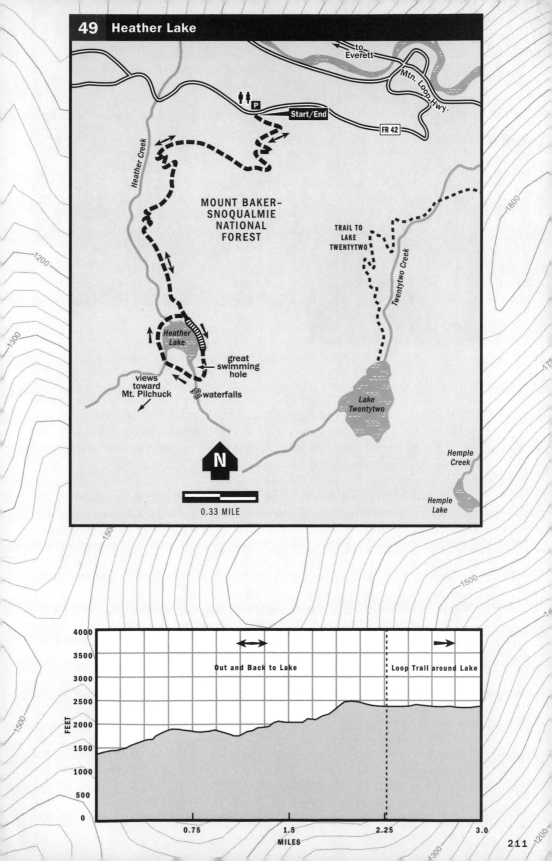

to Everett

Mtn. Loop Hwy.

P

Start/End

FR 42

Heather Creek

MOUNT BAKER-
SNOQUALMIE
NATIONAL
FOREST

TRAIL TO
LAKE
TWENTYTWO

Twentytwo Creek

Heather
Lake

great
swimming
hole

views
toward
Mt. Pilchuck

waterfalls

Lake
Twentytwo

Hemple
Creek

Hemple
Lake

N

0.33 MILE

4000

3500

3000

2500

2000

1500

1000

500

0

FEET

Out and Back to Lake

Loop Trail around Lake

0.75   1.5   2.25   3.0

MILES

Swimming hole at Heather Lake

From the trailhead on the Mount Pilchuck access road, Lake Heather Trail 701 climbs steadily for 2 miles and 1,200 feet to reach its destination. Find the beginning of the trail next to the information board, across the gravel road from the main parking pull-out. On a summer weekend expect to see cars parked along both sides of the road, as hikers aim to reach the lake at the hottest part of the day. Some of the crowds can be avoided by getting an unusually early or late start, but it might prove too cold to swim when you reach the lake.

The trail begins its ascent through a damp second-growth forest, where the moss-laden trees appear velvety and bearded. Scattered along the way are a series of enormous cedar stumps, evidence of what the forest used to be in its old-growth heyday. Many still show the notches where the loggers anchored their springboards as they cut down the trees by hand in the early 20th century. The height of the current trees, a few actually growing out of the stumps themselves, gives some idea of the massive size these ancient wonders would have attained.

Like many trails in this part of the Mount Baker–Snoqualmie National Forest, the path is well-traveled and well taken care of, with waterbars and lining logs where needed. The current route replaces an older trail whose traces are occasionally visible along the way, but there is never any question about which way to go.

The forest floor is littered with deadfall, showing every stage of decay and rebirth imaginable; this includes some old-growth cedars still enduring on either side of the trail near the halfway point to the lake. These impressive trees stand straight as Greek columns, rising far above the surrounding canopy.

The trail narrows to single-track and crosses a creek near the 2,000-foot level. Expect some mud in this section even in the driest part of the year. This is not Heather Creek, the lake's outflow that roughly parallels the trail to the west but which the trail never reaches, despite the frequently audible sound of running water.

With just a quarter mile remaining, reach the trail high-point at 2,500 feet and then start a short descent through a marshy area into the Heather Lake basin. The high trees obscure most of Mount Pilchuck, but glimpses of its rocky ridges are periodically visible through the upper branches. Finally reach the lake at 2,395 feet.

A loop trail continues another 0.75 miles, completing a circuit around the shoreline. All sides of the lake are worth visiting, and you may need to explore on your own to find the best spot. A series of sandy beaches on the northern side of the lake are particularly popular for swimming, but the far end also offers some excellent opportunities where boulders from an old rockslide reach the deep water, allowing for jumping and diving. Segmented snake grass growing out of the water is fun for children, who will enjoy wading among the stems and looking for fish and frogs.

Heather Lake is not particularly deep, but the water never really warms too much, especially in the years when the snow lingers well into July. Even a shallow dive will show the marked difference between the surface water and the icy layers beneath. Although it might be refreshing after a sweaty hike, it could turn hypothermic under the wrong conditions, so be careful, especially with children. A pack towel is a great accessory to bring along for when you are finished.

For the adventurous, a scramble up the rockslide to the south leads to the steep face of the cirque itself. Poke around to find various small waterfalls running down the cliff and into the rocks and look back down for a commanding aerial view of the lake.

▶ **NEARBY ACTIVITIES**

There are multiple amenities and services available in Granite Falls, where the Mountain Loop Highway meets WA 92. As you enjoy a posthike meal or drink, look for Mount Pilchuck, clearly visible towering over the eastern end of town. For more information, visit the Town of Granite Falls Visitor Web site at **www.granitefalls wa.com**.

PINNACLE LAKE AND BEAR LAKE

KEY AT-A-GLANCE INFORMATION

LENGTH: 4 miles (round-trip)

CONFIGURATION: Out-and-back with a short side trip to Bear Lake

DIFFICULTY: Easy to Bear Lake, moderate to Pinnacle Lake

SCENERY: Two different lakes (one surrounded by forested hills and one set below high rocky ridges), old-growth forest

EXPOSURE: Shaded except at Pinnacle Lake

TRAFFIC: Medium

TRAIL SURFACE: Dirt; easy and wide to Bear Lake, rough with rocks, roots, and mud to Pinnacle Lake

HIKING TIME: 3–4 hours

ACCESS: Hikable late-spring–fall (very muddy after rains); Northwest Forest Pass required for parking

MAPS: Green Trails—Granite Falls 109 and Silverton 110; USGS Verlot and Mallardy Ridge

FACILITIES: No restroom at trailhead, but outside toilets at both lakes; no drinking water available

Pinnacle Lake and Bear Lake

Latitude: North 48d03.516m

Longitude: West 121d44.164m

IN BRIEF

Both Bear and Pinnacle lakes offer many of the same attractions as Lake Twenty-Two with smaller crowds, making them great alternate destinations to their glamorous neighbor. The quiet and scenic mountain lakes feel much more remote than they actually are, and the unique forest of old-growth yellow cedar along the way is not to be missed.

DESCRIPTION

It's hard to argue that Lake Twenty-Two is anything but one of the crown jewels of the Stillaguamish River Valley. Thanks to its protected status within the natural area of the same name, all sorts of hikers are attracted to the deservedly popular lake, both by the beauty of the final destination and the exemplary old-growth forest along the way. Yet the intense spotlight on Lake Twenty-Two only minimally spreads to nearby Bear and Pinnacle lakes, despite their obvious similarities.

The hike to the lakes begins on the southern side of the road, behind an information board. From the trailhead at 2,650 feet, follow a short, rocky rise around a corner to the right and pass

DIRECTIONS

From I-5 at the northern end of Everett, take Exit 194, US 2 (east). At the eastern end of the long bridge over the marshlands, take the left-lane exit onto WA 204, which climbs up to the town of Lake Stevens. At the intersection with WA 9, turn left (north) and proceed to a right turn onto WA 92 toward Granite Falls. Continue through Granite Falls and turn left on S Alder Avenue, which becomes the Mountain Loop Highway. After passing Verlot, drive more than 4 miles and turn right onto FR 4020. Just past 2.5 miles from the highway, turn right onto FR 4021 then continue about 3 more miles to the well-signed trailhead.

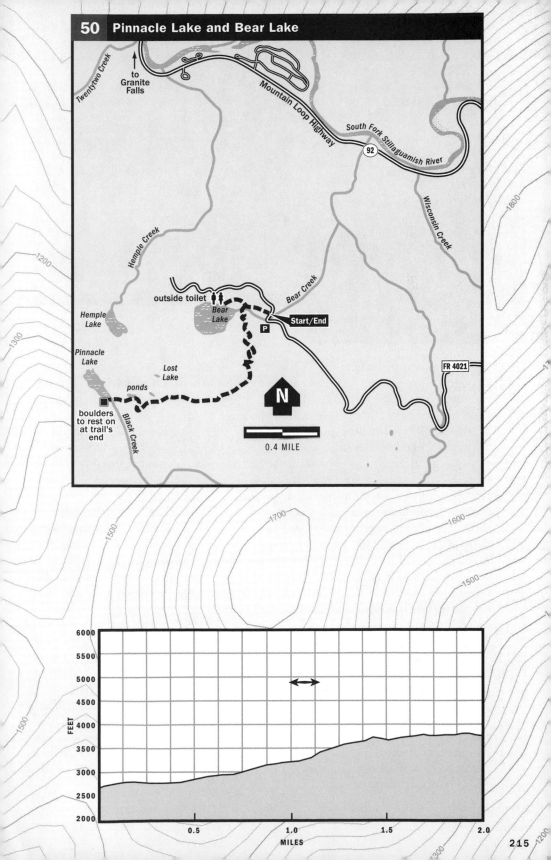

to Granite Falls

Twentytwo Creek

Mountain Loop Highway

South Fork Stillaguamish River

92

Wisconsin Creek

Hemple Creek

Bear Creek

outside toilet

Bear Lake

Hemple Lake

Pinnacle Lake

Lost Lake

ponds

boulders to rest on at trail's end

Black Creek

Start/End

P

FR 4021

N

0.4 MILE

6000
5500
5000
4500
4000
3500
3000
2500
2000

FEET

0.5   1.0   1.5   2.0

MILES

Morning reflection on Bear Lake

through two huge trees, an effective gateway into the forest wonderland beyond. Ancient yellow cedars are scattered throughout the woods, showing their typical distinctive flared bases, drooping branches, and grooved, spiral bark. Sometimes known as Alaska cedar, or Nootka cypress, the trees are not really cedars at all, and are probably most accurately identified by their scientific name, *Chamaecyparis nootkatensis*.

No matter what they are called, though, there is no doubt that the mammoth trees are an awe-inspiring sight. The slow-growing conifer produces the hardest known cedar-type wood in the world, particularly resistant to decay and prized by modern boatbuilders and traditional Native American carvers alike. The fact that these magnificent trees have managed to avoid the saw without special wilderness designation or even the protection given their brothers in the Lake Twenty-Two Research Natural Area just to the west is nothing short of astounding. Even veteran old-growth hikers should find the forest here of particular interest since it is quite different from the standard Douglas-fir-dominated ecosystem so common on the western slope of the Cascades. Indeed, Douglas firs, ancient or not, are difficult to find in the woods here at all.

The flat and gravelly trail runs by occasional viewpoints, providing glimpses of Verlot, the Stillaguamish River, and the obvious summit of Three Fingers (6,854 feet) rising on the far side of the valley. After only a quarter mile, turn right at a signed junction and proceed to Bear Lake at 2,776 feet.

Several good campsites are available directly under the trees on the northeastern shore, where the trail first reaches the water. The lake sits in a wooded bowl, surrounded on all sides by the thick forest. On rare perfect mornings, a mysterious and magical aura is added to the setting when the surface of the water becomes a flawless mirror and a mountain fog rolls up the valley, making the giant cedars stand out like ghostly sentinels in the clouds.

From the previous junction, a path heads toward Pinnacle Lake. Quickly cross the lake's outflow of Bear Creek in a muddy section, the first hint of the wet and sloppy trail that lies beyond.

A series of rough switchbacks leads up the side of an indistinct ridge, where roots, rocks, and other obstacles are the only relief from the mud. The drainage on the slope is hindered by its north-facing aspect and the big trees which keep it in near-perpetual shade. The trail itself serves as a convenient channel for any runoff, which gets trapped by the root wads and then saturates the soil below.

Near 3,400 feet, the ridge becomes more pronounced and Bear Lake becomes visible below to the right. The trail climbs steadily back along the ridgeline and gradually bends to the west in a broad, sweeping curve. The last half mile before the lake could vie for the crown of muckiest trail anywhere in the Cascades, which is quite a claim in this perpetually gray and damp region, to say the least. Nonetheless, this dubious honor is well-deserved, especially if you arrive in anything but the driest part of the year. Several small ponds lie off the trail to the right, but at times you will swear you are walking right through the middle of them instead.

The last of the ponds is rimmed with boulders and studded with rocky islands in the middle. It is easy to mistake the pretty scene for the final destination, but push on past the pond to a short descent through the rocks of the pond's outflow stream. Some easy boulder-hopping may be required to reach Pinnacle Lake at the bottom, elevation about 3,800 feet.

Black Creek drains the lake to the left, running east for several miles before turning back to the north and eventually meeting Bear Creek about 0.7 miles below the trailhead. It ultimately empties into the Stillaguamish River. The rocky prominence on the far shore (probably the source of the Pinnacle name) is actually the eastern end of the Mount Pilchuck ridge, which crests several miles to the west. And the gap to the right looks down on Hemple Lake. It is possible to scramble around the shore and climb to the notch, but the lake sits below considerable cliff bands on the other side and is unreachable. A scramble around either shore is probably unnecessary; the sunny boulders at the head of Black Creek offer the best place to enjoy the lake by swimming, wading, or just relaxing and taking in the scenic mountain environment.

BOULDER RIVER WILDERNESS: BOULDER RIVER TRAIL

KEY AT-A-GLANCE INFORMATION

LENGTH: 8.4 miles (round-trip) to Ford Camp, 2 miles (round-trip) to waterfalls

CONFIGURATION: Out-and-back

DIFFICULTY: Easy to moderate

SCENERY: A low-elevation year-round river trail hike in a wilderness area with old-growth forest, stunning waterfalls, and two trailside backcountry camps

EXPOSURE: Shaded

TRAFFIC: Low to medium

TRAIL SURFACE: Dirt (progressively degrades with distance from trailhead; very muddy in spots, especially after rains)

HIKING TIME: 4–6 hours to Ford Camp; 1–2 hours to waterfalls

ACCESS: Hikable year-round; Northwest Forest Pass required for parking

MAPS: Green Trails—Granite Falls 109; USGS Meadow Mountain

FACILITIES: Restroom along road 2 miles before trailhead; no drinking water available

Boulder River Wilderness:
Boulder River Trail

Latitude: North 48d15.024m

Longitude: West 121d49.041m

IN BRIEF

The Boulder River Trail brings together a great combination of unlikely elements. Old-growth forests and breathtaking waterfalls can be found in many wilderness areas in the Cascades, but the minimal elevation gain and year-round access available here are two pleasant surprises that make Boulder River stand alone.

DESCRIPTION

The Boulder River Wilderness Area juts out from the Mount Baker–Snoqualmie National Forest west of the town of Darrington, separating the north and south forks of the Stillaguamish River. In between, Whitehorse Mountain and Three Fingers reach close to 7,000 feet, centerpiece of a rugged collection of peaks that is crossed by only a single road, the Mountain Loop Highway through Barlow Pass to the east.

Yet the Boulder River Trail penetrates the area via a gentle valley without meeting any significant barriers for almost 5 miles, providing an exceptional opportunity to explore some of the mountain wilderness without the usual toll of sweat and muscle. Better still, the hike is much milder than its location would suggest: In winter, the low elevation keeps the trail mostly snow-free; in summer the forest canopy provides plenty of shade even on the hottest days and the river is always nearby for a quick dip.

Although this is a federally designated wilderness, permits are not required to enter.

DIRECTIONS

From I-5 north of Everett, take Exit 208, WA 530 (east) and drive through Arlington toward Darrington. Just after milepost 41, turn right onto French Creek Road. Continue on this road nearly 4 miles to the end at the parking lot and trailhead for the Boulder River Trail.

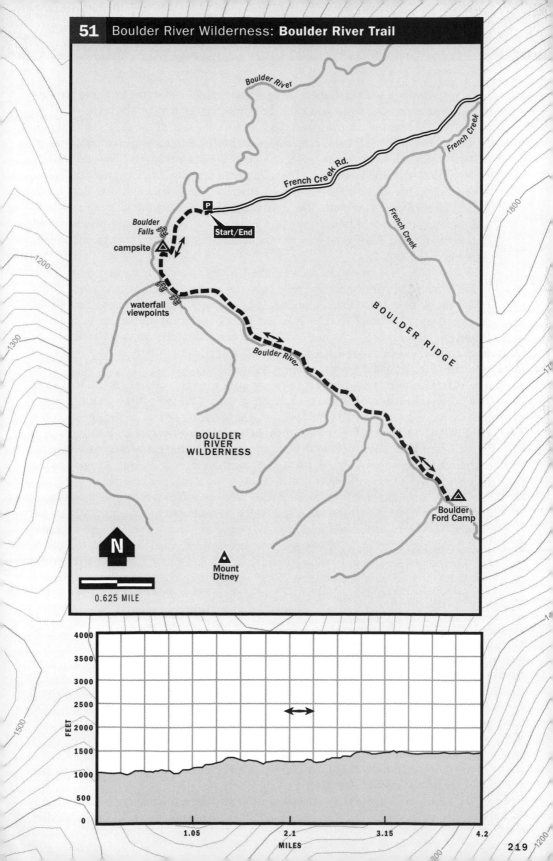

Boulder River

French Creek

French Creek Rd.

French Creek

Boulder Falls

campsite

P

Start/End

waterfall viewpoints

BOULDER RIDGE

Boulder River

BOULDER RIVER WILDERNESS

Boulder Ford Camp

N

0.625 MILE

Mount Ditney

1200

1300

1500

1800

1700

1200

300

4000

3500

3000

2500

2000

1500

1000

500

0

FEET

1.05

2.1

3.15

4.2

MILES

However, there is a self-registration kiosk at the western end of the trailhead parking lot to assist in tracking usage and help the Forest Service manage the area.

The trail starts on an old gravel road cut into the side of the slope by local pioneers. A small rocky cliff band runs alongside on the left, the exposed backbone of Boulder Ridge, which forms the northern side of the Boulder River Valley and reaches its high point at 4,378-foot French Peak. The road actually hangs out over the valley at one point, supported by some heavy timbered beams, although it is difficult to notice unless you look carefully. The river can be heard down the valley to the right, and occasionally seen through gaps in the forest of red alders and moss-covered cedars and maples. Some giant stumps hint at the huge trees that once grew here but were harvested long ago.

The trail bends around to the south and reaches a side trip to an old cabin site in the ferns to the right, about half mile from the trailhead. Not much remains of the cabin, except parts of the foundation, but the clearing where it once stood now serves as a good place to camp. Boulder Falls can usually be heard thundering in the river below, but unfortunately it is not visible from here. An indistinct way trail descends to the water's edge down a steep sandy cliff and provides the best opportunity to view the cascade, but this route is not recommended.

The true wilderness boundary lies just past the campsite, where the trail soon fades to a rocky single-track and gradually approaches the river. After another quarter mile, a spectacular waterfall tumbles down the sheer rocky face of the gorge on the opposite side, split into two distinct forks before meeting the green, churning waters of the Boulder River in a pool at the bottom. The total drop easily exceeds 75 feet as the water plunges down through a hanging garden of moss and plants clinging to the face of the cliff and fed by the constant spray.

Ironically, this noteworthy landmark and possible turnaround point goes unnamed on regional topographic maps, which instead tend to prominently label the hidden Boulder Falls; this can lead to some confusion. And it is not helped by a second, smaller waterfall on another side creek about a quarter mile farther up the valley.

Continue upstream, climbing through roots and rocks until the river is far below. Occasional glimpses of some of the surrounding high peaks appear through the forest, which is now beginning to show some of the signs of true old-growth. The tree species are typical for the lowland Cascades, including silver fir, western hemlocks, and Douglas fir. Watch for a particularly large western red cedar on the right-hand side that has been neatly hollowed out, a natural playhouse in the woods that is irresistible to children. Below the giant trees, the forest floor displays an impressive collection of virtually every type of fern native to the Pacific Northwest, fed by the heavy precipitation and dampness of the river valley. Expect the footing to be muddy and wet, as creeks and streams drain down from Boulder Ridge and frequently flood short sections of the trail.

The hike meanders up and down along the northern bank of Boulder River for several miles altogether, sometimes far above the water level and other times much closer to it. A number of good swimming holes appear below, although they are not always easily or safely accessible.

Ford Camp is the effective turnaround point, where the trail reaches a campsite right next to the river at an elevation of 1,450 feet. Note that this is less than 500 feet higher than the trailhead, although the frequent ups and downs along the way make the total vertical gain closer to twice that amount.

It is theoretically possible to continue beyond the camp and head for Tupso Pass to the south, but that requires fording the river, finding the overgrown and deteriorating trail on the far side, and then essentially bushwhacking steeply uphill for 1.5 miles or more, which few if any hikers would realistically enjoy—or should even consider. The camp does provide a good place to relax, with plenty of good rocks and logs to sit on and watch the river flow. When you are ready, retrace your steps to the beginning.

TACOMA, OLYMPIA, ENUMCLAW, AND WA 410

POINT DEFIANCE PARK

KEY AT-A-GLANCE INFORMATION

LENGTH: 3.6 miles (round-trip)

CONFIGURATION: Loop

DIFFICULTY: Easy

SCENERY: Urban trail through old-growth forest, historic Fort Nisqually, rhododendron garden, sandy beaches; views across Puget Sound

EXPOSURE: Mostly shaded

TRAFFIC: Medium on trails, high at beaches and viewpoints

TRAIL SURFACE: Dirt

HIKING TIME: 2–3 hours

ACCESS: Hikable year-round; no fees for parking or park access

MAPS: USGS Gig Harbor

FACILITIES: Restrooms and water throughout the park

Point Defiance Park

Latitude: North 47d18.2m

Longitude: West 122d31.981m

IN BRIEF

Considered Tacoma's backyard playground by many local residents, Point Defiance offers just about everything any hiker could want: historical sites, great views, deep forest, and sandy beaches, all accessible via an extensive network of trails. A loop around the Outside Perimeter Trail will confirm the park as one of the finest urban green spaces anywhere, a natural treasure not far from Tacoma's downtown core.

DESCRIPTION

Point Defiance got its name when an early explorer noted that the prominent peninsula held such an advantageous position that a fort on the site could stand against any conceivable invading force. The federal government agreed with that assessment, and in 1866 the land was appropriated for defense of the young Washington Territory, which had been carved out of the larger Oregon Territory in 1853. The land remained a military installation for many decades as the city of Tacoma grew just to the south.

By the time Washington had been admitted to the Union as the 42nd State in 1889, however, the possibility of war in Puget Sound against the British or any other significant foreign power was growing increasingly remote, and the need for the continuing fortification of Point Defiance became

DIRECTIONS

From Interstate 5 in Tacoma, take Exit 132, WA 16, toward the Tacoma Narrows Bridge. Exit WA 16 before the Tacoma Narrows Bridge onto Sixth Avenue and then turn right onto Pearl Street (WA 163). Continue on Pearl Street all the way to the main entrance of Point Defiance Park. Drive straight into the park and follow the counterclockwise loop roads to Fort Nisqually and park in the large lot there.

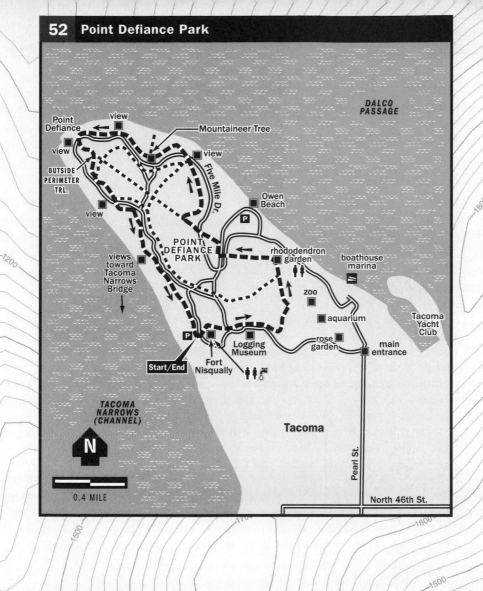

DALCO PASSAGE

Point Defiance

view

view

OUTSIDE PERIMETER TRL.

view

Mountaineer Tree

view

Five Mile Dr.

Owen Beach

P

POINT DEFIANCE PARK

rhododendron garden

boathouse marina

views toward Tacoma Narrows Bridge

zoo

aquarium

Tacoma Yacht Club

Start/End

Fort Nisqually

Logging Museum

rose garden

main entrance

TACOMA NARROWS (CHANNEL)

Tacoma

Pearl St.

N

0.4 MILE

North 46th St.

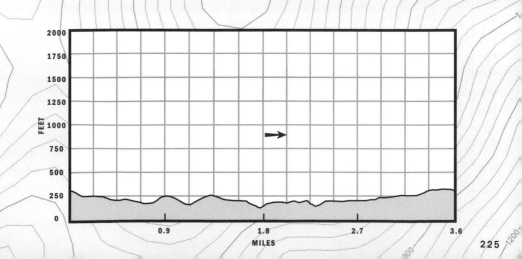

far less apparent. In a victory for local citizens, the land was turned over to the city in 1905 and reborn as a public park, whose first century of existence Tacoma celebrated in 2005.

Ironically, Point Defiance now attracts rather than repels invaders, the multitudes who come every day to take advantage of the park's 700 acres of attractions. On a typical summer weekend Point Defiance is particularly popular, which can make parking difficult, especially near the main entrance. However, there is usually ample space available in the interior along Five Mile Drive. The lot at Fort Nisqually is a good starting point because it typically has room even on the busiest days, although it is possible to begin this hike from anywhere on the loop.

The Outer Perimeter Trail runs on the top of the bluff all the way around the peninsula and can be hiked in either direction, although it is typically traveled counterclockwise, mirroring the general flow of traffic on Five Mile Drive, which follows a similar route.

Look for the start of the trail on the eastern side of the parking lot away from the water, in the trees beyond the bathrooms and picnic area. The trail is generally well-marked with short wooden posts, particularly useful at many points where the hike crosses the road, although some of the posts are concealed by underbrush. Look for a painted square, and possibly an arrow showing the way. Alternate symbols will also appear, a circle for the Spine Trail and a triangle for the Inside Perimeter Trail, both of which intersect the Outer Perimeter Trail and frequently share sections of the route.

After leaving Fort Nisqually, the trail runs gradually downhill through a shady forest of big trees, majestic examples of many signature species of the Pacific Northwest, including hemlocks, cedars, and firs, with a carpet of ferns underneath. After a half mile, pass through the rhododendron garden, where a multitude of azaleas and rhododendrons most generously donated by private citizens are on display. The garden is particularly stunning in spring when the plants are in bloom.

A quarter mile past the rhododendrons, cross the Owen Beach access road, which heads down the hill to the right. The beach is a long stretch of sand with a waterfront promenade and a grassy picnic area, invariably busy on sunny days.

Continue along the eastern side of the peninsula to a view of Vashon Island, just across the stretch of water known as Dalco Passage. Some of the finest old-growth forest in the park stands along this section of the trail, culminating in the impossible-to-miss Mountaineers Tree, a massive, 400-year-old Douglas fir rising more than 200 feet into the sky. Just before the giant tree, watch for a side trail marked with a green square heading down the bluff. It leads to a secluded beach below, great for exploring when the tide is out.

Pass several more viewpoints around the northern tip of the peninsula and then bend back toward the south. Amazingly, although Point Defiance is less than a mile across for most of its length, there is a noticeable difference between the environments on either side. The eastern bluff (which actually faces northeast) is wetter than the western bluff, which has considerable southern exposure. The trail surface underfoot reflects the difference, changing from frequently muddy to more sandy and dry as the trail heads around the point. The plant growth changes as well, with the western side featuring thinner forest and a higher density of the distinctive red-barked madrones.

The Outer Perimeter Trail follows the edge of the bluff on the western side more closely than it does on the eastern, providing repeated views over Puget Sound and the Narrows. The Tacoma Narrows Bridge is visible to the south, gracefully spanning the waters between Tacoma and Gig Harbor. A second bridge parallel to the first is currently under construction, part of a large-scale upgrade not expected to be complete until 2008. It is a safe bet that neither the new concrete structure nor the existing steel one will suffer the fate of the infamous original Tacoma Narrows Bridge, affectionately known as Galloping Gertie, which collapsed from a spectacular torsional failure brought on by high winds in November 1940. Engineering students around the world now study the structure as a lesson in how not to design a suspension bridge.

Finish the loop by hiking along the bluff and reach Fort Nisqually where you began.

▶ NEARBY ACTIVITIES

Point Defiance Park has a host of additional popular attractions, including the Tacoma Zoo and Aquarium, the reconstructed Fort Nisqually site, the Camp Six Logging Museum, an award-winning rose garden, and a boathouse and marina on Commencement Bay. For more information, visit the Point Defiance Park Web site at **www.metroparkstacoma.org**.

NISQUALLY NATIONAL WILDLIFE REFUGE

KEY AT-A-GLANCE INFORMATION

LENGTH: 5.5 miles with a 1-mile boardwalk loop option

CONFIGURATION: Loop with short side trails

DIFFICULTY: Easy to moderate

SCENERY: Wildlife, wetlands, tidelands, forest, old barns.

EXPOSURE: Mostly exposed; a few shaded areas along the Nisqually River and boardwalk sections

TRAFFIC: Busy on weekends and sunny days

TRAIL SURFACE: Mixture of gravel, dirt, and boardwalk

HIKING TIME: 2–3 hours or longer with side trips

ACCESS: Year-round (trails are open during daylight hours, and seasonal closures occur throughout the year); $3 daily fee per family

MAPS: You may find printed maps on the information board near the visitor center, USGS quad Nisqually.

FACILITIES: Restrooms and water outside the visitor center

Nisqually National Wildlife Refuge

Latitude: North 47d03.344m

Longitude: West 122d42.717m

IN BRIEF

Far from its glacial source on the southern side of Mount Rainier, the Nisqually River empties into Puget Sound in a broad delta. Once a working farm, the site has become one of the finest bird-watching locations in the Puget Sound region, although many people come purely to enjoy the natural setting. Whether looking specifically at the birds or not, hikers will find an interesting walk that explores a wide range of habitats and wildlife.

DESCRIPTION

Anyone who has frequented the I-5 corridor between Tacoma and Olympia has sped by the sign for the Nisqually National Wildlife Refuge countless times and probably not given it a second thought. A special place, the refuge was established in 1974 to protect migratory birds. More than 200 separate species, many federally listed as threatened or endangered, have been observed in the refuge's 3,000 acres. Winter brings particularly high numbers of visitors, but there are plenty during the other seasons as well.

The refuge is open year-round from sunrise to sunset, although there are trail closures during the hunting season from October to January. Note that dogs, bicycles, fires, camping, guns, and jogging are all prohibited here, but many of the trails are wheelchair accessible, including boardwalk trails at Twin Barns Loop Trail, Riparian Forest Overlook Trail, and Nisqually Overlook Trail.

Located in a sea of rushes next to the parking lot, the modern-looking visitor center is open

DIRECTIONS

From I-5 south of Tacoma, take Exit 114, Nisqually. Go north for a short distance to an intersection with the Brown Farm Road and go right. The road soon ends at the wildlife refuge visitor center and ample parking.

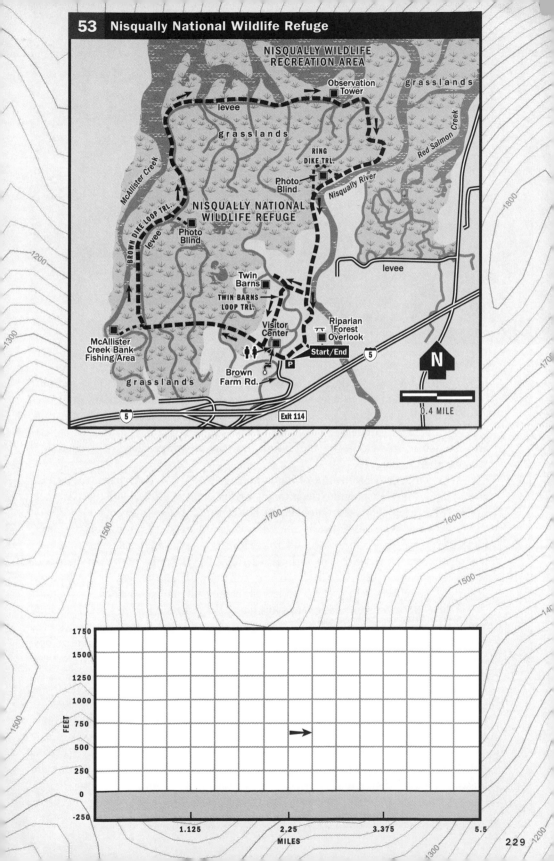

NISQUALLY WILDLIFE
RECREATION AREA

grasslands

Observation
Tower

levee

grasslands

McAllister Creek

RING
DIKE TRL.

Photo
Blind

Nisqually River

Red Salmon Creek

BROWN DIKE LOOP TRL.

levee

Photo
Blind

NISQUALLY NATIONAL
WILDLIFE REFUGE

levee

Twin
Barns

TWIN BARNS
LOOP TRL.

Visitor
Center

Riparian
Forest
Overlook

McAllister
Creek Bank
Fishing Area

Start/End

5

Brown
Farm Rd.

grasslands

N

P

5

Exit 114

0.4 MILE

1800

1200

1300

1500

1700

1600

1500

140

1500

1700

1300

1200

FEET

1750

1500

1250

1000

750

500

250

0

-250

1.125   2.25   3.375   5.5

MILES

Wetlands at Nisqually National
Wildlife Refuge

from 9 a.m. to 4 p.m., Wednesday to Sunday. Pay the day-use fee at a kiosk and pick up a park-information pamphlet with a map. Several display signs at an overlook outside the building describe some of the animals you may see on your trip, and volunteers are frequently available to answer questions. Free lectures from wildlife experts and naturalists are held in the auditorium on many evenings; check the schedule if you are interested.

The refuge is a patchwork of lands managed by the U.S. Department of Fish and Wildlife, the Washington Department of Fish and Wildlife, and the Nisqually Indian Tribe, although you are unlikely to notice these divisions anywhere except on the map. What you will notice is the wide range of habitats throughout the area, including mud flats, shrubs, coniferous forests, freshwater marshes, saltwater marshes, open saltwater, rivers and creeks, mixed grasslands, and riparian woodlands. This habitat diversity leads to the considerable assortment of birds, with waterfowl, songbirds, raptors, and waders all calling the refuge home.

There are two main hiking loops available, the 5.5-mile Brown Farm Dike Trail and the 1-mile Twin Barns Trail. Both start from the visitor center and can be traveled in either direction. If you arrive in the morning, the Brown Farm Dike Trail is best traveled clockwise, which allows you to pass through the early exposed sections before the sun gets too hot. That is how it is described here.

Find the trail on the western side of the visitor center and follow the gravel surface into the grassland. The path is broad, flat, and straight, yielding wide views to either side, including the large twin barns to the right. This is the most open section of the trail, so be prepared for the full force of the sun.

After just 0.75 miles, reach the McAllister Creek Bank Fishing Area. This is the only place in the refuge where fishing from the banks is permitted, although standard Washington State regulations apply. Access is provided by a footpath leading directly down to the shore of the creek and another heading southward along the bank. Unless you plan to cast a line, turn right and follow the main trail north.

The path climbs onto the old dike for which it is named, built to protect the Brown Farm. It no longer serves that specific purpose, but the elevated walkway provides a good vantage point for viewing the surroundings. Depending on the tide, McAllister Creek to the left can appear as a large mud flat or a wide river with a visible flow. On the right, a mix of red earth, green reeds, and yellow grass provides a surprisingly colorful montage. Benches along the way offer resting points to stop and watch for wildlife.

A spur leads to the interior of the refuge and to the first photo blind, a plywood shack with a view over a stretch of flat water. Photography is probably best here early or late in the day, when wildlife is typically more active and there is softer ambient light.

The Brown Dike Trail continues along McAllister Creek and then swings to the right. At 3.3 miles from the parking lot, wooden stairs lead up to an observation platform with a commanding view over the Nisqually Flats and the southern end of Puget Sound, known as Nisqually Reach. This is said to be the best place to spot bald eagles at the refuge; a pair of binoculars would no doubt be helpful for scanning the vast expanse of grass and water.

Near the platform, cool ocean breezes and the start of some shade can mitigate the heat on sunny summer days. The trail soon turns back to the south, and the main channel of the Nisqually River appears through the growth on the left. Despite the many side branches which siphon off the flow, the broad, green river has a noticeable current.

A half-mile side loop called the Ring Dike Trail leads to the second photo blind; the view at times may be unfortunately obscured by high bulrushes. Increasing growth alongside the levee marks the transition into woodlands, and the trail turns from gravel to boardwalk with a half mile remaining.

An additional quarter mile yields the junction with the Twin Barns Loop Trail. Whether you complete the inner loop or not, a side trip to the two barns is well worth the time. These two giant structures show the magnitude of the Brown Farm at its height; its facilities included a creamery, a meat-packing house, and an incubation and brooding house for chickens. The farm was huge for its day, and seems more like a piece of modern, industrial agriculture than its historical roots would indicate.

The barns are now used only for storage, but countless swallows nest under the eaves, aided by mesh netting. Their whirling overhead swarms are an impressive sight.

Continuing on the outer loop trail, another side branch just short of the parking lot heads to the Riparian Forest Overlook. Habitat restoration here, including the culling of non-native plants, is designed to increase the overall wetland acreage. In contrast to the bright sunlight of the flats, the deciduous woods here are thick and dark, with cottonwoods, big leaf maples, and willows. Interpretive signs along the boardwalk provide information on the flora and fauna to be seen. Massive skunk cabbage, with leaves several feet in length, line the muddy creek. Also, watch for otters, mink, and frogs below. Several wooden benches grace the observation platform at the end of the short trail.

When you are ready, return to the main trail and then continue back to your vehicle.

Nisqually Delta view from the Ring Dike Trail

▶ NEARBY ACTIVITIES

The Luhr Beach boat ramp allows access to the northern end of the refuge and to Puget Sound. Canoers, kayakers, and small boaters of all kinds can explore the bottom end of the wetlands outside the Brown Farm Dike. The launch is located at the end of D'Milluhr Road, off 46th Avenue and Meridian Road.

PINNACLE PEAK COUNTY PARK: CAL MAGNUSSON TRAIL

▶ IN BRIEF

Pinnacle Peak is an old favorite of southeast King County hikers that deserves wider attention. The geologically unusual mountain rises straight up from the surrounding farmland, thrust upward like a monument to the powerful volcanic forces that shape the Washington landscape. Although views are limited, the quick climb to the top still makes a worthy outing.

▶ DESCRIPTION

Despite having several alternate names, or perhaps because of it, Pinnacle Peak remains mostly obscure to many Puget Sound hikers. Yet whether it is called Mount Pete, Mount Peak, or Pinnacle Peak (as shown on the USGS topographic map), this singular mountain is worth knowing about.

Pinnacle Peak is just as striking and abrupt in the landscape as some of the cinder cones outside of Bend in central Oregon, although its volcanic origins are not as obvious. Where well-known landmarks like Black Butte and Lava Butte leave no doubt about their fiery beginnings from beneath the earth's crust, the evidence at Pinnacle Peak is more subtle, found in interesting columns of extruded rock near the summit. And

ℹ KEY AT-A-GLANCE INFORMATION

LENGTH: 2 miles (round-trip)

CONFIGURATION: Out-and-back with a loop option

DIFFICULTY: Moderate

SCENERY: Steep hike through dense forest on a stand-alone mountain, unique rock formations, modest views of countryside along the trail

EXPOSURE: Shaded

TRAFFIC: Medium to high

TRAIL SURFACE: Dirt

HIKING TIME: 1–2 hours

ACCESS: Hikable year-round; no fee for parking or park access

MAPS: Green Trails—Enumclaw 237; USGS Enumclaw

FACILITIES: None at trailhead

▶ DIRECTIONS

From I-5 between Seattle and Tacoma, take Exit 142A, WA 18 (east). Travel on WA 18 into Auburn then exit onto WA 164 (east) toward Enumclaw. Continue on WA 164 through Enumclaw to a junction with WA 410 (Roosevelt Avenue) and turn left (east). In less than a mile turn right onto 284th Avenue SE and proceed past King County Fairgrounds to SE 472nd Street on the right. Stay on SE 472nd Street for a half mile to the parking area and trailhead, where the road turns north. Park in the designated head-in spots or along the road out of traffic flow.

Pinnacle Peak County Park:
Cal Magnusson Trail

Latitude: North 47d10.719m

Longitude: West 121d58.425m

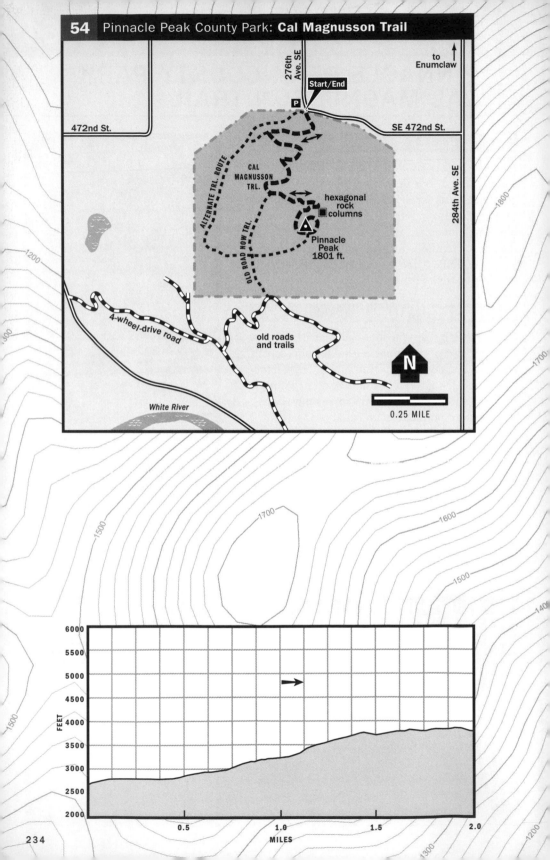

to
Enumclaw

276th
Ave. SE

Start/End

P

472nd St.

SE 472nd St.

ALTERNATE TRL. ROUTE

CAL
MAGNUSSON
TRL.

OLD ROAD NOW TRL.

hexagonal
rock
columns

Pinnacle
Peak
1801 ft.

284th Ave. SE

1200

1300

4-wheel-drive road

old roads
and trails

N

White River

0.25 MILE

1800

1700

1600

1500

1400

1300

1500

1700

1500

1500

1600

1500

1400

FEET

6000
5500
5000
4500
4000
3500
3000
2500
2000

0.5   1.0   1.5   2.0
MILES

Columns of extruded volcanic rock

although at only 1,800 feet it hardly qualifies as a significant climb, nonetheless its visibility and prominence in the Enumclaw region gives Pinnacle Peak a certain "because it's there" satisfaction to all who have reached the top, no matter how easy the trip might be.

Two separate trails originate from the parking area, the wide main trail heading uphill to the left, known as the Cal Magnusson Trail, and a narrower one to the right. Longtime Enumclaw resident Cal Magnusson worked as an engineer for Boeing and then later for REI, developing the company's first quality-control program through a friendship he had with mountaineer Jim Whittaker, the first American to summit Mount Everest in 1963. Magnusson later helped revive interest in backcountry ski touring and climbing through his involvement with The Mountaineers in the 1960s. Despite the similarity in names, Cal Magnusson is no relation to Warren G. Magnuson, who served as a congressman from the state of Washington for more than 40 years and for whom Seattle's Magnuson Park is named.

Both trails lead to the summit, but the alternate trail to the right follows a more rugged and circuitous path, looping around to the far side of the peak before eventually reaching the top. The main Magnusson trail zigzags up the northern side of the mountain and is far more commonly traveled, making it the recommended route.

Start hiking up the steep hill, rapidly climbing above the trailhead at 760 feet. Several long switchbacks cut back and forth across the slope, with an extended traverse leading to a major left-hand turn in the first half mile. A few way trails head off into the trees to the right, connecting to the alternate trail, which runs farther over to the west.

Pinnacle Peak has been logged in the past, and a web of abandoned roads covers most parts of the mountain, especially on the southern side. Nonetheless, a few larger trees remain, including some substantial Douglas firs standing right along the trail.

Reach a major intersection near 1,550 feet with an old road, and stay left. Unmarked social trails abound in this section, but it is always easy to figure out which way to go. Just as in proverbial Rome, virtually every path here heading uphill eventually leads to the top.

Most potential viewpoints are obscured by the trees, which are surprisingly thick and often block GPS signals despite the mountain's considerable isolation from any other high points nearby. Occasional glimpses of the farmland to the north do appear, however, including King County Fairgrounds just over a mile away on the opposite side of 284th Avenue SE.

Watch for some distinctive hexagonal rock columns protruding from the short, steep rise on the right. The viscous stone is molded by great heat and pressure below the surface of the Earth, then it crystallizes and solidifies into these remarkable patterns. Formations like this are generally referred to as columnar basalt, but there are actually four different types of volcanic rock that can be extruded in this way: basalt, andesite, dacite, and rhyolite. Basalt is the most common in the Pacific Northwest and is marked by its dark gray color. The columns at Pinnacle Peak are a much lighter color, though, resembling sandstone, and are likely composed of one of the other kinds of rock which contain higher amounts of silica.

The volcanic rocks are about 0.75 miles from the trailhead and only a quarter mile short of the top. Follow a quick orbit around to the other side of the peak and emerge at the summit, where some more volcanic columns stand vertically below with their geometric ends poking straight up out of the dirt.

A fire lookout once stood here but all that remains are the four concrete blocks that anchored the foundation. The structure was removed in the 1960s, likely because increasing development in the White River Valley made the area much less remote and wildfires would generally be spotted by other means. Unfortunately, there is now almost no view from the top to speak of, as the trees have all grown up around the clearing. It is worth exploring the side trails on the southern and eastern sides of the summit, where better viewpoints can be found looking out toward Mount Rainier and some of the nearby managed forests. These side trails connect to the top of the alternate trail, which provides a good optional descent route and allows for completion of a loop.

The views to the southeast have not gone unnoticed by real estate developers, who hope to acquire some of the land on the mountain's lower flank from the Washington Department of Natural Resources. However, many locals oppose the action, and as of summer 2005 the final fate of the property had not yet been determined. Either way, the hiking trails on the northern side of the peak are likely to remain undisturbed—at least for now.

FLAMING GEYSER STATE PARK

▶ IN BRIEF

An unpretentious state park with a very impressive name, Flaming Geyser presents several basic hiking options on more than 4 miles of trails. Multiple short hikes explore a ridgeline in the forest, the edge of the Green River Gorge, and the unusual geological features advertised in the title.

▶ DESCRIPTION

The words Flaming Geyser can't help but evoke images of the spectacular hydrothermal vents at Yellowstone National Park, or perhaps spurting columns of lava, a little more likely to be seen in the volcanically active Cascade Range. Unfortunately, the geysers here are small, misnamed methane seeps, and their glory is limited, to say the least. No one but the most dedicated geologist is likely to be mesmerized by them for any length of time. At least that explains why visitors from around the world are not flocking to this modest destination.

Nonetheless, Flaming Geyser does hold some attractions for hikers, who can explore a few short loop trails and an out-and-back route along the Green River. The geysers, a unique natural phenomenon in the landscape, are also well worth seeing, as long as expectations are set appropriately.

From the parking lot, head eastward next to the Environmental Learning Center Lodge, just off to the right. Immediately past two concrete

❶ KEY AT-A-GLANCE INFORMATION

LENGTH: 1.5 miles (Ridge Trail), 1.7 miles (River Trail), 0.4 miles (Geyser Loop)

CONFIGURATION: Out-and-back and loop options

DIFFICULTY: Easy to moderate

SCENERY: Three different hiking trails and an interpretive trail, Flaming and Bubbling geysers, Green River Gorge

EXPOSURE: Mostly shaded

TRAFFIC: High visitation to park, only moderate traffic on trails; (get an early start on sunny weekends or parking may fill up)

TRAIL SURFACE: Dirt

HIKING TIME: 1–2 hours

ACCESS: Hikable year-round; Washington State Park Pass required for parking (daily passes available at park)

MAPS: USGS Black Diamond

FACILITIES: Restroom and water at trailhead

▶ DIRECTIONS

From I-5 south of Seattle, take Exit 142, WA 18 (east). After passing through Auburn, turn right (east) onto Auburn–Black Diamond Road then immediately turn right again onto SE Green Valley Road. Continue for more than 8 miles and pass 218th Avenue SE, then look for SE Flaming Geyser Road and the entrance to Flaming Geyser State Park on the right. Drive to the parking lot at the end of the road.

Flaming Geyser State Park

Latitude: North 47d16.351m

Longitude: West 122d01.399m

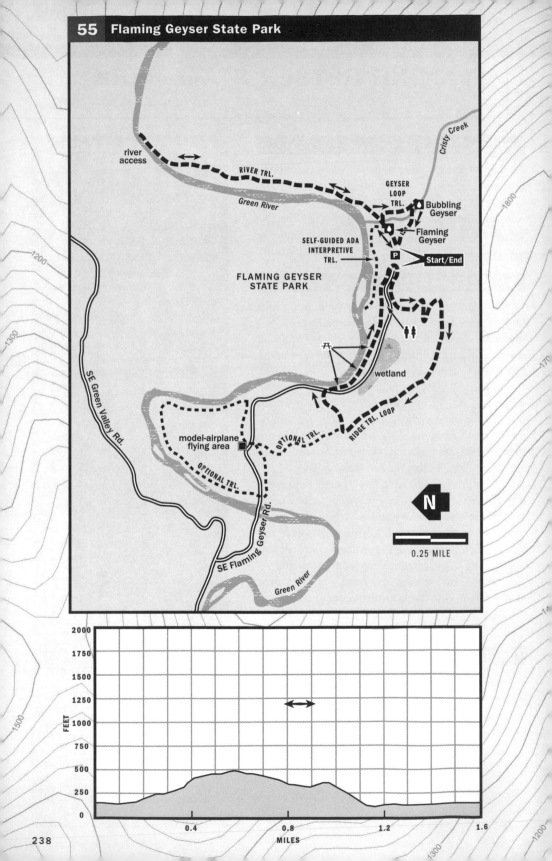

river access

RIVER TRL.

Green River

Cristy Creek

GEYSER
LOOP
TRL.

Bubbling Geyser

Flaming Geyser

SELF-GUIDED ADA
INTERPRETIVE
TRL.

P

Start/End

FLAMING GEYSER
STATE PARK

wetland

SE Green Valley Rd.

model-airplane
flying area

OPTIONAL TRL.

RIDGE TRL. LOOP

OPTIONAL TRL.

SE Flaming Geyser Rd.

Green River

N

0.25 MILE

FEET

2000
1750
1500
1250
1000
750
500
250
0

0.4   0.8   1.2   1.6
MILES

fishponds used as imprinting tanks for steelhead smolts, look for signs with arrows to Flaming Geyser and Bubbling Geyser up the hill to the right. This is the start of a quick loop trail to both of the methane seeps.

The park's namesake Flaming Geyser is practically adjacent to the fishponds. The methane gas escapes from the ground through a concrete cylinder sunk into a stone basin, where it is consumed by a faint, flickering six-inch flame. Once the flame stood much higher, and probably deserved its name, but it largely faded in the 1960s. The most impressive thing about the seep now is the depth of its source underground; the gas rises from more than 1,400 feet below the surface, the by-product of coal-drilling explorations carried out here years ago.

The trail continues uphill along Cristy Creek, and soon reaches a wooden viewing platform at Bubbling Geyser. Here the methane emerges from between some pebbles at the side of the stream, laying a milky-white precipitate in the creek bed. The gas can often be smelled in the air as well.

Cross the creek and descend some stairs along a wooden fence. The stony single-track quickly reaches a junction, and a left turn immediately returns you to the start, for a total trip around the loop of less than a half mile.

Another option from the junction is to head right, joining the River Trail on a wide, muddy surface. A few spurs lead away from the main trail down to the banks of the Green River on the left, frequently used by fly fishermen and others to reach the water's edge.

The River Trail continues through a forest of alders, mossy maples, and some large yellow cedars as it climbs about 50 feet above the shoreline. The river itself becomes increasingly difficult to see down the slope to the left, and a high ridge climbs away to the right. Seams of sedimentary rock are exposed in a small cliff band on the right, with some obvious coal visible in the layered sandstone.

The trail eventually narrows to a muddy single-track, running through some short climbs and drops, sometimes near the river's edge and sometimes farther above it. Eventually, emerge from the brush into some smooth rocks on the banks of the Green. This is the official end of the trail, although it is possible to boulder-hop farther upstream if the water level is low enough.

Across the water, steep rock walls rise 100 feet above the river, the western end of the steep and narrow Green River Gorge. The gorge is at its deepest and most impressive another few miles upstream near the Black Diamond Bridge, but the cliffs here give a small hint of what it is like. The setting on the bank makes a nice place to rest as the water flows by, surprisingly clear and clean. The return on the River Trail is the same as the way you came, a total round-trip of approximately 0.9 miles.

The Ridge Trail starts a quarter mile away on the park road, at the entrance to the final parking lot. Look for the big bathroom building on the river side of the road and an Authorized Vehicles Only sign on a white steel gate on the other side at small traffic turn-out. The trail begins beyond the gate.

Cross the grass at the edge of the field for about 50 yards and look for the Trail sign pointing to the left. Start to climb on a stony surface, a now-abandoned road that heads steeply uphill and begins to bend around to the right. After ascending some 100 feet, the trail flattens out through some high brush, now heading west.

The road is slowly being reclaimed and turned into a trail, narrowing as it continues along the ridge. An easement allows passage here at the edge of some private property, so be sure to stay on the established track. Some very large maples populate the slope to the left, rising far above the trail, which never reaches the top of the ridge despite its name. Some sandstone cliffs are visible up through the trees.

Although the park receives many visitors who use the picnic facilities and playing fields below, up here on the ridge you are likely to have the trail all to yourself, since very few people venture into the woods. You are also far enough above the crowds that the only sounds you typically hear are the birds singing in the trees and the gurgling of several small creeks that run down the slope.

Descend slightly to reach a junction, where a single-track traverses left and a double-track continues down the hill. Follow the double-track past a small wetland area to reach a gravel pull-out on the main park road. Cross the road and then pass through a picnic area to approach the river. A return trail runs along the bank to the right, skirting several more picnic areas and a playfield before returning to the parking lot, a total distance of about 1.5 miles around from where you began.

As a final option, a short interpretive trail runs for less than a quarter mile on the northern side of the parking lot, near the river bank.

MUD MOUNTAIN DAM AND RECREATION AREA: MUD MOUNTAIN LAKE AND WHITE RIVER TRAIL

▶ IN BRIEF

This one-of-a-kind trail follows the White River above Mud Mountain Dam, first on a high bluff and then right along the water, providing the unique opportunity to walk on a part-time lake bed. With year-round access, limited traffic, and a feel more like a riparian zone in eastern Washington than anything in the Cascades, this hike is unlike any other in the region.

▶ DESCRIPTION

Among such Pacific Northwest engineering marvels as the Grand Coulee and Bonneville dams on the Columbia River, Mud Mountain Dam is something of an anomaly. Despite being the tallest dam in the world of its type when it was built in the 1940s, it was designed purely to prevent floods, generating no hydroelectric power and rarely even holding back any water. Instead, the dam acts like a regulator valve for the White River Valley, only allowing a certain volume to pass through and usually doing nothing to impede the river's standard flow. However, during occasional periods of flooding, the river gets backed up behind the dam to form a temporary reservoir, protecting development downstream.

This means that unless you happen to arrive during one of the infrequent periods of extreme

▶ DIRECTIONS

From I-5 between Seattle and Tacoma, take Exit 142A, WA 18 (east). Travel on WA 18 into Auburn, then exit onto WA 164 (east) toward Enumclaw. Continue on WA 164 through Enumclaw to a junction with WA 410 (Roosevelt Avenue), and turn left (east). Stay on WA 410 (east); about 4 miles from Enumclaw turn right onto SE Mud Mountain Road. Follow this road about 2 miles to Mud Mountain Recreation Area and park in the lot outside the park gate.

ⓘ KEY AT-A-GLANCE INFORMATION

LENGTH: 6.5 miles (round-trip)

CONFIGURATION: Out-and-back

DIFFICULTY: Moderate

SCENERY: Walking along the White River on a dry lake bed, viewpoints of valley from Rim Trail and Mud Mountain Dam when the park is open

EXPOSURE: Shaded on Rim Trail, exposed on River Trail

TRAFFIC: Low

TRAIL SURFACE: Mixture of dirt with some gravel

HIKING TIME: 3–4 hours

ACCESS: Hikable year-round (recreation area closed weekends November–March; hours vary year to year); no fees for parking or park access

MAPS: Green Trails—Enumclaw 237; USGS Enumclaw

FACILITIES: None at trailhead; restrooms and water in park when open

Mud Mountain Dam and Recreation Area: Mud Mountain Lake and White River Trail

Latitude: North 47d08.705m

Longitude: West 121d56.035m

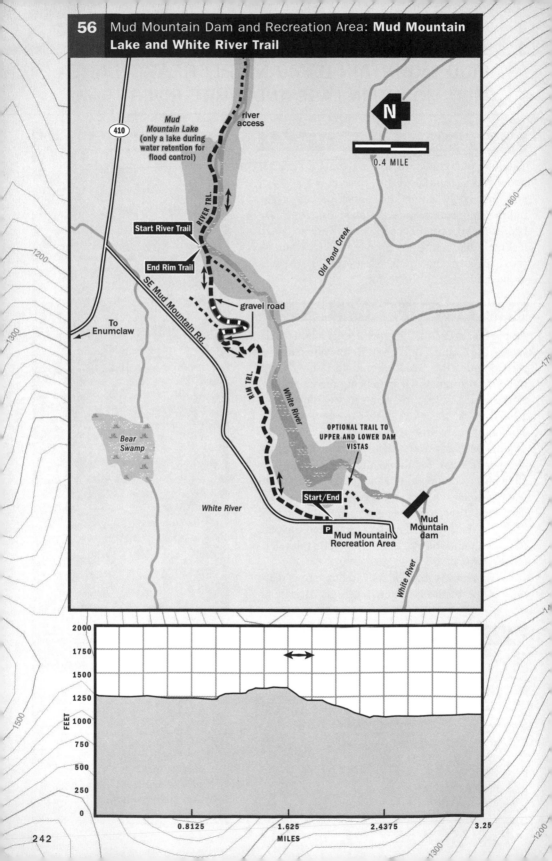

N

0.4 MILE

Mud Mountain Lake (only a lake during water retention for flood control)

river access

410

RIVER TRL.

Start River Trail

End Rim Trail

gravel road

SE Mud Mountain Rd

To Enumclaw

RIM TRL.

White River

Old Pond Creek

OPTIONAL TRAIL TO UPPER AND LOWER DAM VISTAS

Bear Swamp

White River

Start/End

P Mud Mountain Recreation Area

Mud Mountain dam

White River

1800

1700

1200

1300

1500

1300

1200

FEET

2000
1750
1500
1250
1000
750
500
250
0

0.8125   1.625   2.4375   3.25

MILES

White River Valley from Mud
Mountain Recreation Area

high water, the Mud Mountain Dam will be essentially dormant, nothing more than a giant wall waiting to be put into service. Thankfully, it also means that the engaging lower section of the trail above the White River will be dry and accessible, rather than at the bottom of a temporary, man-made lake.

To begin the hike, head east from the parking lot on a gravel path next to the chain-link fence. Turn left at the edge of the gorge, several hundred feet above the White River, which is visible down the steep slope through the trees. Note that the dam itself is just downstream from this location, but it is not visible from here. Although one viewpoint farther along provides a glimpse of the dam, it is necessary to visit the interpretive site inside the adjacent park in order to get a good look at the impressive structure.

The trail quickly meets an unpaved road entering from the left, a secondary access for when the outer gates to the recreation area are closed. To find this alternate starting point, look for a bright-yellow metal gate marked as Mud Mountain Dam Test Well on the left side of the main road, just before the big sign reading Entering Mud Mountain Dam and Recreation Area.

Continue to follow the trail as it heads east along the top of the White River Valley rim. A few gaps in the trees provide views of the water churning far below, and Mount Rainier even makes a token appearance with the crest of Liberty Cap rising just above the ridgeline on the opposite side of the valley.

Turn right at a junction with a dirt road and follow the road until a left turn returns you to the single-track at a sign marked with a hiking icon, two figures with walking sticks.

The trail descends about 40 feet into a forest of large Douglas firs and cedars. Amazingly, these massive and seemingly immovable trees are sometimes uprooted by high winds that howl through the valley during storms. Several sizable specimens lie on either side of the path as it heads through a flat swampy section, where thoughtfully laid wooden planks keep hikers mostly above the mud. Giant skunk cabbages are right at home here in the dampness and shade.

Meet a second dirt road at the end of the flats, and look for a Rim Trail sign tacked to a tree on the far side, just to the right. The trail runs next to the road for about 30 yards before bending back out along the valley rim. You are now much closer to the river than you were before, and the water, laden with the glacial silt that gives it a greenish color, can easily be heard flowing over the rocks. The silt has been carried from far up on Mount Rainier's northeastern flank, where five separate glaciers (including the giant Emmons and Winthrop glaciers) drain into the White River watershed.

Split-rail fencing helps to keep people back from the steep drop-off at a few places where the trail runs right out to the edge. One such point provides the only vantage on the entire trail of Mud Mountain Dam itself, with just a corner visible far downstream through the trees.

At the 2-mile mark, the Rim Trail ends at a gravel road, used by equestrians for access. This is a good turnaround point for hikers seeking a shorter outing. However, the second part of the hike on the banks of the river is well worth the additional effort; for that it is necessary to head downhill on the road to the right.

Follow the road as it loses elevation and bends to the left, dropping through a forest of big leaf maples and then a mix of willows and alders before emerging into a broad clearing. This is in fact the footprint of Mud Mountain Lake, created when the water is sufficiently backed up by the dam, although the thick growth of grasses, bushes, and trees shows the relative rarity of such flooding events. A thick steel cable that spans the entire valley anchors a series of metal pontoons used to trap debris on the surface of the lake before it can reach the dam intake.

The road continues upstream just above the river where the limited shade keeps the footing from becoming too muddy and churned up, even in the winter. Owing to the open terrain, the hike seems more like something in the Yakima River Valley than on the western slope of the Cascades, right down to the abundant reeds and snake grass. The only thing missing is the fragrant sagebrush.

The trail narrows and eventually reaches a small sandy beach on the riverbank, where a creek flows in from the left. This spot provides easy access to the water and a few convenient boulders for sitting and relaxing. Although it is possible to continue exploring upstream, this is likely the best turnaround point for most hikers. From here, it is 3.25 miles back to the start for a 6.5-mile round-trip journey, including a 300-foot elevation gain back up to the rim.

▶ NEARBY ACTIVITIES

The U.S. Army Corps of Engineers operates the Mud Mountain Recreation Area adjacent to the trailhead, offering a public park and playground facilities. An interpretive site at the eastern end of the park provides information about the design and construction of the dam, along with an excellent viewpoint from the rim of the rock and earth structure. A short walk into the canyon leads to a second vista with a much lower viewpoint, accenting the height of the dam. For more information, visit the Mud Mountain Dam Web site at **www.nws.usace.army.mil/PublicMenu/Menu.cfm?sitename=MM& pagename=Tour**.

FEDERATION FOREST STATE PARK

▶ IN BRIEF

A most unlikely oasis in a desert of clear-cuts, Federation State Forest is one of the last stands of significant old-growth anywhere in the White River Valley. This thin stretch of protected land along WA 410 features a lush, lowland forest of Douglas fir, western hemlock, western red cedar, and the relatively uncommon Sitka spruce. Some of the largest trees reach from five to seven feet in diameter and grow several hundred feet high.

▶ DESCRIPTION

Federation Forest State Park was founded in 1949. But it was born centuries before, when many of its giant trees were only seedlings. Since then, the forest has miraculously survived storms, fire, and the chain saw to stand as an impressive reminder of what the entire region was like before modern civilization arrived.

Catherine Montgomery was a pioneer educator and is largely responsible for the preservation of this natural area, organizing and acquiring the park lands through her affiliation with the Washington State Federation of Women's Clubs and keeping the magnificent trees here from meeting the same fate as most of their brothers

▶ KEY AT-A-GLANCE INFORMATION

LENGTH: 4 miles (round-trip)

CONFIGURATION: Loop

DIFFICULTY: Easy

SCENERY: Plant life, old-growth forest, interpretive center and displays, "Hobbit House"

EXPOSURE: Shaded

TRAFFIC: Moderate in summer, low in off-season

TRAIL SURFACE: Dirt

HIKING TIME: 1–3 hours

ACCESS: Hikable year-round; State Park daily fee of $7 required for parking

MAPS: USGS Greenwater

FACILITIES: Restroom and water at interpretive center

▶ DIRECTIONS

From I-5 between Seattle and Tacoma, take Exit 142A, WA 18 (east). Travel on WA 18 into Auburn, then exit onto WA 164 (east) toward Enumclaw. Continue on WA 164 through Enumclaw to a junction with WA 410 (Roosevelt Avenue), and turn left (east). Stay on WA 410 (east) until just before the town of Greenwater, then turn right into a well-signed parking area for the state park. If the parking area near the interpretive center is closed, drive back toward Enumclaw about a half mile to a wide parking area pullout on the southern side of WA 410.

Federation Forest State Park

Latitude: North 47d09.124m

Longitude: West 121d41.299m

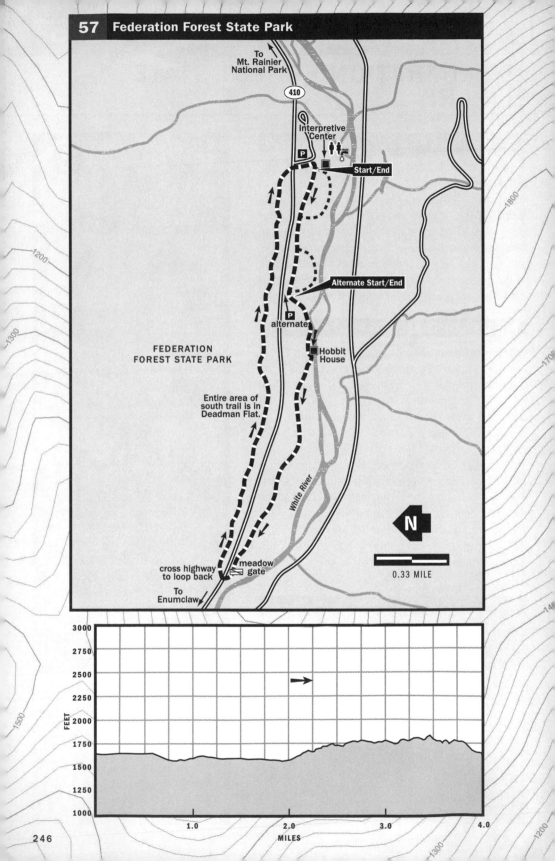

To
Mt. Rainier
National Park

410

Interpretive
Center

P

Start/End

Alternate Start/End

P
alternate

Hobbit
House

FEDERATION
FOREST STATE PARK

Entire area of
south trail is in
Deadman Flat.

White River

N

0.33 MILE

cross highway
to loop back

meadow
gate

To
Enumclaw

FEET

3000
2750
2500
2250
2000
1750
1500
1250
1000

1.0   2.0   3.0   4.0
MILES

The "Hobbit House"

and sisters along the White River. The influence of women on the park can be easily seen in many of the features named in their honor, such as the Ester Maltby Trail, the Jean Caithness Greenlees Grove, and the Ella Higginson Grove, a tribute to the one-time poet laureate of Washington State.

The park's interpretive center now bears Montgomery's name. Although the park's trails are available year-round, the interpretive center is seasonal, open from May 1 through September 30, 9 a.m. to 4 p.m., Wednesday through Sunday. Inside, exhibits detail the various ecosystems visible across the state, from the coastal rain forest to the dry deserts of the east. In front of the building, a garden of plants from throughout the region are displayed, a helpful guide for any would-be naturalist.

The linear park consists of a number of loop trails, many short enough to be suitable for even the youngest children. Multiple hiking options are available. But the best extended hike is detailed here, running between the river and the southern side of WA 410 through some of the largest trees and then returning on the far side of the road.

The trailhead is located on the western side of the parking lot, where a wide gravel path leads into the dark woods. Stay to the right and soon leave the gravel to enter an interpretive forest, where a wide array of plant species is identified. Orange honeysuckle, salal, and sword fern grow through the understory here, along with Oregon grape, the Oregon state flower, which bears blueberry-like fruit and has serrated leaves like holly. The traffic on WA 410 can generally be heard through the trees, but moss-laden vine maples and giant Douglas firs help to create the illusion of deep wilderness.

Despite its status for many as the signature tree of the Pacific Northwest, the Douglas fir is not a true fir and can be identified because its cones hang down (true fir cones grow upwards). Although that is difficult to gauge when looking at a tall tree with cones far above your head, this is the type of useful information the interpretive forest can provide.

Western hemlock (*Tsuga heterophylla*) is another false fir with numerous small cones that hang from the end of its thin branches. It is also known as the Pacific hemlock, or West Coast hemlock, and is marked by a narrow, flexible crown with frequently droopy new growth. A shallow root system makes western hemlocks susceptible to blowdown in high winds, but the tree is also adaptable enough to grow directly on decaying wood.

The western hemlock narrowly beat out the western red cedar to be adopted as the state tree of Washington in 1947. The year before, the prominent Portland *Oregonian* had teased its neighbor to the north about not having a state tree and suggested the hemlock. Many proud Washingtonians did not want anyone from rival Oregon dictating their state tree and instead selected the red cedar. However, when the matter finally came to a vote in the legislature the western hemlock won out in the end.

Of particular interest are the large Sitka spruces, which you will pass as you continue west on the trail. This spruce is the tallest conifer in North America, often reaching 150 to 200 feet high with an estimated life span of up to 800 years. Because of its high moisture requirements, it is typically confined to a narrow coastal fog belt. But it can also grow inland along low elevation rivers and streams, like the ones here.

The fine grain, good strength-to-weight ratio, and long, straight trunk made the wood of the Sitka spruce particularly valuable in the manufacture of airplane wings in World War I, prior to the advent of aluminum, fiberglass, and other modern construction materials. Although the Seattle-based Boeing Corporation had pioneered the use of this local wood, it was rival Howard Hughes' famous Spruce Goose that probably did the most to advertise it as an aircraft construction material. However, Hughes' enormous floating plane was actually built primarily of laminated birch, not spruce, and was considered by many to be nothing more than a manifestation of Hughes' questionable sanity at the time.

At a major, signed junction stay right toward the Jean Caithness Greenlees Grove. Just past the sign is one of the finest collections of old-growth trees in the park. A huge fire swept through this area in 1846; this would have cleared out the understory and left only the biggest trees remaining. Amazingly, some of the ancient trees here still show charred bark, scarred as the unlikely survivors of this epic event that took place more than 150 years ago.

The trail continues through Deadman Flat and eventually reaches the elevated bank of the White River. Below, the milky water reveals its glacial origins as it tumbles over a bed of smooth white rocks. The path winds its way generally along the river, with a surprising series of short ups and downs. Expect some areas to be muddy and wet, although wooden boardwalks with attached metal laths help keep you above the worst of it.

A whimsical "Hobbit House" is neatly tucked below some stumps and roots along the way. And "The Shire" is sure to delight children of all ages, many of whom have left their own contributions to the miniature village.

Past the Hobbit settlement, the trail becomes carpeted with moss and then crosses an open area just before reaching the Meadow Gate to the right. Go through the gate and cross WA 410 to re-enter the forest on the opposite side. Immediately turn right at a T-shaped intersection to head back in the direction you came.

The trail on this side is elevated above the road and more exposed to its traffic and noise, although the forest here is still worth seeing. Fungi of all shapes, sizes, and colors line the route, a very different display than offered by the giant trees but impressive all the same.

After about 1.5 miles, turn right at a sign leading back to the interpretive center. Cross the road in front of the Federation Forest State Park sign and return to the parking lot and your vehicle.

▶ NEARBY ACTIVITIES

The White River Valley along WA 410 beyond Greenwater is renowned for its mountain biking. Some of the better-known rides are Skookum Flats, Sun Top, Dalles Ridge–Ranger Creek, and Crystal Mountain. These are all either physically or technically demanding rides that are often described as epic. If interested, check with a local bike shop or search the Web for directions to these rides.

The Muckleshoot tribe owns and operates the Muckleshoot Casino on their reservation in Auburn. The sprawling facility is located on WA 164, 2 miles south of the junction with WA 18. In addition to gaming, the casino offers a wide variety of amenities, food services, and lodging. For more information, call (800) 804-4944 or visit **www.muckleshootcasino.com.**

MOUNT RAINIER NATIONAL PARK

MOUNT RAINIER NATIONAL PARK:
CARBON RIVER AND CARBON GLACIER

 KEY AT-A-GLANCE INFORMATION

LENGTH: 7.5 miles (round-trip)

CONFIGURATION: Loop

DIFFICULTY: Moderate

SCENERY: Scenic river valley, waterfall, suspension footbridge, a huge glacier close-up; views of Mount Rainier

EXPOSURE: Mostly shaded; exposed beyond the suspension bridge to the glacier

TRAFFIC: Heavy; get an early start to avoid the crowds

TRAIL SURFACE: Dirt

HIKING TIME: 4–5 hours

ACCESS: Summer–fall (check road conditions and snowpack); National Park Pass required

MAPS: Green Trails–Mount Rainier West 269; USGS Mowich Lake

FACILITIES: Restrooms and water at trailhead

Mount Rainier National Park:
Carbon River and Carbon Glacier

Latitude: North 46d58.601m

Longitude: West 121d49.842m

▶ IN BRIEF

This one-of-a-kind trail takes day hikers to the foot of the Carbon Glacier, an experience typically reserved for mountaineers in the high-alpine terrain far above. The glacier is a truly unique geological feature, containing the greatest volume of ice and reaching the lowest elevation of any glacier in the United States outside of Alaska.

▶ DESCRIPTION

Don't wait too long to do this hike. Every year it gets longer as the Carbon Glacier retreats a little farther up the valley, and one day the ice might not be there at all. Fortunately, some delay is probably tolerable; of the 25 major glaciers on Mount Rainier the Carbon has proven one of the most stable in recent history. Owing to its well-shaded position on the northern side of the mountain and its thick layer of insulating rock and debris, the Carbon has seen a much lower melt rate than some of its neighbors.

▶ DIRECTIONS

From Interstate 5 between Seattle and Tacoma, take Exit 142A, WA 18 (East). Travel on WA 18 toward Auburn and exit onto WA 167 (south) toward Puyallup. Before reaching Puyallup, exit onto WA 410 toward Sumner and Mount Rainier National Park. Continue on WA 410 to the town of Buckley. In Buckley, turn right (south) toward Wilkeson on WA 165 and immediately take another right to stay on WA 165. At a Y-shaped intersection, veer left to stay on WA 165 and drive through the small towns of Wilkeson and Carbonado. At another Y-shaped intersection, veer left on paved Forest Road 78 clearly signed for Carbon River (the road on the right is signed for Mowich Lake). Pay the required fee at the National Park boundary and fee station, and then proceed on the rough potholed Carbon River Road to its end at the Ipsut Creek Campground.

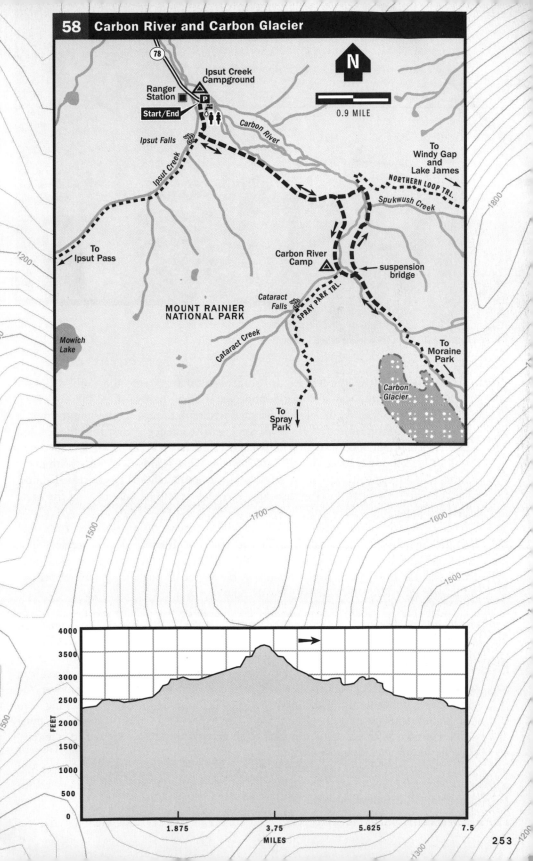

Ipsut Creek
Campground

Ranger
Station

Start/End

Ipsut Falls

Carbon River

To
Windy Gap
and
Lake James

NORTHERN LOOP TRL.

Spukwush Creek

Ipsut Creek

To
Ipsut Pass

Carbon River Camp

suspension
bridge

MOUNT RAINIER
NATIONAL PARK

Cataract
Falls

SPRAY PARK TRL.

To
Moraine
Park

Mowich
Lake

Cataract Creek

Carbon
Glacier

To Spray
Park

N

0.9 MILE

Suspension footbridge over the
Carbon River

At the height of the last ice age some 15,000 years ago, the Carbon Glacier likely reached all the way to Puget Sound, just a small part of the 3,000-foot deep Cordilleran Ice Sheet. As the climate warmed it shrank to near its present position, a process that continues today. However, geological evidence shows that the Carbon has receded a total of only about a half mile over the last few centuries, and there has been little recorded change over the last 75 years. That stands in contrast with many glaciers on the opposite side of the mountain; the South Tahoma has retreated almost 3 miles since 1896 and the Paradise–Stevens has lost half its volume over the same period of time.

Despite the obvious long-term trend, the extensive disappearance of ice from Mount Rainier has been far from linear and consistently defies predictability. Between the late 1960s and early 1980s many glaciers showed considerable advances, and some (such as the Nisqually) have gone through several minor periods of growth and decay over the past few decades.

That would seem to challenge the theory of general global warming now argued by legions of climatologists around the world, but glacial changes are not determined by temperature alone. In general, glaciers grow when more snow accumulates than is able to melt in a given year and shrink when the opposite occurs. Given the climate of the region, it is quite possible that warmer ambient temperatures would result in more humid air rising from the Pacific Ocean and then condensing into snow on the mountain's upper slopes. If the increased snowfall exceeded the rate of melting from the higher temperatures, the glaciers would be expected to grow. Nonetheless, most scientists predict the continued retreat of all glaciers on Mount Rainier for the foreseeable future, including the Carbon.

Begin your hike to the glacier at the Ipsut Creek Campground and Ranger Station, elevation 2,320 feet. The trailhead is in the southeast corner of the vast camping area, at the end of the road.

Many older topographic maps show the trail running parallel to the Carbon River, but it was washed out in recent years when the river changed course. Instead of following the bank, the new route heads south through a damp, mossy forest over a series of creek crossings. The woods here are some of the thickest anywhere inside the National Park boundary, thanks to the low elevation and heavy precipitation.

Within the first quarter mile a worthwhile side trip leads to Ipsut Falls, where Ipsut Creek drops through a narrow gap. The short canyon is noticeably cooler than the surrounding forest, well-shaded by its steep walls and lush growth.

Climb uphill to join the famous Wonderland Trail, a hikers' thoroughfare that circles the entire mountain in just more than 90 miles. The Wonderland was originally built as the primary means for rangers to travel throughout the park and has always been well-maintained, making it broad and easy to follow.

Take the left fork, signed to Carbon River Camp, Carbon Glacier, and Dick Creek Camp. The trail emerges from the woods to reach the edge of the silt-laden Carbon River, the very definition of a braided stream with multiple branches winding through a vast flat of rounded rocks. The river bed here is almost a half mile wide, scattered with logs and debris.

After 2 miles, the Wonderland reaches the first river crossing at the junction with the Northern Loop Trail, signed to Windy Gap and Lake James. This is the recommended return route on the descent. For now, continue climbing on the western side of the river, passing through the Carbon River Camp and crossing Cataract Creek, a nonglacial stream flowing down from the right. Just past the creek another junction leads uphill to Seattle Park and Spray Park; stay left along the river once again.

The second river crossing is on a bouncy suspension footbridge anchored on a glacially scoured slab of bedrock. The rock's polished and striated surface testifies to the Carbon Glacier's historical reach far below its current terminus.

Once you cross the bridge it is only another half mile to the toe of the glacier itself, which is hard to distinguish among the large pile of rocks and mud it carries down the valley. Look for the sun catching the underlying ice to reveal the glacier's true nature. A boulder field at the edge of the moraine makes a great place to rest and observe the wall of ice and the Carbon River flowing out from underneath.

This is the traditional turnaround point, but you can extend your hike by continuing an additional 3 miles one-way to Moraine Park at an elevation of 6,000 feet. The reward for the long climb is an impressive view of the upper glacier, a sea of blue seracs at the foot of the massive Willis Wall.

Descend the way you came, but instead of crossing the suspension bridge a second time, continue along the river's eastern bank to complete a short loop. The route on this side of the river is much less traveled than the Wonderland Trail and is much more peaceful since it is set back from the noise of the running water. Pass underneath high cliffs and tall trees until you reach the junction leading back across the river, signed to Ipsuit Campground.

Unlike the single span of the suspension bridge, the trail here crosses a series of several logs over the various threads of the river. Be careful with your footing, as these logs may be unsteady and are prone to washout during floods. Once safely across, retrace your original steps to your vehicle.

MOUNT RAINIER NATIONAL PARK:
MOWICH LAKE, EUNICE LAKE, AND TOLMIE PEAK LOOKOUT

 **KEY AT-A-GLANCE
INFORMATION**

LENGTH: 6 miles (round-trip)

CONFIGURATION: Out-and-back

DIFFICULTY: Moderate

SCENERY: Plant life and wildflowers, scenic lakes, fire lookout cabin; superb views of Mount Rainier

EXPOSURE: Shaded on about half the route

TRAFFIC: Heavy; get an early start to beat the crowds

TRAIL SURFACE: Dirt

HIKING TIME: 3–4 hours

ACCESS: Summer–fall (check road conditions and snowpack); National Park Pass required

MAPS: Green Trails–Mount Rainier West 269; USGS Mowich Lake and Golden Lakes

FACILITIES: Restroom at trailhead; no drinking water available

Mount Rainier National Park:
Mowich Lake, Eunice Lake, and
Tolmie Peak Lookout

Latitude: North 46d55.97m

Longitude: West 121d51.839m

▶ IN BRIEF

The panoramic view from Tolmie Peak is one of the finest in the entire northwest corner of Mount Rainier National Park. The summit lookout provides a great perspective for studying the giant volcano and its surroundings while Eunice Lake shimmers in a steep alpine bowl directly below.

▶ DESCRIPTION

Most hikers leave Mowich Lake bound for Spray Park, lured up Rainier's northwest flank by the many attractions of the subalpine meadow. However, the best views of the mountain itself are ironically found on some of the high ridges in the opposite direction, far enough away that the entire mountain can be taken in at once. Head up 5,900-foot Tolmie Peak to enjoy such a vista, and possibly escape some of the crowds as well.

▶ DIRECTIONS

From I-5 between Seattle and Tacoma, take Exit 142A, WA 18 (east). Travel on WA 18 toward Auburn, and exit onto WA 167 (south) toward Puyallup. Before reaching Puyallup, exit onto WA 410 toward Sumner and Mount Rainier National Park. Continue on WA 410 to the town of Buckley. In Buckley, turn right (south) toward Wilkeson on WA 165 and immediately take another right to stay on WA 165. At a Y-shaped intersection, veer left to stay on WA 165 and drive through the small towns of Wilkeson and Carbonado. At another Y-shaped intersection, veer right to stay on WA 165, which is clearly signed for Mowich Lake (the road on the left is signed for the Carbon River). Drive 11 miles to the National Park boundary and fee station. After paying the required fees, drive this dirt road (now called Road 79 and Mowich Lake Road) to its end at the Mowich Lake Campground.

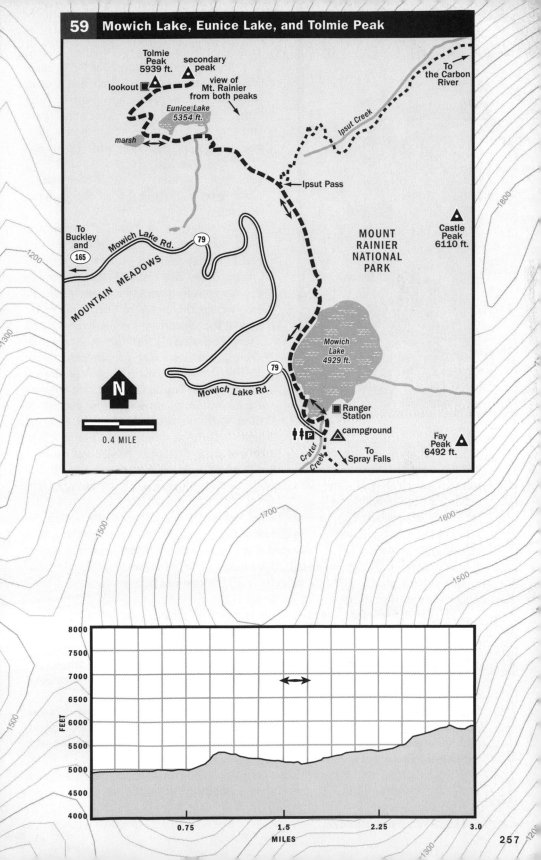

Tolmie Peak 5939 ft.

secondary peak

lookout

view of Mt. Rainier from both peaks

Eunice Lake 5354 ft.

marsh

To the Carbon River

Ipsut Creek

Ipsut Pass

To Buckley and 165

Mowich Lake Rd.

79

MOUNTAIN MEADOWS

MOUNT RAINIER NATIONAL PARK

Castle Peak 6110 ft.

N

0.4 MILE

79

Mowich Lake Rd.

Mowich Lake 4929 ft.

Ranger Station

campground

Crater Creek

To Spray Falls

Fay Peak 6492 ft.

8000
7500
7000
6500
6000
5500
5000
4500
4000

FEET

0.75   1.5   2.25   3.0

MILES

Alpine tarn near Eunice Lake

Tolmie Peak is named for Dr. William Fraser Tolmie, who penetrated this area in 1833 in search of medicinal plants and herbs. Tolmie was likely the first non–Native American man to explore this remote wilderness, less than 30 years after Lewis and Clark had reached the Pacific and long before the founding of either the state of Washington in 1889 or the national park ten years later.

At the time of Tolmie's journey the entire Pacific Northwest was part of the disputed Oregon Territory, claimed by both the United States and Britain. Legal ownership was not resolved until President James K. Polk signed the Treaty of Oregon in 1846, setting the boundary between the United States and Canada on the 49th parallel, where it still lies today. The agreement with the British turned expansionist Polk into yet another politician unable to deliver on campaign promises; he had been elected in 1844 with the slogan "Fifty-four forty or fight!," pledging to annex the entire region between the California border and latitude 54°40°, near the current Canadian city of Prince George. However, Polk was already facing war with Mexico, so he backed away from hostilities with Britain and agreed to divide the land.

Tolmie is believed to have reached a high point somewhere in the vicinity of Mowich Lake, but probably not on the peak that now bears his name. His botanical expedition would have to be considered a success, as he is credited with discovering Tolmie's saxifrage (*Saxifraga tolmiei*). Also known as alpine saxifrage, the hardy, flowering plant is typically found in high-elevation meadows or in loose rocks and scree throughout most of the mountainous west.

A host of formal and informal trails explore the southern end of Mowich Lake near the campground. Most of these eventually join the Lakeshore Trail that runs along the western side of the lake, with a signed trailhead near the parking lot entrance. Head north along the shoreline, following signs to Ipsut Pass. Larger and larger sections of Mount Rainier become visible to the southeast as the mountain emerges from behind Fay Peak.

The trail climbs out of the lake bowl at the northern end and continues beneath a rocky ridge for another half mile. A view opens down a valley to the left, looking out over Mountain Meadows and Meadow Creek as it descends toward its junction with the Mowich River.

Stay right at the next junction to explore a short detour to Ipsut Pass, well worth the negligible effort. The pass offers a great view down the steep Ipsut Creek

Valley, bounded by the sharp spires of Castle Peak and Mother Mountain to the south. At one time legions of "round-the-mountain" hikers crossed through here on the Wonderland Trail, part of their long loop around Rainier. However, although this is still officially part of the route, most long-distance hikers choose to bypass this section by climbing up through Spray and Seattle parks and then rejoining the Wonderland down along the Carbon River to the east.

Return to the junction and go down the slope toward Tolmie Peak, heading northwest below some rocky cliffs. After a quarter mile climb, back uphill to reach Eunice Lake, elevation 5,354 feet. Be careful to stay on the trail as it passes through fragile subalpine meadows along the lake's southern shore. Camping used to be allowed here, but has since been restricted due to excessive damage to plant growth. Expect a colorful display both in the spring from blooming wildflowers and in the autumn from fall colors among the stunted evergreens, mostly grand firs.

Tolmie Peak guards the northern side of Eunice Lake above steep cliffs of columnar basalt. The summit lookout can be seen perched on the western end of the high ridge, 600 feet above. Follow around to the western end of the lake to begin the hardest ascent of the entire route, unfortunately right at the end. Hikers accustomed to life at sea level are likely to feel the altitude, now over 1 mile high.

The trail winds up several switchbacks to reach the summit ridge and the lookout about a half mile beyond the lake. The grand view here stretches to all points of the compass and includes the Olympic Mountains, Glacier Peak, Mount Stuart, Mount Baker, and even an unusual glimpse right into the crater of Mount Saint Helens to the south. Eunice Lake lies almost straight below and a corner of Mowich Lake where you started can be seen through the trees.

Nonetheless, it is Mount Rainier that dominates the skyline. There are few better places to study the mighty glaciers, cliffs, and ridges of the mountain's northwestern aspect than here, although the true summit at Columbia Crest (14,410 feet) is hidden behind Liberty Cap (14,112 feet) at the top of the Willis Wall. Arriving particularly early or late in the day will improve the view as the lower-angle light from the sun will bring the crevasses and gullies into sharper relief.

For the adventurous, an easy scramble route continues eastward along the ridge to a second summit, slightly higher than the lookout. Otherwise, return the way you came.

MOUNT RAINIER NATIONAL PARK: SPRAY FALLS AND SPRAY PARK

 KEY AT-A-GLANCE INFORMATION

LENGTH: 4.5 miles (round-trip) to Spray Falls; 7 miles (round-trip) with optional hike up to Spray Park

CONFIGURATION: Out-and-back

DIFFICULTY: Moderate to Spray Falls, difficult to Spray Park

SCENERY: Stunning waterfall, meadows and wildflowers (in Spray Park); views of Mount Rainier

EXPOSURE: Mostly shaded; exposed in Spray Park

TRAFFIC: Heavy; lower in off-season and beyond the falls.

TRAIL SURFACE: Dirt

HIKING TIME: 3–8 hours

ACCESS: Summer–fall (check road conditions and snowpack); National Park Pass required

MAPS: Green Trails—Mount Rainier West 269; USGS Mowich Lake

FACILITIES: Restroom at trailhead, no drinking water available

Mount Rainier National Park:
Spray Falls and Spray Park

Latitude: North 46d55.97m

Longitude: West 121d51.839m

▶ **IN BRIEF**

This deservedly popular hike finds its way on a moderate walk through the woods to one of the highest and most beautiful waterfalls in the state of Washington—or anywhere else, for that matter. Past the falls, a challenging 600-foot ascent in the next half mile leads to majestic Spray Park, a vast subalpine meadow on Mount Rainier's northwest flank. In the spring, the meadow is a sea of wildflowers, complementing the wide views of the mountain and the surrounding landscape.

▶ **DESCRIPTION**

Like most of nature's finest spectacles, words alone cannot adequately convey the power and beauty of the cascade at Spray Falls. There is simply no substitute for the direct experience of standing below the torrent as it tumbles over the rocks, to hear its deafening roar, to feel the mist

▶ **DIRECTIONS**

From I-5 between Seattle and Tacoma, take Exit 142A, WA 18 (east). Travel on WA 18 toward Auburn, and exit onto WA 167 (south) toward Puyallup. Before reaching Puyallup, exit onto WA 410 toward Sumner and Mount Rainier National Park. Continue on WA 410 to the town of Buckley. In Buckley, turn right (south) toward Wilkeson on WA 165 and immediately take another right to stay on WA 165. At a Y-shaped intersection, veer left to stay on WA 165 and drive through the small towns of Wilkeson and Carbonado. At another Y-shaped intersection, veer right to stay on WA 165, which is clearly signed for Mowich Lake (the road to left is signed for the Carbon River). Drive 11 miles to the National Park boundary and fee station. After paying the required fee, drive this dirt road (now called Road 79 and Mowich Lake Road) to its end at the Mowich Lake Campground.

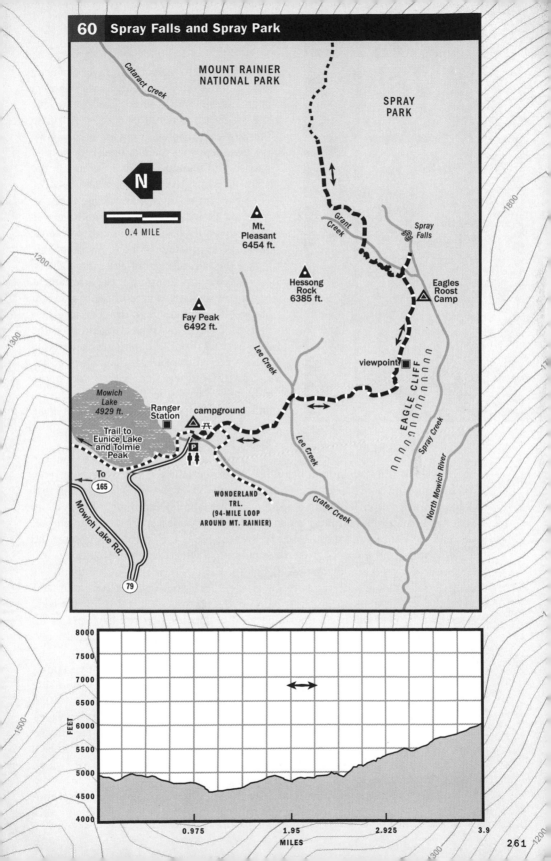

MOUNT RAINIER
NATIONAL PARK

SPRAY
PARK

Cataract Creek

N

0.4 MILE

Grant Creek

Spray Falls

Mt.
Pleasant
6454 ft.

Hessong
Rock
6385 ft.

Eagles
Roost
Camp

Fay Peak
6492 ft.

Lee Creek

viewpoint

EAGLE CLIFF

Mowich
Lake
4929 ft.

Ranger
Station

campground

Spray Creek

Trail to
Eunice Lake
and Tolmie
Peak

P

Lee Creek

North Mowich River

To

165

WONDERLAND
TRL.
(94-MILE LOOP
AROUND MT. RAINIER)

Crater Creek

Mowich Lake Rd.

79

FEET

8000
7500
7000
6500
6000
5500
5000
4500
4000

0.975   1.95   2.925   3.9
MILES

Spray Falls

and wind, and to marvel at the ever-changing vista as the white water finds its way through countless alternate routes, like champagne spilling over a pyramid of glasses. A trip to the falls is an absolute must for anyone visiting this section of the National Park, a truly outstanding natural feature even among the many for which the park is famous.

Not surprisingly, Spray Falls tends to attract a crowd; don't expect to have this place to yourself on a summer weekend. What is surprising is how many people ignore the falls altogether and pass right by on their way up to Spray Park, a testament to the true embarrassment of riches this trail has to offer. Nonetheless, the total foot traffic is still much less than it would be if the hike started from the popular and easily accessible visitor centers at Paradise or Sunrise on the southern and eastern sides of the mountain. Thanks to its lack of amenities and unpaved approach road, Mowich Lake sees far fewer park users than the other major access points.

Start hiking at the trailhead on the southern side of the campground behind some picnic tables. The trail unexpectedly starts downhill on some steps and reaches a junction in 0.4 miles, indicating that you have already been following a section of the Wonderland Trail. Although the Wonderland technically continues along Mowich Lake to descend toward the Carbon River through Ipsut Pass, the route up and over the Spray Park divide has become the de facto Wonderland for most "round-the-mountain" hikers, the same path you will be following. Stay left at the junction, signed for Eagles Roost and Spray Park.

The trail gradually descends to cross Lee Creek after another half mile, and then reaches its low point at just less than 4,600 feet, some 300 feet below the lake. Cross a boulder field and begin to gain back all of the elevation you have lost so far, as the trail heads uphill on a series of switchbacks, climbing through a mixed forest of young and old trees.

The trail skirts the top of Eagle Cliff, eventually reaching an excellent viewpoint on a marked spur to the right near the 1.5-mile mark. Be sure to make this short side trip for a commanding view. From the overlook, the mountain rises almost 10,000 feet in a horizontal distance of about 6 miles and the steep walls of the Spray Creek Valley drop another 1,500 feet straight down, for a total of about 11,500 feet of visible vertical relief. Even with a good topographic map and a practiced eye, it can be a real challenge to positively identify every feature of the terrain in view, which includes seven major glaciers and countless ridges and rocky points.

Another half mile yields first the Eagles Roost campsite (typically used by Wonderland through-hikers) and then the Grant Creek crossing (a log footbridge over a pleasant stream that flows down through a series of boulders in a small waterfall). This waterfall is no match for what is to come, however, as the junction for Spray Falls lies just on the other side of the creek.

Head right at the junction, cross another small bridge, and then traverse a talus field of small white rocks to emerge after 0.1 mile below the mighty falls. It's easy to see where the falls got its name, as curtains of spray and mist repeatedly sweep across everyone and everything below. If the prevailing winds and volume of water are favorable, you may be able to find a dry spot to relax and take a picture, but there is no guarantee. Scramble up through the boulders to get a better sense of the true size of the 350-foot cascade, although this is likely to expose you to an even greater wetness.

The stream sweeps around a broad curve, keeping the top essentially invisible from the base. However, the majesty of the falls lies in the 80-foot width across the fan and the white water contrasting against the reddish volcanic rock underneath.

For many hikers, the falls make a suitable day-hike destination, but additional rewards await anyone continuing uphill to Spray Park. To reach the subalpine meadow, return to the main trail and turn right to enter a tough uphill grind through a long chain of switchbacks. Your effort will be rewarded when you finally escape the trees near the 5,700-foot line.

Many hikers consider Spray Park the finest place to view wildflowers anywhere at Mount Rainier, as the fields are carpeted with white avalanche lilies through much of the late spring and summer. Less heralded but equally impressive is the view in autumn, when fiery reds, oranges, and yellows ignite the landscape and the biting insects have mostly disappeared.

The trail continues uphill for another mile to reach a saddle at 6,400 feet that separates Spray Park from Seattle Park. This high point is as far as most day-hikers are likely to venture, about 4 miles total from the trailhead, but anyone with greater ambitions can continue on eastward as far as they wish. More typically, hikers will be captivated by the many pleasures of Spray Park and seek to explore it on their own. Scramblers may pursue multiple peak-bagging opportunities to the northwest in the vicinity of Hessong Rock and Mount Pleasant, rock hounds might investigate the pumice and other volcanic rocks at the higher elevations, botanists and naturalists can enjoy the wildflower displays and other subalpine life, and many people may simply wish to relax and soak in the fantastic views of both Mount Rainier itself and the landscape stretching away to the north, as far as the northern Cascades on a clear day.

60 Hikes
within 60 MILES

SEATTLE
INCLUDING BELLEVUE, EVERETT, AND TACOMA

APPENDIXES
AND INDEX

APPENDIX A:
HIKING STORES

▶ LOCATION/CITY

Feathered Friends
119 Yale Avenue N
Seattle, WA 98109
(206) 292-2210
www.featheredfriends.com

Outdoor & More
510 Westlake Avenue N
Seattle, WA 98109
(206) 340-0677
www.outdoormore.com

Outdoor Emporium
1701 Fourth Avenue S
Seattle, WA 98134
(206) 624-6550
www.outdooremporium.net

Pro Mountain Sports
5625 University Way NE
Seattle, WA 98105
(206) 522-1627
www.promountainsports.com

REI–Online
www.rei.com

REI–Seattle
222 Yale Avenue N
Seattle, WA 98109
(206) 223-1944
(888) 873-1938

REI–Alderwood
3000 184th Street SW, Suite 952
Lynnwood, WA 98037
(425) 640-6200

REI–Redmond
7500 166th Avenue NE
(Redmond Town Center)
Redmond, WA 98052
(425) 882-1158

REI–Southcenter/Tukwila
240 Andover Park W
Tukwila, WA 98188
(206) 248-1938

REI–Tacoma
3825 S Steele Street
Tacoma, WA 98409
(253) 671-1938

Second Ascent
5209 Ballard Avenue NW
Seattle, WA 98107
(206) 545-8810
www.secondascent.com

APPENDIX B:
PLACES TO BUY MAPS

▶ LOCATION/CITY

Metsker Maps of Seattle
1511 First Avenue
Seattle, WA 98101
(206) 623-8747
(800) 727-4430
www.metskers.com

Metsker Maps/Janssen Inc.
9616 40th Avenue SW
Lakewood, WA 98499
(253) 588-5222
(866) 588-5222
www.metskermaps.com

Metsker Maps of Tacoma
7030 Tacoma Mall Boulevard
Tacoma, WA 98409
(253) 474-6277

World Wide Books and Maps
4411A Wallingford Avenue N
Seattle, WA 98103
(206) 634-3453
(888) 534-3453
www.seattletravelstore.com

Green Trails Maps
Seattle, WA 98101
(206) 546-6277
www.greentrails.com

REI Stores
(see above)

APPENDIX C:
HIKING CLUBS

▶ LOCATION/CITY

The Mountaineers–Seattle branch
300 Third Avenue W
Seattle, WA 98119
(206) 284-6310
www.seattlemountaineers.org

The Mountaineers–Everett branch
www.everettmountaineers.org

The Mountaineers–Kitsap branch
www.kitsapmountaineers.org

The Mountaineers–Olympia Branch
www.olympiamountaineers.org

The Mountaineers–Tacoma Branch
www.tacomamountaineers.org

Issaquah Alps Trail Club
P.O. Box 351
Issaquah, WA 98027
www.issaquahalps.org

Washington Trails Association
2019 Third Avenue, Suite 100
Seattle, WA 98121
(206) 625-1367
www.wta.org

INDEX

INDEX

INDEX

INDEX

INDEX

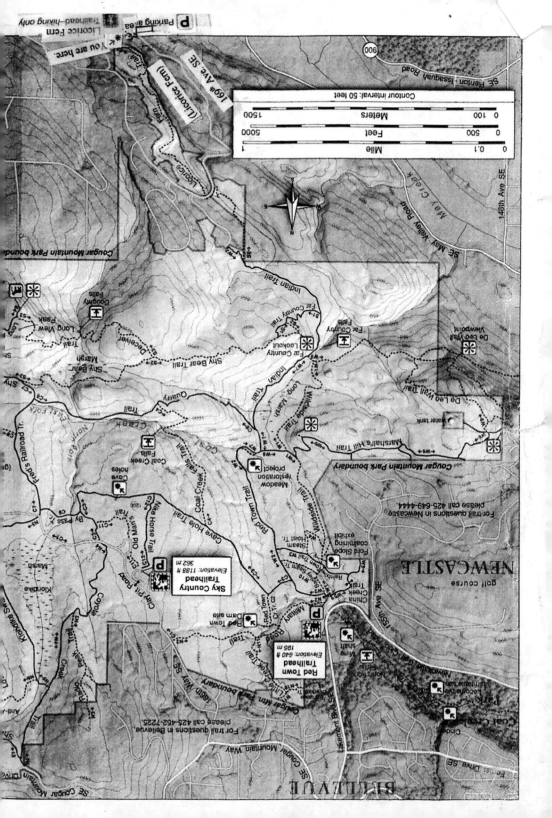

Opportunities

What's There To Do?

- Play with your kids and friends or have a picnic. There are 10 picnic tables located on the open, grassy meadow at the old radar site at the Anti-Aircraft Peak trailhead.

- Hike on more than 35 miles of wooded trails.

- Ride your horse on 12 miles of equestrian trails.

- Portable toilets are located at each of the trailheads.

Quick Facts

Area .... 3,012 acres
High point (Wilderness Peak) ...... 1,500 feet
Hours....................................... 8:00AM to dusk
King County Parks and
Recreation Division 206-296-4232
www.metrokc.gov/parks
To schedule an event or
interpretive walk 206-205-7532
King County Parks
Volunteer Coordinator 206-296-2990
www.metrokc.gov/parks/volunt/volunt1.htm
Emergency contact............... 911 or 206-296-8100

Information in this brochure is available in alternative formats upon request. Please call 206-296-4232 or 1-800-324-6165 ext. 6-4232. Washington Relay Service 1-800-833-6388.

Old "Coal Creek" at Cougar Mountain

Experience what remains of the coal-mining town that once thrived on the lower slopes of Cougar Mountain. Interpretive signs describe the life and work of the miners and loggers. Walk the trails of old "Coal Creek" townsite.

Volunteer—Help a Trail!

There are opportunities every month to help maintain park trails and natural areas. Each event has a crew leader who will coach you on safety, tools and maintenance techniques. You will "learn by doing," and have fun with a great bunch of people. It's a safe way to discover new trails, meet new friends and to "give something back." Imagine hiking a trail with your child and being able to say, "I helped build this." To learn about upcoming events and register for a work party that matches your schedule, contact the parks volunteer coordinator at 206-296-2990.

Trail work volunteers

Meadow project volunteers

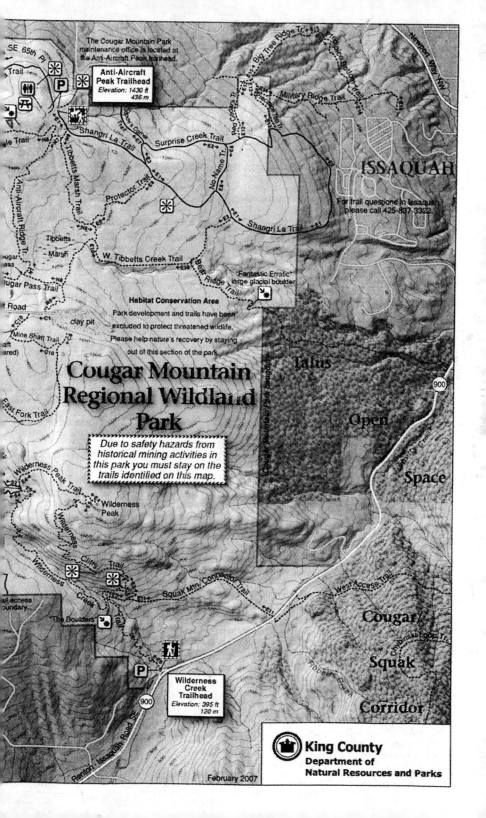

Map Legend *(map on reverse)*

Due to safety hazards from historical mining activities in this park you must stay on the trails identified on this map.

Trailhead–*horseback riding and hiking*		Trail–*horseback riding and hiking*	
Trailhead–*hiking only*		Trail–*hiking only*	
Picnic area			
Point of interest		Major arterial street	
Viewpoint		Other street or road	
Waterfall			
Hitching rail			
Parking area		Cougar Mountain Park	
Restrooms			
Gates		Other park land	

For information about King County Parks, please call 206-296-4232. Visit King County Parks on the Internet at www.metrokc.gov/parks.

Map created by the King County Parks and Recreation Division and the King County GIS Center: www.metrokc.gov/gis.

©2007 King County, Washington.

Printed on recycled paper.

This information is available
in alternative formats upon request.
Please call 206-296-4232
or 1-800-324-6165 ext. 6-4232.
Washington Relay Service: 1-800-833-6388.

Getting There

Red Town Trailhead

From I-90 Take Exit 13 and drive south or Lakemont Boulevard SE for 3.1 miles. Look gravel entrance to the Red Town Trailhead o left side of the road.

From I-405 Take Exit 10 and follow Coal C Parkway SE 2.4 miles to the shopping cente left at the light onto SE 72nd Place and then again at Newcastle Golf Club Road. Follow t 1.9 miles. The gravel entrance to the Red To Trailhead is on the right side of the road just the big bend.

Sky Country Trailhead

From I-90 Take Exit 13 and drive south or Lakemont Boulevard SE for 2.5 miles. Turn l SE Cougar Mountain Way and then right on Way SE. The road will change to gravel, and end on the right is the Sky Country Trailhead parking lot, which includes space for horse tr

Anti-Aircraft Peak Trailhead

From I-90 Take Exit 13 and drive south on Lakemont Boulevard SE for 2.5 miles. Turn l onto SE Cougar Mountain Way. Follow the d yellow line (The road will first swing left and become 168th Place SE, and then right to be SE 60th Street.) Turn off 60th Street uphill on dead end road, SE Cougar Mountain Drive. road will change to gravel, and at the very en the Anti-Aircraft Peak Trailhead, where you w restrooms, picnic tables, and a playfield.

Wilderness Creek Trailhead

From I-90 Take Exit 15 and drive south on Highway 900 (17th Avenue NW and then Renton-Issaquah Road SE) for 3.3 miles. Lo the trailhead sign and an asphalt driveway th goes uphill to the right.

Trail Lengths in Miles

Calculated from current digital data; older trail signs may indicate different values.

N2	Military Road Trail	0.7	W7	Indian Trail	1.3
N3	Radio Peak Trail	0.4	*W8*	*abandoned for habitat restoration*	
N4	Coyote Creek Trail	1.1	W9	De Leo Wall Trail	1.1
N5	Klondike Swamp Trail	0.9	W10	Bagley Seam Trail	0.2
N6	Lost Beagle Trail	0.7	C1	Clay Pit Road	1.3
N7	Anti-Aircraft Ridge Trail	0.7	C2	Red Town Creek Trail	0.2
N8	Cougar Pass Trail	0.3	C3	Cave Hole Trail	1.2
N9	Tibbetts Marsh Trail	1.0	C4	Coal Creek Falls Trail	0.7
N10	Primrose Overlook Trail	0.2	*C5*	*abandoned for habitat restoration*	
N11	Little Creek Trail	0.4	C6	Quarry Trail	1.0
W1	Wildside Trail	1.0	C7	Fred's Railroad Trail	0.6
W2	Red Town Trail	0.8	C8	East Fork Trail	0.7
W3	Rainbow Town Trail	0.3	C9	By Pass Trail	0.2
W4	Steam Hoist Trail	0.2	C10	Mine Shaft Trail	0.3
W5	China Creek Trail	0.3	C11	Old Man's Trail	0.3
W6	Marshall's Hill Trail	1.1	C12	Nike Horse Trail	0.3
			E1	Shangri La Trail	1.7
			E2	Surprise Creek Trail	0.6
			E3	Bear Ridge Trail	1.5

E4	Wilderness Peak Trail
E5	Wilderness Cliffs Trail
E6	Wilderness Creek Trail
E7	Goode's Corner Trail
E8	No Name Trail
E9	Protector Trail
E10	West Tibbetts Creek Trail
E11	Squak Mtn. Connector Tr.
E12	Red Cedars Trail
E13	Precipice Top Trail
E14	Military Ridge Trail
E15	Big Tree Ridge Trail
E16	Precipice Bottom Trail
S1	Far Country Trail
S2	Shy Bear Trail
S3	Deceiver Trail
S4	Long View Peak Trail
S5	Ring Road Trail
S6	Licorice Fern Trail